Before You Start

Follow These Four Steps

Step 1

Spend time in prayer, asking God to guide you. Go through the list of 135 statements on the questionnaire found on pages 4–8. For each one, mark on the answer sheet to what extent the statement is true of your life: MUCH = 3, SOME = 2, LITTLE = 1, or NOT AT ALL = 0.

> **Warning:** Do not score according to what you think *should* be true or what you hope might be true in the future. For the best results, be honest and score only on the basis of past experience. In most cases, your first thought on what the answer should be will be the most accurate. If you are a young Christian, the results will need extra care in interpretation.

Step 2

When you are finished, score the questionnaire according to the instructions on the scoring sheet.

Step 3

Study the gift definitions and Scripture references found on pages 9–12. The capital letters next to the definitions correspond with the lettered rows on the scoring sheet.

Step 4

Complete the exercises on pages 13–14 to gain a tentative evaluation of where your gifts may lie and to explore the implications for your ministry in the Body of Christ. If possible, get together with other believers who know you and talk about your survey results.

Step 1

Wagner-Modified Houts Questionnaire

For each statement, mark to what extent it is true of your life:

Much = **3**, Some = **2**, Little = **1**, or Not at All = **0**.

1. I have a desire to speak direct messages that I receive from God in order to edify, exhort or comfort others.

2. I have enjoyed ministering to a certain group of people over a long period of time, sharing personally in their successes and their failures.

3. People have told me that I have helped them learn biblical truths in a meaningful way.

4. I have applied spiritual truth effectively to critical situations in my own life.

5. Others have told me I have helped them to discern key and important facts of Scripture.

6. I have verbally encouraged and helped the wavering, the troubled or the discouraged.

7. Others in my church have noted that I am able to see through phoniness before it is evident to other people.

8. I find I manage money well in order to give liberally to the Lord's work.

Much = **3**, Some = **2**, Little = **1**, or Not at All = **0**.

9. I have assisted Christian leaders to relieve them for concentrating on their essential jobs.

10. I have a desire to work with those who have physical or mental problems in order to alleviate their suffering.

11. I feel comfortable relating to people of other cultures, and they seem to accept me.

12. I have led others to a decision for salvation through faith in Christ.

13. My home is always open to people who need a place to stay.

14. When in a group, I am the one to whom others often look for vision and direction.

15. When I speak, people seem to listen and agree.

16. When a group I am in is lacking organization, I love to step in to fill the gap.

17. Others can point to specific instances in which my prayers have resulted in visible miracles.

Much = **3**, Some = **2**, Little = **1**, or Not at All = **0**.

18. In the name of the Lord, I have been used in curing diseases instantaneously.

19. I have spoken in tongues.

20. Sometimes when a person speaks in tongues, I seem to know what God is saying through them.

21. I could live more comfortably, but I choose not to in order to identify with the poor.

22. I am single and enjoy it.

23. I spend at least an hour a day in prayer.

24. I have spoken directly to evil spirits, and they have obeyed me.

25. I enjoy being called on to do odd jobs around the church.

26. A number of pastors and/or ministry leaders have told me that they desire to minister and to be held accountable under my spiritual covering.

27. I have an insatiable appetite for the presence of God.

28. Through God I have been used to reveal to others specific things that will happen in the future, and they have come to pass.

29. I have enjoyed assuming the responsibility for the spiritual well-being of a particular group of Christians.

30. I feel I can explain the New Testament teaching about the health and ministry of the Body of Christ in a relevant way.

31. I can intuitively arrive at solutions to fairly complicated problems.

32. I have had insights relating to spiritual truth that others have said helped bring them closer to God.

Much = **3**, Some = **2**, Little = **1**, or Not at All = **0**.

33. I can effectively motivate people to get busy and do what they are supposed to do.

34. I can "see" the Spirit of God resting on certain people from time to time.

35. My giving records show that I contribute considerably more than 10 percent of my income to the Lord's work.

36. Other people have told me that I have helped them become more effective in their ministries.

37. I have offered to care for others when they have had material or physical needs.

38. I feel I could learn another language well in order to minister to those in a different culture.

39. I have shared joyfully how Christ has brought me to Himself in a way that is meaningful to nonbelievers.

40. I enjoy taking charge of church suppers or social events.

41. I have believed God for the impossible and seen it happen in a tangible way.

42. Other Christians have followed my leadership because they trusted me.

43. I enjoy handling the details of organizing ideas, people, resources and time for more effective ministry.

44. God has used me personally to perform supernatural signs and wonders.

45. I enjoy praying for sick people because I know ahead of time that many of them will be healed as a result.

46. I have spoken an immediate message of God to His people in a language I have never learned.

47. I have interpreted public tongues with the result that the Body of Christ was edified, exhorted or comforted.

Much = **3**, Some = **2**, Little = **1**, or Not at All = **0**.

48. Living a simple lifestyle is an exciting challenge for me.

49. Other people have noted that I feel more indifferent about not being married than most.

50. When I hear an urgent prayer request, I pray for that need for several days at least.

51. I have actually heard a demon speak in a loud voice.

52. I don't have many special skills, but I volunteer to do what needs to be done around the church.

53. I am known as a leader of leaders.

54. I intuitively know what should happen next in a worship service.

55. People have told me that I have communicated timely and urgent messages that must have come directly from the Lord.

56. I feel unafraid of offering spiritual guidance and direction to a group of Christians.

57. I can devote considerable time to learning new biblical truths in order to communicate them to others.

58. When other people have a problem, I can frequently guide them to the best biblical solution.

59. Through study or experience I have discerned major strategies or techniques that God seems to use in furthering His kingdom.

60. People come to me in their afflictions or suffering because they know that I will listen to them and understand.

61. I can tell with a fairly high degree of assurance when a person is afflicted by an evil spirit.

62. When I am moved by an appeal to give to God's work, I usually can find the money I need to help.

Much = **3**, Some = **2**, Little = **1**, or Not at All = **0**.

63. I have enjoyed doing routine tasks that have allowed more effective ministry on the part of others.

64. I enjoy visiting in hospitals and/or retirement homes, and feel I do well in such a ministry.

65. People of a different race or culture have been attracted to me, and we have related well.

66. Non-Christians have noted that they feel comfortable when they are around me, and that I have a positive effect on them toward developing a faith in Christ.

67. When people come to our home, they indicate that they "feel at home" with us.

68. Other people have told me that I had faith to accomplish what seemed impossible to them.

69. When I set goals, others seem to accept them readily.

70. I have been able to make effective and efficient plans for accomplishing the goals of a group.

71. God regularly seems to do impossible things through my life.

72. Others have told me that God healed them of an emotional problem when I ministered to them.

73. I can speak to God in a language I have never learned.

74. I have prayed that I may interpret if someone begins speaking in tongues.

75. I am not poor, but I can warmly identify with poor people.

76. I am glad I have more time to serve the Lord because I am single.

77. Day in and day out, intercessory prayer is one of my favorite ways of spending time.

Much = **3**, Some = **2**, Little = **1**, or Not at All = **0**.

78. Others call on me when they suspect that someone is demonized.

79. Others have mentioned that I seem to enjoy routine tasks and do well at them.

80. Christian leaders seem pleased to work under my leadership, and they respect my authority when we undertake a common task.

81. During worship, I can often tell if there is a spiritual force attempting to hinder our connection with God.

82. I sometimes have a strong sense of what God wants to say to people in response to particular situations.

83. I have helped fellow believers by guiding them to relevant portions of the Bible and praying with them.

84. I feel I can communicate significant truths to others and see resulting changes in knowledge, attitudes, values or conduct.

85. Some people indicate that I have perceived and applied biblical truths to the specific needs of fellow believers.

86. I study and read quite a bit in order to learn new biblical truths.

87. I have a desire to effectively counsel those in need.

88. I can recognize whether a person's teaching or actions are from God, from Satan, or of human origin.

89. I am so confident that God will meet my financial needs that I do not hesitate to give to His work sacrificially and consistently.

90. When I do things behind the scenes and others are helped, I am joyful.

91. People call on me to help those who are less fortunate.

Much = **3**, Some = **2**, Little = **1**, or Not at All = **0**.

92. I would be willing to leave comfortable surroundings if it would enable me to share Christ with less-fortunate people.

93. I get frustrated when others don't seem to share their faith with nonbelievers as much as I do.

94. Others have mentioned to me that I am a very hospitable person.

95. There have been times when I have felt sure I knew God's specific will for the future growth of His work, even when others have not been so sure.

96. When I am part of a group, others seem to back off and expect me to take leadership.

97. I am able to give directions to others without using persuasion to get them to accomplish a certain task.

98. People have told me that I was God's instrument that brought supernatural change in lives or circumstances.

99. I have prayed for others and instantaneous physical healing has often occurred.

100. When I give a public message in tongues, I expect it to be interpreted.

101. I have interpreted tongues in a way that seemed to bless others.

102. Others tell me that I sacrifice too much materially in order to fulfill God's calling.

103. I am single and have little difficulty controlling my sexual desires.

104. Others have told me that my prayers for them have been answered in tangible ways.

105. Other people have been instantly delivered from demonic oppression when I have prayed.

106. I prefer being active and doing something rather than just sitting around talking or reading or listening to a speaker.

Much = **3**, Some = **2**, Little = **1**, or Not at All = **0**.

107. I regularly receive revelation from God as to what the Holy Spirit is currently saying to the Church.

108. Others have told me that my worship helps them enter into the presence of God.

109. I frequently feel that I know exactly what God wants to do in ministry at a specific point in time.

110. People with needs have told me that I have helped them be restored to the Christian community.

111. Studying the Bible and sharing my insights with others are very satisfying for me.

112. I have felt an unusual presence of God and personal confidence when important decisions needed to be made.

113. I have the ability to discover new truths for myself through reading or observing situations firsthand.

114. I have helped others find a biblical solution to their affliction or suffering.

115. I can tell whether a person speaking in tongues is genuine.

116. I have been willing to maintain a lower standard of living in order to benefit God's work.

117. When I serve the Lord, I truthfully don't care if someone else gets the credit for what I do.

118. I frequently enjoy spending time with a lonely, shut-in person or with someone in prison.

119. More than most, I have had a strong desire to see peoples of other countries won to the Lord.

120. I am attracted to nonbelievers mainly because of my desire to win them to Christ.

Much = **3**, Some = **2**, Little = **1**, or Not at All = **0**.

121. I have desired to make my home available to those in the Lord's service whenever needed.

122. Others have told me that I am a person of unusual vision, and I agree.

123. When I am in charge, things seem to run smoothly.

124. I have enjoyed bearing the responsibility for the success of a particular task within my church or in the workplace.

125. In the name of the Lord, I have been able to help blind people receive their sight.

126. When I pray for the sick, either I or they feel sensations of tingling or warmth.

127. When I speak in tongues to a group, I believe it is edifying to the Lord's Body.

128. I have interpreted tongues in such a way that the message appeared to be directly from God.

129. Poor people accept me easily because I choose to live on their level.

130. I readily identify with Paul's desire for others to be single as he was.

131. When I pray, God frequently speaks to me, and I recognize His voice.

132. I regularly cast out demons in Jesus' name.

133. I respond cheerfully when asked to do a job, even if it seems menial.

134. When I call Christian leaders to come together for a certain purpose, a significant number of them respond.

135. I have a compelling desire to lead others into an experience with God.

Answer Sheet
Instructions

Go through the list of 135 statements on the questionnaire on pages 4–8. For each one, mark to what extent the statement is true of your life:

MUCH = 3
SOME = 2
LITTLE = 1
NOT AT ALL = 0

If the statement is true of MUCH of your life, then darken circle 3 (MUCH). If the statement is true of SOME of your life, then darken circle 2 (SOME). If the statement is true of LITTLE of your life, then darken circle 1 (LITTLE). If the statement is NOT AT ALL true of your life, then darken circle 0 (NOT AT ALL).

Warning! Do not score according to what you think should be true or hope might be true in the future. Be honest and score only on the basis of past experience.

Step 2

Wagner-Modified Houts Scoring Sheet

Add scores across the sheet to determine your total for each gift.

Total Gift Score

1. ③ ② ① ⓪	28. ③ ② ① ⓪	55. ③ ② ① ⓪	82. ③ ② ① ⓪	109. ③ ② ① ⓪	A. Total _____
2. ③ ② ① ⓪	29. ③ ② ① ⓪	56. ③ ② ① ⓪	83. ③ ② ① ⓪	110. ③ ② ① ⓪	B. Total _____
3. ③ ② ① ⓪	30. ③ ② ① ⓪	57. ③ ② ① ⓪	84. ③ ② ① ⓪	111. ③ ② ① ⓪	C. Total _____
4. ③ ② ① ⓪	31. ③ ② ① ⓪	58. ③ ② ① ⓪	85. ③ ② ① ⓪	112. ③ ② ① ⓪	D. Total _____
5. ③ ② ① ⓪	32. ③ ② ① ⓪	59. ③ ② ① ⓪	86. ③ ② ① ⓪	113. ③ ② ① ⓪	E. Total _____
6. ③ ② ① ⓪	33. ③ ② ① ⓪	60. ③ ② ① ⓪	87. ③ ② ① ⓪	114. ③ ② ① ⓪	F. Total _____
7. ③ ② ① ⓪	34. ③ ② ① ⓪	61. ③ ② ① ⓪	88. ③ ② ① ⓪	115. ③ ② ① ⓪	G. Total _____
8. ③ ② ① ⓪	35. ③ ② ① ⓪	62. ③ ② ① ⓪	89. ③ ② ① ⓪	116. ③ ② ① ⓪	H. Total _____
9. ③ ② ① ⓪	36. ③ ② ① ⓪	63. ③ ② ① ⓪	90. ③ ② ① ⓪	117. ③ ② ① ⓪	I. Total _____
10. ③ ② ① ⓪	37. ③ ② ① ⓪	64. ③ ② ① ⓪	91. ③ ② ① ⓪	118. ③ ② ① ⓪	J. Total _____
11. ③ ② ① ⓪	38. ③ ② ① ⓪	65. ③ ② ① ⓪	92. ③ ② ① ⓪	119. ③ ② ① ⓪	K. Total _____
12. ③ ② ① ⓪	39. ③ ② ① ⓪	66. ③ ② ① ⓪	93. ③ ② ① ⓪	120. ③ ② ① ⓪	L. Total _____
13. ③ ② ① ⓪	40. ③ ② ① ⓪	67. ③ ② ① ⓪	94. ③ ② ① ⓪	121. ③ ② ① ⓪	M. Total _____
14. ③ ② ① ⓪	41. ③ ② ① ⓪	68. ③ ② ① ⓪	95. ③ ② ① ⓪	122. ③ ② ① ⓪	N. Total _____
15. ③ ② ① ⓪	42. ③ ② ① ⓪	69. ③ ② ① ⓪	96. ③ ② ① ⓪	123. ③ ② ① ⓪	O. Total _____
16. ③ ② ① ⓪	43. ③ ② ① ⓪	70. ③ ② ① ⓪	97. ③ ② ① ⓪	124. ③ ② ① ⓪	P. Total _____
17. ③ ② ① ⓪	44. ③ ② ① ⓪	71. ③ ② ① ⓪	98. ③ ② ① ⓪	125. ③ ② ① ⓪	Q. Total _____
18. ③ ② ① ⓪	45. ③ ② ① ⓪	72. ③ ② ① ⓪	99. ③ ② ① ⓪	126. ③ ② ① ⓪	R. Total _____
19. ③ ② ① ⓪	46. ③ ② ① ⓪	73. ③ ② ① ⓪	100. ③ ② ① ⓪	127. ③ ② ① ⓪	S. Total _____
20. ③ ② ① ⓪	47. ③ ② ① ⓪	74. ③ ② ① ⓪	101. ③ ② ① ⓪	128. ③ ② ① ⓪	T. Total _____
21. ③ ② ① ⓪	48. ③ ② ① ⓪	75. ③ ② ① ⓪	102. ③ ② ① ⓪	129. ③ ② ① ⓪	U. Total _____
22. ③ ② ① ⓪	49. ③ ② ① ⓪	76. ③ ② ① ⓪	103. ③ ② ① ⓪	130. ③ ② ① ⓪	V. Total _____
23. ③ ② ① ⓪	50. ③ ② ① ⓪	77. ③ ② ① ⓪	104. ③ ② ① ⓪	131. ③ ② ① ⓪	W. Total _____
24. ③ ② ① ⓪	51. ③ ② ① ⓪	78. ③ ② ① ⓪	105. ③ ② ① ⓪	132. ③ ② ① ⓪	X. Total _____
25. ③ ② ① ⓪	52. ③ ② ① ⓪	79. ③ ② ① ⓪	106. ③ ② ① ⓪	133. ③ ② ① ⓪	Y. Total _____
26. ③ ② ① ⓪	53. ③ ② ① ⓪	80. ③ ② ① ⓪	107. ③ ② ① ⓪	134. ③ ② ① ⓪	Z. Total _____
27. ③ ② ① ⓪	54. ③ ② ① ⓪	81. ③ ② ① ⓪	108. ③ ② ① ⓪	135. ③ ② ① ⓪	AA. Total _____

Study the gifts and definitions on pages 9–12 based on your highest scores.
The capital letters before the gift definitions correspond with rows A through AA.

Step 3

Gift Definitions and Scripture References

The following three pages contain **suggested** definitions of the spiritual gifts. While not meant to be dogmatic or final, these definitions and supporting Scriptures do correspond to characteristics of the gifts as expressed in the Wagner-Modified Houts Questionnaire.

A. Prophecy. The gift of prophecy is the special ability that God gives to certain members of the Body of Christ to receive and communicate an immediate message of God to His people through a divinely anointed utterance.

> Luke 7:26 • Acts 15:32 • Acts 21:9–11 • Romans 12:6 • 1 Corinthians 12:10, 28 • Ephesians 4:11–13

B. Pastor. The gift of pastor is the special ability that God gives to certain members of the Body of Christ to assume a long-term personal responsibility for the spiritual welfare of a group of believers. (**Note:** The term "pastor" is commonly used to describe the leader of a local congregation; however, many who lead churches have dominant gifts other than pastor [e.g., leader or teacher]. Those leaders who do not have the dominant gift of pastor may augment their role using volunteers or staff members.)

> John 10:1–18 • Ephesians 4:11–13 • 1 Timothy 3:1–7 • 1 Peter 5:1–3

C. Teaching. The gift of teaching is the special ability that God gives to certain members of the Body of Christ to communicate information relevant to the health and ministry of the Body and its members in such a way that others will learn.

> Acts 18:24–28 • Acts 20:20–21 • Romans 12:7 • 1 Corinthians 12:28 • Ephesians 4:11–13

D. Wisdom. The gift of wisdom is the special ability that God gives to certain members of the Body of Christ to know the mind of the Holy Spirit in such a way as to receive insight into how given knowledge may best be applied to specific needs arising in the Body of Christ. (**Note:** Pentecostals and charismatics often use the term "word of wisdom," meaning a revelatory message God gives to bring resolution to a certain situation. I feel the charismatic "word of wisdom" is really a subset of the gift of prophecy, not the gift of wisdom. A judge, on the other hand, would be one who has the gift of wisdom.)

> Acts 6:3, 10 • 1 Corinthians 2:1–13 • 1 Corinthians 12:8 • James 1:5–6 • 2 Peter 3:15–16

E. Knowledge. The gift of knowledge is the special ability that God gives to certain members of the Body of Christ to discover, accumulate, analyze and clarify information and ideas that are pertinent to the well-being of the Body.

Acts 5:1–11 • 1 Corinthians 2:14 •
1 Corinthians 12:8 • 2 Corinthians 11:6 •
Colossians 2:2–3

F. **Exhortation.** The gift of exhortation—sometimes called the gift of counseling—is the special ability that God gives to certain members of the Body of Christ to minister words of comfort, consolation, encouragement and counsel to other members of the Body in such a way that they feel helped and healed.

Acts 14:22 • Romans 12:8 • 1 Timothy 4:13 •
Hebrews 10:25

G. **Discerning of Spirits.** The gift of discerning (or discernment) of spirits is the special ability that God gives to certain members of the Body of Christ to know with assurance whether certain behavior purported to be of God is in reality divine, human or satanic.

Matthew 16:21–23 • Acts 5:1–11 •
Acts 16:16–18 • 1 Corinthians 12:10 •
1 John 4:1–6

H. **Giving.** The gift of giving is the special ability that God gives to certain members of the Body of Christ to contribute their material resources to the work of the Lord liberally and cheerfully, above and beyond the tithes and offerings expected of all believers.

Mark 12:41–44 • Romans 12:8 •
2 Corinthians 8:1–7 • 2 Corinthians 9:2–8

I. **Helps.** The gift of helps is the special ability that God gives to certain members of the Body of Christ to invest the talents they have in the life and ministry of other members of the Body, thus enabling those others to increase the effectiveness of their own spiritual gifts. (**Note:** The gift of helps may be confused with the gift of service. Someone with the gift of helps usually aids one individual [e.g., an administrative assistant], while a person with the gift of service is willing to do whatever is necessary for a cause or project.)

Mark 15:40–41 • Luke 8:2–3 • Acts 9:36 •
Romans 16:1–2 • 1 Corinthians 12:28

J. **Mercy.** The gift of mercy is the special ability that God gives to certain members of the Body of Christ to feel genuine empathy and compassion for individuals (both Christian and non-Christian) who suffer distressing physical, mental or emotional problems, and to translate that compassion into cheerfully done deeds that reflect Christ's love and alleviate the suffering.

Matthew 20:29–34 • Matthew 25:34–40 •
Mark 9:41 • Luke 10:33–35 • Acts 11:28–30 •
Acts 16:33–34 • Romans 12:8

K. **Missionary.** The gift of missionary is the special ability that God gives to certain members of the Body of Christ to minister whatever other spiritual gifts they have in a second culture. (**Note:** The gift of missionary should not be confused with the gift of apostle. Some apostles have the gift of missionary and do cross-cultural ministry [e.g., the apostle Paul], while other apostles do not have the missionary gift and therefore they minister monoculturally [e.g., the apostle Peter].)

Acts 8:4 • Acts 13:2–3 • Acts 22:21 •
Romans 10:15 • 1 Corinthians 9:19–23 •
Ephesians 3:6–8

L. **Evangelist.** The gift of evangelist is the special ability that God gives to certain members of the Body of Christ to share the Gospel with nonbelievers in such a way that they become Jesus' disciples and responsible members of the Body of Christ.

Acts 8:5–6 • Acts 8:26–40 • Acts 14:21
• Acts 21:8 • Ephesians 4:11–13 •
2 Timothy 4:5

M. **Hospitality.** The gift of hospitality is the special ability that God gives to certain members of the Body of Christ to provide an open house and a warm welcome to those in need of food and lodging.

> Acts 16:14–15 • Romans 12:9–13 •
> Romans 16:23 • Hebrews 13:1–2 • 1 Peter 4:9

N. Faith. The gift of faith is the special ability that God gives to certain members of the Body of Christ to discern with extraordinary confidence the will and purposes of God for His work.

> Acts 11:22–24 • Acts 27:21–25 •
> Romans 4:18–21 • 1 Corinthians 12:9 •
> Hebrews 11

O. Leadership. The gift of leadership is the special ability that God gives to certain members of the Body of Christ to set goals in accordance with God's purpose for the future and to communicate these goals to others in such a way that they voluntarily and harmoniously work together to accomplish those goals for the glory of God.

> Luke 9:51 • Acts 7:10 • Acts 15:7–11 • Romans 12:8 • 1 Timothy 5:17 • Hebrews 13:17

P. Administration. The gift of administration is the special ability that God gives to certain members of the Body of Christ to understand clearly the immediate and long-range goals of a particular unit of the Body of Christ and to devise and execute effective plans for the accomplishment of those goals.

> Luke 14:28–30 • Acts 6:1–7 • Acts 27:11 •
> 1 Corinthians 12:28 • Titus 1:5

Q. Miracles. The gift of miracles is the special ability that God gives to certain members of the Body of Christ to serve as human intermediaries through whom it pleases God to perform powerful acts that are perceived by observers to have altered the ordinary course of nature.

> Acts 9:36–42 • Acts 19:11–20 • Acts 20:7–12 •
> Romans 15:18–19 • 1 Corinthians 12:10, 28 •
> 2 Corinthians 12:12

R. Healing. The gift of healing is the special ability that God gives to certain members of the Body of Christ to serve as human intermediaries through

whom it pleases God to cure illness and restore health apart from the use of natural means.

> Acts 3:1–10 • Acts 5:12–16 • Acts 9:32–35 •
> Acts 28:7–10 • 1 Corinthians 12:9, 28

S. Tongues. The gift of tongues is the special ability that God gives to certain members of the Body of Christ (a) to speak to God in a language they have never learned and/or (b) to receive and communicate an immediate message of God to His people through a divinely anointed utterance in a language they have never learned.

> Mark 16:17 • Acts 2:1–13 • Acts 10:44–46
> • Acts 19:1–7 • 1 Corinthians 12:10, 28 •
> 1 Corinthians 14:13–19

T. Interpretation of Tongues. The gift of interpretation is the special ability that God gives to certain members of the Body of Christ to make known in the vernacular the message of one who speaks in tongues.

> 1 Corinthians 12:10, 30 • 1 Corinthians 14:13
> • 1 Corinthians 14:26–28

U. Voluntary Poverty. The gift of voluntary poverty is the special ability that God gives to certain members of the Body of Christ to renounce material comfort and luxury and adopt a personal lifestyle equivalent to those living at the poverty level in a given society in order to serve God more effectively.

> Acts 2:44–45 • Acts 4:34–37 •
> 1 Corinthians 13:1–3 • 2 Corinthians 6:10 •
> 2 Corinthians 8:9

V. Celibacy. The gift of celibacy is the special ability that God gives to certain members of the Body of Christ to remain single and enjoy it; to be unmarried and not suffer undue sexual temptations.

> Matthew 19:10–12 • 1 Corinthians 7:7–8

W. Intercession. The gift of intercession is the special ability that God gives to certain members of the Body of Christ to pray for extended periods of time on a regular basis and see frequent and specific answers to their prayers, to a degree much greater than that which is expected of the average Christian.

> Luke 22:41–44 • Acts 12:12 • Colossians 1:9–12 • Colossians 4:12–13 • 1 Timothy 2:1–2 • James 5:14–16

X. **Deliverance.** The gift of deliverance is the special ability that God gives to certain members of the Body of Christ to cast out demons and evil spirits. (**Note:** This gift has also been referred to as the gift of exorcism; however, that term has been degraded due to its frequent use by those practicing occult exorcism, a counterfeit form of deliverance.)

> Matthew 12:22–32 • Luke 10:12–20 • Acts 8:5–8 • Acts 16:16–18

Y. **Service.** The gift of service—sometimes called the gift of volunteer—is the special ability that God gives to certain members of the Body of Christ to identify the unmet needs involved in a task related to God's work, and to make use of available resources to meet those needs and help accomplish the desired results. (**Note:** The gift of service may be confused with the gift of helps. See note on helps for clarification.)

> Acts 6:1–7 • Romans 12:7 • Galatians 6:2, 10 • 2 Timothy 1:16–18 • Titus 3:14

Z. **Apostle.** The gift of apostle is the special ability that God gives to certain members of the Body of Christ to assume and to exercise divinely imparted authority in order to establish the foundational government of an assigned sphere of ministry within the Church. An apostle hears from the Holy Spirit and sets things in order accordingly for the Church's health, growth, maturity and outreach. (**Note:** "Church" refers to the believers who gather weekly and also to the believers scattered in the workplace.)

> Luke 6:12–13 • 1 Corinthians 12:28 • Ephesians 2:20 • Ephesians 4:11–13

AA. **Leading Worship.** The gift of leading worship is the special ability that God gives to certain members of the Body of Christ to accurately discern the heart of God for a particular public worship service, to draw others into an intimate experience with God during the worship time and to allow the Holy Spirit to change directions and emphases as the service progresses.

> 1 Samuel 16:23 • 1 Chronicles 9:33 • 2 Chronicles 5:12–14

Step 4

Gifts and Ministries

1. Using the results of the Wagner-Modified Houts Scoring Sheet and the corresponding list of gifts on pages 9–12, enter below in the "Dominant" section your three highest-rated gifts. Then enter in the "Subordinate" section the next three highest-scoring gifts. This will give you a tentative evaluation of where your gifts may lie.

   Dominant: 1. _____

   2. _____

   3. _____

   Subordinate: 1. _____

   2. _____

   3. _____

2. What ministries are you *now* performing—formally or informally—in the Body of Christ?

   _____

   _____

   _____

   _____

   _____

3. Are there any of these ministries that you are not especially gifted for? If so, God may be calling you to consider changes.

   _____

   _____

   _____

   _____

4. Is your vocational status lay or clergy?

_____

5. In light of your gift cluster and vocational status, what are some ministry models or roles suitable for you? For what specific roles in the Body of Christ has God possibly gifted you?

_____
_____
_____
_____
_____
_____
_____

6. Discuss your findings with other believers who know you in order to evaluate your conclusions. Record their comments in the space provided.

_____
_____
_____
_____
_____
_____
_____
_____
_____
_____
_____
_____
_____
_____
_____
_____
_____
_____
_____

Editors' Introduction

Reconsidering Gender, Violence, and the State

As emerging feminist scholarship and queer-of-color critique make clear, archives contain surprising histories about gender, sexuality, and violence, stories that challenge axiomatic, gendered oppositions of power and vulnerability. More than simply repositories of untold stories, archives reproduce, obscure, engender, and distort histories of violent subjugation, conditional accommodation, and creative resistance. This issue of *Radical History Review* unearths and deconstructs such bodies of knowledge in order to reassess conflicting narratives of victimization, subjection, retaliation, and self-defense that arise under, coincide with, and partially constitute forms of state authority.

Events and developments over the last two centuries reveal complex histories of race, gender, and violence. Long-term trends, such as the expansion and dissolution of empires, the growth and subsequent mitigation of racial slavery, the rise of the carceral state, and the emergence of decolonization movements, as well as more contemporary issues, such as the torture and abuse at Abu Ghraib and the recent mass kidnapping of girls in Chibok, Nigeria, reveal the state's complex, evolving role as enforcer, perpetrator, and/or protector. These histories remind us that gendered violence and gendered understandings of violence are political and intersectional topics of lasting significance. Indeed, during the months that this issue of *Radical History Review* was in production, activist scholars in the United States created the African American Policy Forum and launched the "Say Her Name" campaign to incorporate black women's historical and contemporary experiences into the growing movement against the nation's militarized police forces and their concomitant forms of brutality. The intervention represented by this project represents a complex admixture of historical longevity and politicized evolution characteristic of all of these stories of gender, violence, and the state.

Radical History Review

Issue 126 (October 2016)   DOI 10.1215/01636545-3594359

© 2016 by MARHO: The Radical Historians' Organization, Inc.

We came to this issue of *Radical History Review* with a number of interrelated questions: How have historically shifting conceptions of masculinity and femininity informed the persistence of and punishments for gendered violence? What do the archives reveal about the larger structural factors that perpetuate and engender violence? How have feminist and queer organizing efforts to protect and/or avenge victims further complicated legal, penal, and legislative efforts to address gendered violence?

The questions owe an enormous debt to earlier scholarship about gender, violence, and the state. Judith Walkowitz's path-breaking analysis of the Contagious Diseases Acts in 1860s England, *Prostitution and Victorian Society* (1982), alerted scholars to the unintended consequences of state action and regulation of female sexuality, showcasing the state's penchant for overreach, the resulting incarceration of suspected prostitutes, and the license such laws gave to harassment of women in the public sphere. In the United States, efforts to curb domestic violence foundered on stereotypes of the inherent "brutishness" of working-class men in the late nineteenth century and focused disproportionately on bourgeois interventions of "uplift," to a large extent sidestepping the social and economic roots of violence. Simultaneously, African American women developed a powerful critique of white rape of black women, and of its counterpoint, the rape-lynching narrative that posited all black men as rapists. A growing body of scholarship on the history of the US carceral state makes clear that more complicated readings of gender, violence, and the state are critical to any reconsideration of the state's power to coerce and control through gendered violence and the proposed abolition of the prison-industrial complex.[1]

Meanwhile, scholars of empire, ethnicity, and postcolonial studies have generated new understandings of the ways in which gender, violence, and the state interact. Scholars engaging in queer-of-color critique have laid bare the connections between the expansive western (neo)liberal state and the concurrent acceptance of violent suppression of "others" as suspected terrorists, as noncitizens, as postcolonial subjects.[2] Building on the longer history and contemporary debates and conversations about feminism, its evolving critique of violence, and some of its blind spots, the goal of this issue is to reanimate conversations about gender, violence, resistance, victimization, and the role of the state as arbiter among these categories.

Five separate but complementary sections explore these questions from different angles. Three feature essays dig deep into the historical intertwining of gender, violence, and the state in three discrete time periods and settings. Three interventions on antiviolence activism and the state explore the sometimes conflicting individual, state, and community approaches to antiviolence work. The five compact articles in "Ways of Seeing and Knowing Violence" offer new findings and new interpretive insights into existing and future archives of violence. A visual essay questions the validity of photographic documentary "evidence" of state violence against its own citizens. Finally, the issue's Curated Spaces contribution showcases a creative new approach to the project of antiviolence documentation. Together, these varied perspectives, approaches, and methodologies sketch out new lines of inquiry and sites of intervention. They demonstrate what can be gained by approaching the archives with new eyes and probing previous assumptions in ways that challenge received wisdom and familiar historiographies. While in some cases the authors push the limits of what the archives reveal, they nevertheless insist that we reconsider the vexing intersections between gendered violence and state power.

The three feature articles collected here introduce the key themes explored throughout this issue. The articles in this section uncover the role of violence in the carceral and militarized state, and they examine moments when women enact violence upon others, placing these actions in the service of political or personal agendas. They also raise critical questions about the ways in which some forms of media have employed narratives about violence to create and shore up ideals of femininity, masculinity, family, and heteronormativity. Together they investigate the mutual constitution and/or imbrication of gender, violence, and the state, with an awareness of intersectional factors that connect the three categories. Further, each provides detailed analysis of a place in time and a highly specific context, while reconsidering broader themes about the interrelationships among gender, violence, and the state.

The violent treatment of female prisoners was both inherent and invisible to the early development of the penitentiary system in New York State, as Jen Manion reveals through a close reading of two notorious incidents of violence used against female prisoners in the early 1800s. During this time, the idea of a penitentiary was in transition from one of a nonviolent, reflective space designed to promote redemption through reflection and prayer to that of the more familiar and punitive model that infused the modern prison system. Protestant reformers, imbibing romanticism and the Second Great Awakening's emphasis on individual redemption through self-improvement and good works, advocated "punishment without violence," a regime that included solitude (at the time deemed a nonviolent treatment), silence, and prayer as a means of "humane" correction of criminals, particularly female ones. Very soon, however, both male guards and female wardens found rationales, in the "masculine" or nonsubmissive behaviors of their Irish and African American prisoners, for the imposition of violence as an essential tool for prison control. Sentimental notions of female delicacy, in other words, gave way to the infliction of ever-harsher punishments, even for women, at times meted out by (female) authorities who banded together to protect their professional standing and authority and prevent legal oversight for their actions. In this case, the state eschewed its own highly gendered regulations governing the administration of violent punishments for and by women.

In a very different setting, Tomoko Seto shows how, nearly a century later, police authorities used violent means to contain Japanese anarchist and socialist women protesting during the 1908 Red Flag Incident in late Meiji Japan. Dubbed "anarchist beauties" by the Japanese press, a few radical, nonconformist women dramatized their defiance of conventional feminine gender roles with unconventional clothing and hairstyles and with unfeminine speech and behavior on the street, asserting their visibility within the socialist/anarchist movement. Their accounts of violent abuse by the police, evident at the time and further detailed in court testimony months later, exposed numerous contradictions in popular and media perceptions (and prescriptions) about legitimate gender roles, specifically relating to political power, visibility in public, and/or legitimacy as mouthpieces of a radical ideology and socioeconomic critique. Ironically, state overreach in punishing (i.e., jailing) the radical women generated lively media commentary that—at least in the short term—expanded the reach and inflated the importance of the anarchist critique, in the process attracting young (male) students intrigued by the activities and descriptions of female radicals. The enthusiasm proved short-lived, however; in 1910, the state cracked down on political radicals after the High Treason Incident and imposed a traditional gender order that effectively suppressed the women's expressions of political radicalism.

Josh Cerretti's article on domestic militarism examines the engendering of violence from a late twentieth-century US perspective, tracing the US government's rationales for military intervention abroad and military-style suppression at home. Through strategic invocation of threats to women and children, he argues, the government introduced something akin to a "civic family," enforced by masculine warriors and sanctioned by the state. To document this "militarization of heterosexuality," Cerretti juxtaposes four geographically diverse events: the Gulf War in Iraq (1990–94); the Los Angeles riots (1992); the siege in Waco, Texas (1993); and the bombing of the federal building in Oklahoma City (1995). In each case, Cerretti tests how well the idea of state "protection" of the innocent and vulnerable offered political cover for military or quasi-military responses to threats foreign and domestic. So, US intervention to prevent Iraq's invasion of US ally Kuwait was framed as a necessary response to the sensational (but later discredited) news accounts of the "slaughter" of infants in a hospital ward in Kuwait, rather than as a strategic deployment to secure access to oil-rich territory in the Gulf. Similarly, military-style crackdowns against unrest in Los Angeles following the acquittal of police officers involved the Rodney King beating invoked protection of communities and restoration of order from lawless rioters rather than suppressing legitimate outrage against a questionable verdict. Likewise, the FBI justified its siege and attack on the Waco Branch Davidian compound with (later discredited) stories of child abuse. Cerretti reads these disparate cases together as evidence that the US state frequently employs the protection of women and children to deflect criticism of a variety of militaristic responses to complex conflicts both abroad and at home. The twin ideas—the warrior as protector, the "womenandchildren" as victims—he suggests, have disguised the rise of domestic militarism in the United States.

The three essays in the "Antiviolence Activism and the State" section ask us to reconsider the efficacy and/or legitimacy of state solutions to gendered violence in the US context. They differ in approach, analysis, and range of solutions posited over recent decades: self-protection, community organizing, and reexamination of opportunities lost in the state takeover of antiviolence intervention through punishment. For example, Catherine O. Jacquet explores a period in the early 1970s when some activist women, inspired by the militancy of the Black Panthers and other radical organizations of the time, embraced a philosophy of self-defense as a means to female empowerment. Frustrated by the lack of organized protest against sexual violence and rape, and disgusted by the state's well-documented failure to win prosecutions in individual cases, a few women's organizations advocated female self-defense as an alternative to state legislation or prosecution. They believed that, through acquisition of personal skills (e.g., martial arts training, marksmanship), women could develop autonomy and reject governing cultural logics that conflated female subjectivity and victimhood. Rhetorically, these movements posited personal militancy as one possible route to political and social equality.

The personal approach emerged, in part, as a reaction to failed state efforts to tackle gendered violence during the same period. As Raphael Ginsberg demonstrates, anti-domestic violence initiatives since the mid-1970s abandoned the original community-based, structural critique for a law-and-order approach of state punishment. A 1978 consultation of the US Civil Rights Commission, influenced by feminists and antibattering activists, identified the root cause of domestic violence firmly within the traditional, patriarchal family structure and the dearth of economic opportunities and support structures for women outside the home. Conservatives quickly rejected the report's recommendations for federal, state, and local funding for services (safe houses, job training, and housing support for domestic violence survivors), however, as antithetical to traditional family. They pushed instead for a criminal justice approach that focused on punishment of offenders, without consideration of the ability of survivors (typically women and children) to survive outside of marriage, creating an inherent conflict between the need for protection from physical violence and the need for economic survival. Recently, activists have challenged both the state interventions and punishment ethos that took root in the 1994 Violence Against Women Act, instead advocating for renewed attention to a societal, structural approach to domestic violence.

Other recent efforts to address structural inequality, however, threaten to resuscitate rather than avoid the heteronormative patriarchal ideal. Xhercis Méndez explores community activism as an alternative to state-sanctioned efforts to bolster the patriarchal family structure, this time with a primary focus on the African American community. President Barack Obama's My Brother's Keeper initiative, designed to provide training, counseling, and other support services for young African American men at risk, she notes, ironically revives the largely discredited patriarchal bias of the 1965 Moynihan Report. Critics at the time, and since, have questioned Daniel Patrick Moynihan's assumption of a "pathological" black family structure as a cause for poverty, low educational status, and crime. My Brother's Keeper's embrace of Moynihan's approach, its espousal of a version of individual "uplift" for African American men, does little to challenge the structural causes of inequality. Community-based organizations such as Black Lives Matter and social critics like Julieta Paredes, by contrast, see addressing these root causes—high rates of incarceration for African American men, underfunded and/or highly segregated public education, limited training and job opportunities, a lack of affordable housing, and so forth—as central to efforts to address poverty and unequal justice. Again, it is clear that the state's primary investment in the patriarchal family, and a simultaneous commitment to punishment—the carceral-industrial complex—diverts precious resources from positive infrastructure alternatives and contributes to the failures of modern US antiviolence policies.

The five case studies in the "Ways of Seeing and Knowing Violence" section explore surprising new findings and/or critical reinterpretations of older materials in the archive of violence and antiviolence work. By focusing on the archive as a site of knowledge production, these articles recognize its role in shaping current understandings of gender, violence, and the state and its lasting imprint on future quests for restitution or reconciliation. These authors highlight the importance of critical (re)evaluation of archives and archive building, demanding a full reconsideration of what rightfully belongs in the archive, what has been excluded or overlooked, and/or what can be read in a more critical light. In the process, they caution scholars of the inherent unreliability and instability of existing documentation of violence and the need for greater attention to and intentionality in their compilation.

Reading case files from colonial South Africa's Cape Colony in the early 1800s, for example, Carla Tsampiras brings to light stories of enslaved women resisting and/or "provoking" unsanctioned violence at the hands of their purportedly feminine women slave owners. In the 1820s and 1830s, a series of measures designed to "ameliorate" the Cape Colony's slavery system, emerging from London, officially lessened and finally outlawed violence against female slaves. The measures rested on a highly sentimentalized rationale of domesticity and femininity emerging in England and throughout the empire during this period. In the remote frontier town of Graaff-Reinet, however, such restrictions collided with more ambiguous gender norms. Local officials charged with upholding the new rules lamented the newly empowered slaves (the "stubborn, masculine women") who resisted slavery's subjection. Far from embracing the prescriptions of feminine docility emanating from the metropole, mistress and slave alike fought hard, both physically and in court, to exercise and/or resist slavery's violent control. Enslaved women took their mistresses to court under the new measures, often at great personal risk or hardship, so as to highlight the violence administered by female owners in violation of colonial regulations. Read alongside the new regulations, these cases suggest that, in this remote stock-raising region at least, there was a profound gulf between expected and actual behaviors relating to gender and violence.

Likewise, Deana Heath explores the disconnect in twentieth-century colonial India between prescribed and actual practices of gendered violence, through her discovery of an anomalous presence in the archive: the sexual assault of an Indian man documented in legal records that otherwise avoided explicit mention of male rape. In 1915, the rape (and subsequent death) of Rahmat Musalli, tortured at the hands of minor local officials, was downplayed and ignored by the British magistrate and again on appeal, and it entered the legal archive on second appeal only because the Punjab Chief Court questioned the ruling, thus preserving details of the torture for the historical record. Sexual violence against men was neither uncommon nor unknown (if unnamed) in the colonial setting; it was not imported from Britain, Heath argues, but rather emerged in the process of colonization and assertion of imperial control over India, mirroring the gendered violence in comparable colonial settings designed to turn colonized men and women into obedient colonial subjects. The logic of colonial gendered power relations made it virtually impossible to admit that sexual assault of Indian men occurred because, in the hierarchy of authority, male rape called into question the masculinity and virility of the British imperialist and thus could not be named. As desire was transformed into discipline, however, so acts of sexual violation could be dismissed as torture. Only an oppositional reading of the details of that torture at the time allowed this particular case of rape to be preserved for later discovery in the archive.

In their study of twentieth-century Ireland, Jennifer Yeager and Jonathan Culleton provide another way to challenge the distortions imposed by a partial and/or incomplete archive. The erasure from the national archives of the Irish "Magdalenes," or women confined in religious Magdalene Laundries for pregnancy or other sexual transgressions, they argue, fosters a kind of cultural amnesia about the violence the women endured. Testimonies from oral histories gathered in the Waterford Memories Project and elsewhere do more than challenge the official suppression of the laundries from official Irish histories. More important, the oral histories make evident how laundry survivors themselves have begun to insist on their inclusion in the archive; their importance to the process of national remembering, acknowledgment, and healing; and the value of undoing the silence around their economic exploitation and incarceration in the name of Irish family values. The women's oral histories detail and corroborate years of coercive violence against women, but also they demand that scholars handle official archival materials with caution; only a full accounting and recognition of the "work" done by the laundries will allow the nation to come to terms with its own history of oppression of women.

Jessie Kindig also proposes a more critical approach to the imperial archive, in this case through a close, contextualized visual analysis of souvenir snapshots taken by US servicemen in post–World War II Japan and Korea. Using a single collection of more than 120 Kodak instant snapshots, she analyzes their exposure of the "violent embrace" of the two occupied nations by US military power in general and US servicemen in particular. The images appear to show men with Asian "girlfriends," but attention to the wider context reveals "what is outside the snapshots' frame," thus enabling the viewer to see beyond the camera's coercive lens. Read against the high incidence of rape, the photos, and their hand-written captions about "good pieces," force a clearer understanding of the role of the US military in promoting and defending servicemen's (transactional and/or violent) access to Asian women and the efforts of Korean and Japanese women to resist violent sexual subjugation. This kind of reexamination of seemingly benign memorabilia in the archives makes it possible to retrieve the unstated and unmentioned sexual violence underlying the banal and chilling phrases like "rest and relaxation" or "rape and restitution." Further, it demands that scholars remain vigilant in decoding gendered power relationships during wartime, particularly when the archives contain such partial evidence.

The need for care in extracting evidence of gendered violence from the archive is also vividly evident in Benjamin N. Lawrance's analysis of contemporary African asylum narratives and claims. Writing as an expert witness and legal historian, he reflects on the power of mimesis as a narrative strategy, allowing asylum seekers to invoke a current threat—Boko Haram—to bolster their claims of past abuse and/or future jeopardy. Perusal of a personal collection of letters from asylum seekers and their lawyers reveals the growing insertion of Boko Haram into asylum cases, even those coming from regions lacking Boko Haram activity, or citing past harms that predate the organization's existence. Asylum seekers' use of mimetic devices to strengthen their claims portrays Africa in ways that conform seamlessly to western stereotypes about Africa. Meanwhile, media accounts of dramatic (and typically unsuccessful) asylum claims constitute a parallel popular archive in process of formation, one that further reproduces and embeds the Boko Haram mimesis within the context of other, unconnected fears (e.g., genital cutting). The very present reality of the Boko Haram threat becomes obscured, as it comes to stand in for a host of other, unrelated potential harms, even as claimants insert "evidence" of gendered violence into the archive in ways that pander to western fears.

The collection's visual essay deepens this questioning and reexamination of the archive of violence through the refabrication of discredited photographs of "false positives" that the military in Colombia used to document alleged rebel militancy. By questioning the reliability of photographic documentation, the drawings make visible a scandal in which young men were killed, put into uniform, and left in public spaces for civilians to "document" (for reward money) the military's successful campaign against rebels. As Claudia Salamanca points out, the hand-drawn reproductions (by artist Luis Morán) highlight the photographs' illegitimacy—their demonstrable falsity, in other words—thus establishing an alternative archive to a body of photographic "evidence" that may yet be redeployed to validate future military brutality. If the photographs transformed the typically marginal and often developmentally disabled boys and young men, enticed away from distant homes with promises of jobs and other enticements, into hypermasculine "warriors" replete with the gear and costumes of war, Morán's new, more obviously fictive archive of drawings allows future historians to displace the discredited photos, together with the military brutality they were meant to legitimate. By highlighting the staged quality of the photographed bodies, as well as the discrepancies, or "anomalies," within each image, both artist and author insist on a more capacious archive, one that inspires reflection and critique of unchecked state power.

The significant role of the visual in antiviolence work is evident in Efeoghene Igor's Curated Spaces essay, a powerful conception of what an alternative to the archive of violence might look like. In an exploration of a series of photographs by South African photographer Zanele Muholi, titled *Phases and Faces* (2006–14), Igor reveals the artistic, expressive, and political value of establishing a new archive of violence, resistance, and subjectivity, one that both problematizes and resists oppressive readings and suppressive "disappearing" of antilesbian violence in postapartheid South Africa. The photographs attest to the presence of lesbian women in South Africa, while hinting at a history of sexual violence largely ignored or unprosecuted by the state. Rather than reproducing pain, violence, and suffering, the photos detach the subjects from the national and local context, focusing instead on the faces, the subtle nuances of gaze and expression, as mute interrogators of viewers' failure to act, intervene, and/or protest. The portraits constitute a wholly new archive, one that emphasizes the subjectivity of the faces in the frame. Muholi's images and Igor's commentary remind us of the crucial importance of tending to the archive in process, building of bodies of evidence that truly acknowledge past injustices while gesturing toward a future of restitution and reconciliation.

Together, the histories, reflections, interventions, and imagery collected in this issue of *Radical History Review* reveal how gender and violence are mutually constituted categories of personal, political, cultural, and legal subjectivity. They further demonstrate how violence—and narratives of violence—have been used (and misused) to uphold, resist, or reshape the ordering structures of the state in a variety of national, geopolitical, and socioeconomic contexts. Finally, the pieces here challenge readers, viewers, and scholars to interrogate the archive as a site of knowledge and a body of sources, in order to construct a more accurate, and usable, past.

—Lisa Arellano, Erica L. Ball, and Amanda Frisken

Notes

1. See, for example, Judith Walkowitz, *Prostitution and Victorian Society: Women, Class, and the State* (New York: Cambridge University Press, 1982). On US antiviolence legislation, see Linda Gordon, *Heroes of Their Own Lives: The Politics and History of Family Violence—Boston, 1880–1960* (Champaign: University of Illinois Press, 2002); and Elizabeth Pleck, *Domestic Tyranny: The Making of American Social Policy against Family Violence from Colonial Times to the Present* (Champaign: University of Illinois Press, 2004). On antirape efforts of African American women from the 1890s, see, for example, Mia Bay, *To Tell the Truth Freely: The Life of Ida B. Wells* (New York: Hill and Wang, 2010); Gail Bederman, *Manliness and Civilization: A Cultural History of Gender and Race in the United States, 1880–1917* (Chicago: University of Chicago Press, 1996); Lisa Duggan, *Sapphic Slashers: Sex, Violence, and American Modernity* (Durham, NC: Duke University Press, 2000); and Rebecca M. McLennan, *The Crisis of Imprisonment: Protest, Politics, and the Making of the American Penal State, 1770–1941* (New York: Cambridge University Press, 2008). There is an abundant literature on the rise of the carceral state; for a few recent examples, see Michelle Alexander, *The New Jim Crow: Mass Incarceration in the Age of Colorblindness* (New York: New Press, 2012); and Talitha LeFlouria, *Chained in Silence: Black Women and Convict Labor in the New South* (Chapel Hill: University of North Carolina Press, 2015). On the new abolition movement, see Angela Y. Davis, *Abolition Democracy: Beyond Empire, Prisons, and Torture* (New York: Seven Stories, 2005).

2. See, for example, Chandan Reddy, *Freedom with Violence: Race, Sexuality, and the US State* (Durham, NC: Duke University Press, 2011); Jasbir Puar, *Terrorist Assemblages: Homonationalism in Queer Times* (Durham, NC: Duke University Press, 2007); and Christina B. Hanhardt, *Safe Space: Gay Neighborhood History and the Politics of Violence* (Durham, NC: Duke University Press, 2013).

Gendered Ideologies of Violence, Authority, and Racial Difference in New York State Penitentiaries, 1796–1844

Jen Manion

In January 1826 an Irish woman named Rachel Welch died in Auburn State Penitentiary, just one year into her three-year prison sentence for petty larceny.[1] Her death led to an investigation that exposed the chaos and violence characteristic of the early penitentiary. She became pregnant while serving time in what was supposed to be solitary confinement, and she was whipped by guards despite a legal prohibition on the flogging of women in prison.[2] The ordeal put the penitentiary on trial at a crucial moment in its history. Despite substantial evidence of abuse and mismanagement, investigators refused to conclude that Welch was a victim of wrongdoing. Rather, they relieved guards of responsibility and blamed Welch for disrupting the gendered and sexual order of the penitentiary.

A generation of reformers in the postrevolutionary period called for sympathy and reform for suffering and destitute prisoners. Thirty years into the great experiment in enlightened justice, there was a new subject in need of compassion: the white male prison keepers and guards who ran the penitentiaries.[3] One keeper reported that four women in prison made "more trouble" than the ninety-three men also under his charge. The same account also quoted the superintendent of New York's Auburn Prison, suggesting his predicament was even worse: "I have (says he) under my care, about four hundred and fifty male prisoners, and *nine* females; and I

Radical History Review
Issue 126 (October 2016)   DOI 10.1215/01636545-3594321
© 2016 by MARHO: The Radical Historians' Organization, Inc.

could cheerfully undertake the care of an *additional four hundred and fifty men* to be rid of the nine women."[4] These accounts circulated amid growing public debate over the purpose of punishment and harsh conditions faced by women in prison. The importance of addressing women's needs and rights in an institution chiefly designed for men was publicly mocked, while the white male guards gained public support and sympathy.

This essay examines the roots and legacy of violence against women in prison at the hands of guards and matrons during the first fifty years of the penitentiary in New York State. Though officially prohibited by law, whipping female inmates was practiced by numerous matrons and guards who were subject to formal investigations. While immigrant and black women were disproportionately victims of institutional violence, US-born white men and women dominated the staff.[5] News of violent encounters involving women generated voluminous and sensational headlines that outpaced coverage of the more pervasive and widespread violence against men. Coverage also raised questions about the merits of flogging, the discretion of guards, the competency of supervisors, and the rights of inmates. Two major incidents—one in 1826 and one in 1839—threatened to bring the system to its knees. Instead, investigators privileged guard discretion over law and authorized the expansion of the system. None of this happened without great conflict—internal to the prison and within the community at large—when inmates, guards, inspectors, reformers, and state officials squared off. The public debates over these two scandals helped establish broad support for state-sanctioned violence against prisoners—especially black and immigrant women and men, the central targets of the carceral state from the beginning.

In much of the voluminous scholarship on the origins of the penitentiary system, the particulars of racial hierarchies, gender roles, and sexual norms are deemed negligible in the quest to understand the expansion of state power. Important scholarship that establishes labor and profit as cornerstones of punishment in New York State, for instance, neglects the vital role of race and gender in shaping the institution.[6] Prisoners were compelled to work diligently and silently through force, coercion, and violence. Authority was asserted in a highly racialized and gendered way that reinforced white patriarchal supremacy, especially on the bodies of black women.

This essay contributes to a growing body of work by historians of race, gender, and sexuality who are rewriting this narrative. Estelle Freedman and Nicole Hahn Rafter first showed that women were subject to terrible neglect and abuse as tenants of the nation's first jails and penitentiaries. Many have looked to the work of female reformers and matrons who experimented with hard labor, redemptive suffering, phrenology, and domesticity in managing women in prison.[7] An imagined sisterhood among female inmates, matrons, and reformers, however, was never meant to be, as studies of African American women in prison reveal the persistence of racism in punishment. Racist ideologies defined to justify enslavement were later used to criminalize free blacks.[8] From early republican Pennsylvania through postbellum Georgia to Progressive Era New York, Chicago, and Philadelphia, black girls and women were disproportionately incarcerated and more harshly treated.[9] Research in the new fields of sexology and criminology were anchored in and also further promoted negative associations between African American women and masculinity, female masculinity and sexual deviance, and sexual deviance and criminality.[10] By examining the racial dimensions of the use of violence against women in prison during this formative period, we can better understand how racialized gender norms of patriarchal white supremacy structured the penitentiary, making the promise of American justice so elusive for black and immigrant women.

. . . . .

In the final decade of the eighteenth century and early years of the nineteenth, penitentiaries opened throughout the United States with a mission to reform criminals, abandon corporal punishment, and reduce reliance on capital punishment.[11] When statesmen, lawyers, judges, and reformers came together to devise a distinctly American form of punishment in the postrevolutionary period, the whole point was to eschew violence. Inspired by similar developments in neighboring Pennsylvania, New York revised its criminal law in 1796, called for the establishment of two state penitentiaries, and aspired to make punishment "proportioned to the different degrees of guilt."[12] This work was led by Quaker Thomas Eddy, who helped design and oversee Newgate Prison, opened in 1797 in Greenwich Village. Auburn Prison was later opened in 1818, organized around a system of congregate labor in silence by day and separate confinement by night. By 1823, the "Auburn Plan" was heralded as a model and adopted in numerous states throughout the country. This "success" inspired state officials to authorize construction of yet another prison. This new prison, opened at Mt. Pleasant in the town of Ossining in 1828, was built by prisoners themselves under strict supervision and threat of violence.[13]

Eddy, New York's leading prison reformer, was deeply engaged in the international debates among reformers and statesmen from across the United States and England. For Eddy, the key was to "govern" offenders through "kind treatment" and humanity while inculcating them with "industrious habits and moral sentiments."[14] The law stipulated that keepers were authorized to punish convicts only by putting them in solitary confinement—assumed to be a nonviolent punishment— and restricting their diet to bread and water. Even this punishment needed to be approved by two inspectors so as to prevent abuse and ensure that numerous reasonable people agreed to the proper length of the punishment.[15] The policy also stated explicitly, "No keeper or assistant-keeper is permitted to strike a prisoner." Punishment without violence would be the hallmark of democracy.

Eddy also served as Newgate's first agent and expected the keeper and his assistants to embrace their work "with a heart warmed by the feelings of benevo-lence" combined with an ability to be firm, resolute, dignified, and commanding.[16] Eddy offered an elaborate explanation of the particular way he wanted the keeper to punish inmates who broke the rules: "In the infliction of punishment, he should be calm and inflexible, without anger, so that he may convince the offender that he acts not from passion or vengeance, but from justice."[17] In fact, keepers and assistants were held to the highest standards of conduct, including refraining from "impropri-ety of speech and conduct" so they might serve as role models for inmates.[18] A spe-cial kind of person was needed to work in the prison, as the weight of the entire proj-ect of penal reform—and potentially the stability and order of the nation—would rest on the shoulders of the poorly paid white men (and later women) who would staff the prison. It was no secret that early reformers believed that "hard-hearted" keepers needed to be replaced with men of feeling who understood the sentimental project of prison reform.[19]

Even though guards were specifically prohibited from whipping inmates in the early decades, the system of oversight was still anchored in violence. One inmate was chosen to whip others into obedience—a disciplinary strategy commonly used against enslaved people. This "captain" served as the eyes and ears of the jailer. Elizabeth Munro Fisher, imprisoned for forgery and sentenced to five years in 1801, recounted that inspectors Thomas Eddy and John Murray "put the women prisoners under my command" during one of their visits.[20] Eddy confirmed this, stating, "One woman is appointed by the keeper to preserve order, and is styled the captain, and she exercised the whip on her fellow-prisoners at discretion."[21] Elizabeth, a white woman, would have overseen the thirty-five other women in prison at that time, including fifteen African American women.[22]

The formal ban on corporal punishment was overturned by a law passed on April 2, 1819, authorizing keepers to whip any prisoners who "shall refuse to comply with the rules of the institutions, or refuse to perform their daily task, or shall resist any of the officers of either of the prisons in their lawful authority, or shall willfully destroy any of the property." There were two conditions to the use of force: it was to be applied only to men and required the approval and presence of two inspec-tors.[23] This policy change coincided with a leadership change at Auburn. The new principal keeper was Elam Lynd, a military man who introduced stricter discipline. In June 1818 inmates rebelled against his changes, causing an uproar that required the military to quell. Over one hundred men were put in solitary confinement—an untenable situation.[24] Prison officials used the rebellion as evidence that greater use of force was needed to maintain control of the prison. Governor DeWitt Clinton wanted to build yet another prison more suitable for a "mild system of criminal jurisprudence," but the inspectors defended the wishes of their new keeper and prevailed in advocating for "a more *energetic* discipline."[25] The law granted consid-erable latitude for state-sanctioned violence against prisoners but left several questions unanswered, including how strictly the policy would be enforced and what consequences there would be for violations.[26]

. . . . .

The public responded to rumors of excessive flogging of inmates at Auburn Prison because it contradicted the promise of the penitential ideal: that punishment would be predictable, controlled, and rational—a counter to barbaric punishments of old Europe.[27] News that a woman had been flogged evoked even greater anger because it undermined the paternalistic vision of punishment. Anchored in Anglo-American republican family values, this view promised the largely immigrant, black, and poor white women prisoners protection from the white male state in exchange for embracing female domesticity, submission, and dependency.[28] Inspectors George Tibbits and Samuel M. Hopkins were ordered to lead the investigation of alleged prisoner abuse in 1826. In an investigation of unprecedented scope, they interviewed nearly seventy witnesses.[29] They found evidence of twenty-one instances of punishment "of a character to deserve investigation" in a nine-month span defined by the tenure of Mr. Goodell as chief agent of the prison. They concluded that eight of the cases were "justifiable and proper," while fourteen of the total were "severe," and four were "abusive and unjustifiable" (30). Even this degree of accountability was remarkable given the parameters of the investigation, as the investigators refused to hear the testimony of any convicts, stating, "We inflexibly overruled every attempt, to make use of the testimony of convicts; whether urged as testimony on oath, or as hearsay" (2). So even though the aggrieved victims were denied a voice, the violence committed against them was so great that other witnesses—chiefly prison staff with great incentive to protect each other and the state—testified on behalf of inmates.

Inspectors argued that it was for the public's own safety that the keepers resorted to violent means on so many different occasions. When an inmate named Rosenburgh "called out for liberty" in the dining hall, he was "struck down by a keeper." The inspectors chastised the citizens of Auburn who complained, and warned them that "if the prison had been broken, their houses, families and property" would have been destroyed (13). With each incident reported, the inspectors justified the actions of the guards in their report. After recounting horrific treatment of a man named Mastison, they suggested that people were naive to the real evil of prisoners who were cunning, manipulative, passionate, and the embodiment of "giant strength and demoniac fury" that must be properly disciplined and channeled (14–15). In this damning statement, the inspectors undermined the very principles of reformative incarceration that stood at the heart of the penitentiary project.

Only one of the twenty-one instances of abuse reported concerned violence against a woman, but the outstanding circumstances of the situation compelled the inspectors to dedicate twelve pages to recounting the details (19–30). In the middle of a vast report about a long line of abuses against men, they noted that the singular account of violence against a woman was "by far the most important" because it had considerable "influence upon the public feeling." Even without her direct testimony, reports of the treatment of Rachel Welch were indisputably terrible. Welch was born in Ireland. She sailed to Quebec in 1824. At some point she traveled to Rochester, New York, where she was convicted of larceny and sent to Auburn Prison on January 5, 1825, to serve her term. Welch was sentenced to a term of solitary confinement and became pregnant while living in isolation. Later, after she returned to the cell with other women, a turnkey punished her by "beating or whipping" her during her sixth or seventh month of pregnancy. She gave birth December 5, 1825, and died shortly after. Nothing is said about the fate of her child (4, 19).

Inspectors reported that the extraordinary circumstances of Welch's confinement were a result of the challenge faced by guards to find a proper space inside the prison for her term of solitary confinement. One testified, "For she must be kept in a room constantly warm, and yet without access to fire; and it is obvious that she must receive her food, and that some necessary offices about her room must be performed by men, or else women must be brought from a remote part of the prison to perform them" (19). Because women made up a minority of inmates, their presence challenged penal authorities, who could not figure out where to house them or how to treat them. Unable to enforce both the total isolation of Welch (per her sentence) and complete segregation from male inmates (per prison policy) they settled on cell 15, "a large room over keeper's hall" that also served as a storage space for "tools, cordate, lead," and other materials. According to testimony of the master carpenter, Samuel C. Dunham, this space was far from solitary but in fact functioned as a thoroughfare for keepers, turnkeys, and workers. He stated, "The turnkeys resorted to it often, for articles wanted; the deputy keeper passed through it often, to put away and take out convicts' clothes. I passed through it often for tools and other articles, and to repair the roof of the building." Despite this long list of workers who had unregulated access to the room, responsibility for getting Welch pregnant was laid on an inmate (137).

One of the inmates who worked as a cook was an Irish immigrant named John White who most commonly delivered Welch her meals. Several reports suggest that the guard charged with White's speedy entry and exit into Welch's quarters was not particularly vigilant, leaving ample time for the two to develop a relationship and also potentially have sex. Evidence that Rachel gave John a gift (a pair of knit suspenders with needlework that said "a gift of love from R.W. to J.W.") was used as proof that the two were intimate. The monogrammed suspenders carried tremendous weight in the testimony by suggesting that Rachel loved John. If this was the case, it was easier for authorities to assume that she consented to sexual intimacies with John rather than accept she may have been the victim of sexual assault by him, another inmate, or a guard. The interrogation into who had access to her room and why revealed numerous weaknesses in internal security and inconsistencies in prison policy (20).

Once the likely circumstances for Welch's pregnancy were established, questions turned to her beating and death. Accounts of Welch's aggressive behavior were recalled again and again to justify the actions of the keeper who beat her, Ebenezer B. Cobb. Welch was said to behave in a way of "outrageous passion, insult, and abuse, towards her keeper, accompanied with language in the highest degree provoking, profane, and indecent" (21). Cobb reported that others encouraged him to whip Welch, including Mr. Parks, the deputy keeper, as well as Dr. Tuttle and Dr. Bigelow. As Cobb's supervisor, Parks very well may have ordered him to whip her. His testimony showed he was unsympathetic toward Welch and actually held another woman responsible for the entire episode: Mrs. Goodell, wife of chief keeper Goodell. Hughes McCallen, a thirty-five-year-old contractor who worked at the prison for two years, testified to overhearing Mr. Parks complain, "Mrs. Goodell and her adopted daughter had been fussing about Rachel, bringing her tea and good things, which made her take airs, and caused all the difficulty" (115). Cobb had other excuses as well. Dr. Tuttle encouraged him to discipline her, stating, "Damn her, whip her, she is a troublesome, outrageous hussey; whip her," while Dr. Bigelow reported that Cobb asked him if "flogging would do her more good than medicine," to which he replied "in reality it might" (22). As if he needed another excuse, Cobb also contended that he did not know whipping women was prohibited by law (101).

There is no disputing that Cobb whipped Welch, only questions about the circumstances in which he did so, including which parts of her body he flogged, how hard he hit her, whether or not he drew blood, and if two black male prisoners pinned her down (she claimed they did; he claimed they did not) (23). Cobb reported that he used the two men as bodyguards for fear she might attack him. Welch's account of the encounter is recorded in the testimony of Dr. Tuttle, who reported, "She said she was held down by two big negroes, and whipped almost to death." Tuttle claimed this account was corroborated by Cobb himself, who confessed to that fact (24). This seemingly trivial point took on greater significance because the idea that a woman of European descent—even a poor unruly Irish immigrant—would be restrained by two black men signaled even further violation of the norms of racialized gender hierarchy that organized society.

Accounts from various keepers and doctors disputed the extent of Welch's injuries. The chaplain noticed that Welch seemed very sick and shortly decided "it proper to address her in some serious conversations" despite the fact that she generally laughed at him and lacked "female delicacy" (93–94). Her room was informally divided by "hanging up blankets" and shared by several other women, including an English girl named Betsy, an old Welsh woman named Elizabeth, and an old woman named Sarah who enjoyed talking with the chaplain. Dr. Tuttle reported her skin was broken in some places and "from her neck to below her shoulders, or towards the small of her back" was black and blue (25). Dr. Tuttle, the only one who seemed to support Welch and communicate her voice, was fired for his drinking shortly before the investigation. This fact was used to discredit his testimony (27). Dr. Bigelow blamed Welch herself for the injuries, stating, "I have no doubt she hurt herself as much or more by her struggles at the time, and raving and agitation afterwards, than the punishment hurt her" (26). He reported markings that were more contained and less dramatic. The inspectors concluded that the whipping did not cause her death.

Reports of Welch's flogging forced the public to reconsider violence against women by the state. The press was divided: some spoke of Welch's plight with passionate outrage and called for the firing of everyone involved, while others defended the right of guards to use violence in maintaining order. Use of corporal punishment for a whole host of subjects, from children and wives to those imprisoned or enslaved, was up for debate during the period.[30] Concern for the imprisoned and enslaved was part of a broader cultural shift in attitudes toward pain, including an awareness of the power of violence to elicit both excitement and revulsion.[31] Flogging was so tainted by its association with the brutality of slavery that prison officials increasingly felt the need to explain how judiciously and carefully it was administered. For those whose imaginations conjured up visions of bloody lacerations, the reports qualified that flogging was "never [administered] with such severity as to draw blood."[32] If slave floggings were brutal, irrational, and deadly, penal floggings would be fair, reasoned, and nondeadly. Just as abolitionists selected images of brutal violence for their antislavery tracts, those concerned about the excessive use of force in punishment turned to incidents of flogging to draw attention to prison management and state violence.

Men deeply invested in humanitarian reform efforts fiercely debated the ethics, utility, and consequences of corporal punishment inside the penitentiary. This was captured in numerous public exchanges between British and American reformers. Phrenologist Charles Cardwell entered into a debate between Philadelphia's Roberts Vaux and England's Edward Livingston to argue against lashing because of the effects that flogging had on the flogger, rather than the victim. Cardwell was unflinching in his view that this practice was terrible not only for penal authority but also for society at large. He wrote that flogging "tends to the extinguishment of all high, amiable, and honorable feelings in the hirelings who pursue it, almost as inevitably as in the convicts who are the subjects of it." To Cardwell, flogging represented humanity's basest animal instincts and pushed men farther away from the desired ideals of morality, virtue, and feeling.[33] While both state officials and reformers in Pennsylvania agreed with Cardwell's assertions, New York prison officials were not convinced that whipping inmates was the worst thing or that the cultivation of sentiment was a valued part of punishment.[34]

In concluding the investigation into Rachel Welch's death, the inspectors blamed neither the inmates nor the keepers but the project of reformative incarceration itself. This was a startling conclusion to a deeply disturbing investigation that was regularly reported in the press over a number of months. The inspectors decided that the attempt to make punishment less violent and more humane—and more appropriate for a modern democracy—was foolhardy. They blamed the chief keeper Mr. Goodell for being "too far infected by the feelings of those well meaning men in Europe and America, who, without actual acquaintance with the character of criminals, have framed theories grounded upon the good qualities of convicted felons." They chastised Goodell and Cobb not for breaking the law but for being too soft and naive.[35] Their inability to manage women prisoners was held up as even greater evidence of the failure of humane punishment. The idea that women were too much to handle and invited abuse, something widely promoted by inspectors, keepers, and doctors in Welch's case, prevailed.[36] This discrepancy between ideals of womanhood anchored in white middle class values—such as submission—and the behavior of actual women imprisoned created great anxiety and conflict for keepers and inspectors. It pushed Cobb to the brink, for if only Welch had obeyed him and submitted to his wishes, he would not have beaten her. Too many white men in authority believed in the unrestricted right of white men to expect total submission from women. Here we see an abandonment of the principles of reformative incarceration just as the movement began.[37]

In this single case, the optimism and hope that had defined prison management just a generation earlier was now replaced by a defensive cynicism that privileged the rights of keepers over other ideals such as humanitarianism. Though some states actively questioned the efficacy of corporal punishment, especially Pennsylvania, New York State commissioners reasserted "the power to administer prompt correction with the rod" was central to maintaining order.[38] But social order was violated by the very fact of imprisonment. Everyone understood that the idea of captivity as punishment was compelling only because of humanity's great desire for freedom.[39] The structure of carceral punishment was so unnatural and dehumanizing that it compelled human resistance. Enforcement of penal order required even greater violence to command total submission and obedience of its subjects. The belief that violence was the only way to maintain order in the penitentiary of the antebellum period was embraced to devastating and deadly ends.

. . . . .

Despite this turn, a group of reformers refused to abandon their effort to improve women's conditions in prison. They reported that the women in Auburn Prison were kept "in a large single room in the attic" with no ventilation. Over twenty women were crowded together in this room, "of all ages, colours, and crimes, without the means of discipline or useful employment." They recommended to Governor Clin-

ton the establishment of a distinct institution for women.[40] White female reformers, inspired by the famed Dorothea Dix, also joined the movement and argued
that matrons should oversee women instead of male guards. This idea was part of
a larger movement to embrace "separate spheres" for men and women, an ideology
that was anchored in distinctly racialized gender norms that marked white middle-
class women as fundamentally peaceful, virtuous, and maternal.[41]

Officials relented and invited women into prison management, with mixed
results. Reports of daily living conditions in the women's section were contradictory.
The chaplain from 1836 to 1839 claimed women did not have access to religious
services or reading lessons, while the matron claimed they received both.[42] Women
were fed a diet of bread and meat for breakfast and dinner that was sometimes sup-
plemented by potatoes, pea soup, or bean soup. Supper consisted of mush or bread
and tea.[43] The women were definitely put to work more consistently and rigorously
than previously. In 1839, of the forty-six women inmates, thirty-two labored on con-
tract "binding and trimming hats" or "stitching, closing, and binding boots," while
the others took up the domestic tasks of the prison, such as washing, hall work, and
making all of garments for both male and female inmates.[44] None of this did anything to stop the expansion of violence in punishment. The system of discipline and
authority ordered by the penal state would prove too great, violent, and debased for
even the most virtuous of matrons.

In January 1839, the state legislature debated whether they should inquire
about the accusations that prison punishments were cruel and unusual.[45] Alexander H. Wells, publisher of the *Hudson River Chronicle*, submitted a petition for a
committee "to inquire into the management of the Mount Pleasant State Prison."[46]
Numerous former male inmates who published pamphlets detailing their time in
New York's state penitentiaries cited many abuses throughout the 1830s.[47] The press
published rumors of abuses, including accusations that the agent profited from prisoners' labor, prisoners were starved, prisoner deaths were swept under the rug, and
vicious means of corporal punishment were used by the guards from "the scourging
of men with hot irons" to "the laying open of heads with three foot rules."[48] A law
passed in 1834 allowed for wider latitude on the part of keepers in punishment by
"stripes upon their naked back with the cat" for any convicts who "willfully or obsti-
nately" violated the rules of the prison. Certain parts of the body were off limits,
including "the head, face, or eyes," along with special consideration to general health
and limbs.[49] Articles calling for an investigation never challenged the need for prisons or punishment itself but emphasized the importance of consistency—that punishments be "fixed by law" and not left to the discretion of a keeper.[50] The investigation of Mount Pleasant began February 28, 1839.[51]

Once again, violence against women was a small fraction of the terrible
abuses levied against prisoners, but it merits particular attention because it was
committed chiefly by the female matron and her assistants—people hired explic-

itly to protect women from abuse. Numerous male guards were questioned about the behavior of the matron and the whipping of female inmates. Barton W. Powell, assistant keeper from December 1834 until May 1839, testified that he asked matron Isabella Bard how she kept order without flogging. He claimed she replied, "She could not get along without" the flog and that she did the flogging herself with either a rawhide or rattan.[52] Upon cross-examination, the counsel for the prison aimed to justify Bard's illegal action by establishing that she acted in self-defense of a black woman who was large, strong, and frightening. The prison counsel asked Powell, "Did she not tell you that the convict came at her with great violence to take hold of her, and that she caught up the instrument she used, and struck the convict in her defense?" and "Did she not say that the black woman was a large and strong person?"[53] Powell confirmed none of these things, leaving open the possibility that Mrs. Bard was lying. Most of the women incarcerated were convicted of larceny and were without histories of violence or violent tendencies. If they posed a threat to the matrons, it was likely their time in prison made them violent or threatening.[54]

Bard was no middle-class Protestant reformer. Born Isabella McNichol in Nova Scotia, Canada, in 1790, she married James Bard of Dublin, Ireland, in New York City in 1808.[55] Her husband died in 1828 at the age of thirty-seven, leaving her alone with seven children ranging in ages from three to nineteen. She kept a lodging house for "gentlemen" that served breakfast and tea for a number of years in New York City. Bard brought a libel case against a former tenant and ex-sheriff of London, who gave "her house and establishment a bad name" and declared her "a more worthless character." She won the case along with $6,500 in damages, no small sum.[56] The publicity also established Bard as a hardworking, astute, and respectable woman who was described in one account as "a widow lady of irreproachable character, and the mother of a large family."[57] She was hired as the matron because her son-in-law, Robert Wiltse, was the principal keeper at Sing Sing from 1830 to 1840, but she had proved herself more than capable. By the time scandal rocked the prison in 1839, it was no secret that management of the prison was a family affair. Wiltse married Bard's middle daughter Mary Romeyn Bard, and together they named their baby girl Isabella after her grandmother.[58] When the baby died at just fourteen months of age, a notice went out in the local paper inviting friends of the family to attend the funeral—at the prison.[59]

Robert Lent had worked at Sing Sing for nine years in various capacities, first as a carpenter and then as an assistant keeper in the stone shop, when he was called to testify before the committee.[60] He gave a detailed account of the violent abuse toward Jane Coffin, a black inmate, at the hands of assistant keeper Miss Green. Lent stated, "I saw a black female convict, tied up by her wrists to the gallery floor," at which point he went outside within earshot. He heard about a half dozen whips and returned to see "one of the female keepers standing by her, about a good striking distance from the convict, with a rattan in her hand, and I saw blood on the clothes of the convict on her back in two spots."[61] Not only did Lent provide a crucial eye-witness testimony for this graphic scene involving Miss Green, but he also verified the worst of it: Mrs. Bard, the head matron, not only authorized and witnessed Green's actions but also abused other women herself.[62]

If the testimony of the male keepers offered legitimacy to the complaints, the testimony of the women themselves, matron Isabella Bard and assistant matron Harriett Clark, provided powerful insights into the justification for violence.[63] Clark had worked at the prison since 1837 in several capacities, both as assistant matron and as instructor of women's work "in stitching and binding boots." When Mr. Wells questioned Clark, she admitted that she, Miss Green, and Mrs. Bard all punished female convicts by "tying them up merely." It should be noted that when women were tied up, it was often "in such a manner that their toes barely touched the floor."[64] When asked directly, "Did you ever see blows inflicted upon a female convict; and if so, by whom?" she replied, "I have, by Mrs. Bard and Miss Green, and I have myself." The questioning turned to the role of a male keeper, Courtland Lawrence, in punishing female convicts. Clark said he didn't really punish women but that the matrons called him to assist them in subduing another black woman named Sarah Rose Harris. Clark declared that Harris "rose upon us and declared she would kill us, and called for a large pair of scissors and declared she would stab us, both Mrs. Bard and myself" and that this is what occasioned them to reach out to Lawrence. Clark again contradicted herself when asked about the extent of Lawrence's violence against women. She said she never saw him kick or strike a woman but then detailed the violent encounter between him and Harris, stating, "I saw him strike at the same one I have mentioned, with a rattan he happened to have in his hand about a foot long." While the investigators sought to expose instances of violence against women, prison council used their cross-examination to justify use of violence, asking, "Was not Sarah Harris a strong, powerful woman?"

Isabella Bard was the matron of the women's prison for two years and was interviewed last. Bard testified to overseeing forty-six inmates, twenty of whom were African American. When asked, "What is the method of punishing the female convicts?" she replied, "I confine them in a dark cell, and sometimes tie them up." She stated whipping was only used for a three-month period of her tenure, at which point she "occasionally used a small rattan over all their clothes." Here Bard invoked a sense of maternal authority and feeling, suggesting she viewed inmates as part of her family in that she did not punish them any more severely than she did her own children. She maintained an exception, however, for black women, two of whom she said "now appear to be so refractory as to require punishment."[65] Maternal feelings had limits when the matrons were unable to pity or sympathize with their charges but rather retained a cold, fearful distance, as Bard did with the black women in her care.

Bard was asked about the beating of Jane Coffin by Miss Green that Robert

Lent described. She denied the beating and the blood but also sought to justify Coffin's punishment, saying "this black woman had been very abusive and insulting to her, and Miss Green reported her conduct to me." As days passed and Miss Green reported "she could stand it no longer," Bard claimed she "ordered Miss Green to tie her up, or have her tied up." Bard took the unusual position of claiming that even though she was very sure Green did not whip Coffin, even if she had, Bard was certain there would not have been blood.[66] Bard's denial saved her own career and showed that white women could rely on racist ideologies about black women as threatening to justify their own incompetence and violent behavior. Even though Bard tried to protect Miss Green with her testimony, Green was immediately fired. Rumors suggested Green was "too talkative" and shared secrets from behind the prison's walls too freely.[67]

The governor addressed the state senate about the contents of the report on April 16, 1839. He cited a long list of the most egregious abuses and condemned the entire situation. "If our system of imprisonment, with solitary dormitories and social labor, cannot be maintained without the constant infliction of such punishments as are disclosed by this report, it was established in error, and ought to be immediately abandoned."[68] Never were truer words spoken, had he stopped there. But the governor could not imagine an alternative and so proceeded to justify the extension and expansion of this disaster, concluding, "But such is not the case. . . . Equality and justice, kindness and gentleness, combined with firmness of temper, would, with very few exceptions, assure the cheerful obedience even of the tenants of our State Prisons." With this statement, the governor reasserted what Michel Foucault referred to as the "techno-politics of punishment"—the imperative that law must treat in a "humane" way the outlaw—the person who is "outside nature." This was not based on an idea of humanity that the law concedes in the outlaw but, rather, "a necessary regulation of the effects of power"—a power, in this case, strengthened by softening its public face and its enforcement.[69]

Coincidentally, just months after the findings were reported, New York opened the first women's prison in the country in June 1839. The new facility was first authorized in 1828 by Governor Clinton in the aftermath of the 1826 scandal that killed Rachel Welch. Women were ordered removed from the main jail and relocated to the women's prison, which would focus on the "softening and subduing" of the female inmates in a new, special environment.[70] Despite damning testimony aired during the interrogation, Isabella Bard was put in charge, creating a divided response. One news story declared Bard to be "a lady whose assiduous attention to the duties of her station, and successful employment and control of the wretched beings committed to her care, have elicited the most unqualified expressions of approbation and pleasure from all who have known them."[71] Her whiteness, along with her defense of the state, played an important role in her own promotion.[72] Other reports expressed outrage and disbelief that she remained in her position, stating, "It was proved that Mrs. Bard inflicted not only *cattings*, but *cainings*, upon female convicts, although the law expressly declares that female convicts shall not be struck or scourged."[73] They felt the inspectors went against public opinion in keeping her on.[74] In the grand scheme of the controversy, Bard was low-hanging fruit as the matron of the women's ward. The original investigation into prisoner abuse was stoked in 1838 by the Whig press in an attempt to overthrow the Democratic administration. The dismissal of Robert Wiltse satisfied most critics, as Wiltse would have been Bard's superior whose example she followed.[75]

It was also becoming clear that any system of imprisonment was too harsh and violent to be tamed. While Miss Green was dismissed, the justification of the future of punishment required the defense, protection, and ultimately promotion of Mrs. Bard, who was making $650 a year in 1841.[76] White women were increasingly hired as matrons in prison to care for the predominantly black and immigrant women imprisoned. The fact that they turned to violence themselves signaled betrayal for those who believed esteemed female matrons would provide council and a positive example for prisoners to emulate. The cult of white womanhood proved no match for the violent system of punishment that brought out the worst in everyone.[77] This dynamic was greatly shaped by slavery's legacy—a view that black women were strong, masculine, and a threat to white women. This legacy justified a great many abuses against black women in prison by white keepers, male and female.[78] The weight of this racist logic was so great that the newspaper trying to demand state accountability even neglected to report that one of the female victims was black in an attempt to gain more sympathy from a readership who might not see black women as vulnerable or innocent.[79]

Years later, a young assistant matron named Georgina Kirby captured some of the contradiction in white attitudes toward the plight of African Americans and the justice system in America. In one breath, she expressed outrage that black women were generally convicted to long sentences "on the flimsiest testimony," while in the next breath she described the black women inmates she worked with in overtly racist, animalistic, and even satanic terms: "They had the air of Amazons, with their dilated eyes and distended nostrils. When they threw their heads back with an impatient gesture, one almost expected them to paw the ground with their hoofs. Their eyes had the unreflecting character of the animal, indicating neither reason nor memory."[80] And so white women continued to dehumanize, vilify, and violate black women while boasting of their own benevolence in working as prison matrons.

The violence against black women that occurred under Bard's care and at the hands of her assistants, Clark and Green, was preserved in the historic record of the state senate but completely overlooked (or ignored) by white female reformers. The popular myth that women in New York prisons were never whipped was reasserted just a few years later and became etched in popular memory through the widely circulated words of the famed prison reformer Dorothea Dix. In her account of the treatment of women in Mount Pleasant, Dix celebrated the fact that "the lash is never used."[81] With the scandal erased from popular narrative, Dix and others like her could reassert white women as saviors of black and immigrant women in prison.

The plight of African American women in America's jails has been inhumane for a very long time.[82] Prisons in the postbellum South notoriously enacted multiple violences on their disproportionately black female inmates, much of this ill treatment justified using "preconceived ideas about black female promiscuity" that enabled abusers to blame the women themselves.[83] Violence is so common inside women's prisons in the United States that Amnesty International issued a report in 1999 citing a long list of human rights violations, from the denial of reproductive medical care and excessive use of restraints to sexual exploitation and humiliation in the name of security.[84] As we look back on an institution over two hundred years old, we can see a cycle of violence, outrage, and investigation repeat countless times, often resulting in a reassertion of punitive authority and an expansion of carceral reach. We wonder how a system named "justice" could continue to function as a source of injustice for so long. Prison abolitionists are challenging everyone to wake up—to see the fact that the system is *not* broken but, rather, is doing *exactly* what it was intended to do.[85]

Notes

Parts of this essay were first presented as a paper at the Organization of American Historians annual meeting in 2011. I am grateful for the remarks of the panel chair, Cornelia Dayton, as well as the comments made by those present, and the constructive feedback from the peer reviewers for the *Radical History Review*.

1. "(No. 1) List of Convicts Discharged from the State Prison, Auburn, by Expiration of Sentence, Death and Escape, from 1st January to 31st December, 1826," *Annual Report of the Inspectors of the State Prison at Auburn* (Albany, 1827).
2. "Appendix A, Report of the Commissioners, Directed by the Act of 17th April, 1826, to Visit the State Prison at Auburn. Made to the Senate, January 13, 1827," *Journal of the Senate of the State of New York at Their Fiftieth Session* (Albany, 1827), 19.
3. On suffering and redemption, see Karen Halttunen, "Humanitarianism and the Pornography of Pain in Anglo-American Culture," *American Historical Review* 100, no. 2 (1995): 303–34; and Jennifer Graber, *The Furnace of Affliction: Prison and Religion in Antebellum America* (Chapel Hill: University of North Carolina Press, 2011).
4. "Anecdote for the Ladies," *Bachelors' Journal*, July 3, 1828; *Socialist*, July 18, 1828.
5. For example, in 1827, fifteen of seventeen guards employed by Auburn State Penitentiary were described as "American born." "Appendix A," *Journal of the Senate*, 31.
6. Rebecca M. McLennan, *The Crisis of Imprisonment: Protest, Politics, and the Making of the American Penal State, 1770–1941* (New York: Cambridge University Press, 2008). McLennan challenges long-standing arguments that the prisons were not profitable, especially prior to the Civil War, but largely neglects race. Pennsylvania prisons were not profitable; see Mary Ellen Curtin, "State of the Art: The New Prison History," *Labor: Studies in Working-Class History of the Americas* 8, no. 3 (2011): 106–7. See also Michael

Meranze, *Laboratories of Virtue: Punishment, Revolution, and Authority in Philadelphia, 1760–1835* (Chapel Hill: University of North Carolina Press, 1996), 226–27; and Jen Manion, *Liberty's Prisoners: Carceral Culture in Early America* (Philadelphia: University of Pennsylvania Press, 2015), 33–47.

7.   Estelle Freedman, *Their Sisters' Keepers: Women's Prison Reform in America, 1830–1930* (Ann Arbor: University of Michigan Press, 1984); Nicole Rafter, *Partial Justice: Women, Prisons, and Social Control* (Boston: Northeastern University Press, 1985); Estelle Freedman, *Maternal Justice: Miriam Van Waters and the Female Reform Tradition* (Chicago: University of Chicago Press, 1996); Anne Butler, *Gendered Justice in the American West: Women Prisoners in Men's Penitentiaries* (Champaign: University of Illinois Press, 1997); L. Mara Dodge, *"Whores and Thieves of the Worst Kind": A Study of Women, Crime, and Prisons, 1835–2000* (DeKalb: Northern Illinois University Press, 2006); Susan Branson, *Dangerous to Know: Women, Crime, and Notoriety in the Early Republic* (Philadelphia: University of Pennsylvania Press, 2008).

8.   See Jeannine Marie DeLombard, *In the Shadow of the Gallows: Race, Crime, and American Civic Identity* (Philadelphia: University of Pennsylvania Press, 2012).

9.   Leslie Patrick-Stamp, "Numbers That Are Not New: African Americans in the Country's First Prison, 1790–1835," *Pennsylvania Magazine of History and Biography* 119, no. 1/2 (1995): 95–128; Kali Gross, *Colored Amazons: Crime, Violence, and Black Women in the City of Brotherly Love, 1880–1910* (Durham, NC: Duke University Press, 2006); Cheryl D. Hicks, *Talk with You Like a Woman: African American Women, Justice, and Reform in New York, 1890–1935* (Chapel Hill: University of North Carolina Press, 2010); Tera Agyepong, "Aberrant Sexualities and Racialised Masculinisation: Race, Gender and the Criminalisation of African American Girls at the Illinois Training School for Girls at Geneva, 1893–1945," *Gender and History* 25, no. 2 (2013): 270–93; Talitha LeFlouria, *Chained in Silence: Black Women and Convict Labor in the New South* (Chapel Hill: University of North Carolina Press, 2015).

10.   Lisa Duggan, *Sapphic Slashers: Sex, Violence, and American Modernity* (Durham, NC: Duke University Press, 2000); Cesare Lombroso, Geglielmo Ferrero, Nicole Hahn Rafter, and Mary Gibson, *Criminal Woman, the Prostitute, and the Normal Woman* (Durham, NC: Duke University Press, 2004); Regina Kunzel, *Criminal Intimacy: Prison and the Uneven History of Modern American Sexuality* (Chicago: University of Chicago Press, 2008); Kali Gross, "African American Women, Mass Incarceration, and the Politics of Reform," *Journal of American History* 102, no. 1 (2015): 25–33. Also see Kali N. Gross and Cheryl D. Hicks, eds., "Gendering the Carceral State: African American Women, History, and the Criminal Justice System," special issue, *Journal of African American History* 100, no. 3 (2015).

11.   There is an extensive literature on the transformation of punishment in early America. See David Rothman, *Discovery of the Asylum: Social Order and Disorder in the New Republic* (Boston: Little, Brown, 1971); Michael Ignatieff, *A Just Measure of Pain: The Penitentiary in the Industrial Revolution, 1750–1850* (New York: Pantheon, 1978); Michael S. Hindus, *Prison and Plantation: Crime, Justice, and Authority in Massachusetts and South Carolina, 1767–1878* (Chapel Hill: University of North Carolina Press, 1980); Meranze, *Laboratories of Virtue*; Mark Kann, *Punishment, Prisons, and Patriarchy: Liberty and Power in the Early American Republic* (New York: New York University Press, 2005); McLennan, *Crisis of Imprisonment*; and Michele Lise Tarter and Richard Bell, eds., *Buried Lives: Incarcerated in Early America* (Athens: University of Georgia Press, 2012).

12.   New York State, *Collection of Penal Laws and Laws Concerning the State Prison* (New York, 1799), 3.

13. Orlando F. Lewis, *The Development of American Prisons and Prison Customs 1776–1845* (Albany, NY, 1922), 109.

14. *A View of the New York State Prison in the City of New-York by a Member of the Institution* (New York, 1815), 15.

15. New York State, *Collection of Penal Laws*, 17.

16. Thomas Eddy, *An Account of the State Prison or Penitentiary House in the City of New York* (New York, 1801), 25–26.

17. Ibid., 26–27.

18. Ibid., 28.

19. In Philadelphia, inmates tried to exploit the gap between keepers and inspectors by instigating conflict between the two. See Jennifer Lawrence Janofsky, "'Hopelessly Hardened': The Complexities of Penitentiary Discipline at Pennsylvania's Eastern State Penitentiary," in Tarter and Bell, *Buried Lives*, 106–23. For more on class struggle, see Heather Ann Thompson, "Rethinking Working-Class Struggle through the Lens of the Carceral State: Toward a Labor History of Inmates and Guards," *Labor Studies in Working-Class History of the Americas* 8, no. 3 (2011): 26.

20. Elizabeth Munro Fisher, *Memoirs* (New York, 1810), 40–41.

21. Thomas Eddy, Peter Augustus Jay, John H. Hobart, and J Morton, "Report, December 26, 1809," *Theophilanthropist*, February 1, 1810.

22. "New York, March 9. Abstract of the Annual Account of Prisoners in the State Prison," *Gazette of the United States*, March 12, 1802. By 1817, there were nineteen white women and twenty-nine black women. "Annual Census," *Commercial Advertiser*, May 14, 1817.

23. "Appendix A," *Journal of the Senate*, 5.

24. Scott Christianson, *With Liberty for Some: Five Hundred Years of Imprisonment in America* (Boston: Northeastern University Press, 1998), 111–12.

25. "No. 120 in Senate, April 11, 1846, Report of the committee on State prisons, on petitions praying for a law abolishing the sue of the whip in our penitentiaries," *Documents of the Senate of the State of New York, Sixty-Ninth Session, 1846* 4 (Albany, 1846): 4–5.

26. "Appendix A," *Journal of the Senate*, 6–7.

27. Michael Meranze, "Penitential Ideal in Eighteenth-Century Philadelphia," *Pennsylvania Magazine of History and Biography* 108, no. 4 (1984): 419–50.

28. Manion, *Liberty's Prisoners*, chap. 2; Kann, *Punishment, Prisons, and Patriarchy*.

29. "Appendix A," *Journal of the Senate*, 4. Further cites to this work in this section appear in parentheses in text.

30. Myra C. Glenn, "Wife-Beating: The Darker Side of Victorian Domesticity," *Canadian Review of American Studies* 15, no. 1 (1984): 17–33; Kelly Birch and Thomas C. Buchanan, "The Penalty of a Tyrant's Law: Landscapes of Incarceration during the Second Slavery," *Slavery and Abolition* 34, no. 1 (2013): 22–38.

31. Halttunen, "Humanitarianism."

32. "Auburn State Prison," *Ohio Monitor*, June 2, 1830.

33. Charles Caldwell, *New Views of Penitentiary Discipline, and Moral Education and Reform* (Philadelphia, 1829), 4.

34. Graber, *Furnace of Affliction*, 107.

35. "Appendix A," *Journal of the Senate*, 30.

36. One way to deflect accountability among men is to hold "female victims responsible for their role in their own victimization"; see Nancy Berns, "Degendering the Problem and Gendering the Blame: Political Discourse on Women and Violence," *Gender and Society* 15, no. 2 (2001): 269.

37. In Rothman's *Discovery of the Asylum*, this movement had just begun. Michael Meranze shows the movement's origins in the revolutionary period in *Laboratories of Virtue*. Most studies look to the origins and expansion of reformative justice throughout the nineteenth century and consider its failings in the twentieth.

38. Pennsylvania reformers published extensively on the use of whipping and flogging. See *Pennsylvania Journal of Prison Discipline* 1 and 2 (1845 and 1846); and "Appendix A," *Journal of the Senate*, 8.

39. Benjamin Rush, *An Enquiry into the Effects of Public Punishments upon Criminals and upon Society. Read in the Society for Promoting Political Enquiries* (Philadelphia, 1787).

40. *Annual Report of the Inspectors of the Auburn State Prison: Made to the Senate, January 26, 1829* (Albany, 1829), 7.

41. "Separate spheres" ideology was highly raced and classed; see Carroll Smith-Rosenberg, "Female World of Love and Ritual," *Signs: Journal of Women in Culture and Society* 1, no. 1 (1975): 1–29; Nancy Cott, *Bonds of Womanhood: "Woman's Sphere" in New England, 1780–1835* (New Haven, CT: Yale University Press, 1977); and Jacqueline Jones, *Labor of Love, Labor of Sorrow: Black Women, Work, and the Family from Slavery to the Present* (New York: Basic Books, 1985).

42. "Testimony Taken by the Committee Appointed by the Senate to Investigate the Affairs of the Auburn and Mount Pleasant State Prison," *Documents of the Senate of the State of New York, Sixty-Third Session* 2, no. 48 (1840): 297.

43. Ibid., 296.

44. Ibid., 300.

45. "Legislature of New-York. In Senate-Thursday, Jan. 24," *Commercial Advertiser*, January 26, 1839.

46. "In Assembly—Jan 24," *Hudson River Chronicle*, February 5, 1839.

47. Graber, *Furnace of Affliction*, 113.

48. "Sing Sing, Feb 7, 1839," *Hudson River Chronicle*, February 12, 1839.

49. "Testimony," *Documents of the Senate*, 104.

50. "Sing-Sing State Prison."

51. "State Prison Investigation," *New York Spectator*, March 21, 1839.

52. "Testimony," *Documents of the Senate*, 148, 150.

53. Ibid., 152.

54. Nicole Hahn Rafter, "Prisons for Women, 1790–1980," *Crime and Justice* 5 (1983): 143.

55. Isabella Bard, 1860 and 1870 United States Federal Census, Village of Sing Sing, Town of Ossining, Westchester County, New York, Ancestry.com (December 8, 2015).

56. "United States Circuit Court New York Isabella Bard vs. Joseph W. Parkins," *Daily National Intelligencer*, April 16, 1833; "Slander," *Boston Commercial Gazette*, April 15, 1833.

57. "Slander," *Alexandria Gazette*, April 16, 1833.

58. George Hill Bottome, *An Unvested Sister: Recollections of Mary Wiltse* (New York, 1891).

59. "Died," *Hudson River Chronicle*, August 28, 1838.

60. "Testimony," *Documents of the Senate*, 176.

61. Ibid., 179.

62. Ibid., 181.

63. Ibid., 173–74.

64. W. David Lewis, "The Female Criminal and the Prisons of New York, 1825–1845," *New York History* 42, no. 3 (1961): 231.

65. "Testimony," *Documents of the Senate*, 299–301.

66. Ibid., 300.

67. "How Is This?," *Hudson River Chronicle*, March 19, 1839, and *Eason Gazette*, April 20, 1839.

68. "Sing-Sing State Prison. The Governor's Message to the Senate," *Albany Evening Journal*, April 26, 1839.

69. Michel Foucault, *Discipline and Punish: The Birth of the Prison* (New York: Vintage, 1995), 92.

70. "Female State Prison," *Commercial Advertiser*, June 24, 1839.

71. "Female State Prison," *New York Spectator*, June 27, 1839.

72. Black women with claims to respectability through marriage, employment, or faith often struggled to be seen as sympathetic figures in the face of state violence. See Hicks, *Talk with You like a Woman*, 73–80.

73. "We have received a long and well written communication," *Hudson River Chronicle*, November 17, 1840.

74. "Hon. Frederick A. Tallmadge," *Hudson River Chronicle*, February 16, 1841.

75. W. David Lewis, *From Newgate to Dannemore: The Rise of the Penitentiary in New York, 1796–1848* (Ithaca, NY: Cornell University Press, 1965), 204–9.

76. "Hon. Frederick A. Tallmadge."

77. Carroll Smith Rosenberg, "Beauty, the Beast, and the Militant Woman: A Case Study of Sex Roles and Social Stress in Jacksonian America," *American Quarterly* 23, no. 4 (1971): 562–84; Nancy A. Hewitt, "Taking the True Woman Hostage," *Journal of Women's History* 14, no. 1 (2002): 156–62; Stephanie Camp, "'Ar'n't I a Woman?': In the Vanguard of the History of Race and Sex in the United States," *Journal of Women's History* 19, no. 2 (2007): 146–50.

78. Hicks, *Talk with You like a Woman*, 66, 125–27.

79. "How Is This?," *Easton Gazette*, April 20, 1839.

80. Georgiana Bruce Kirby, *Years of Experience: An Autobiographical Narrative* (New York, 1887), 200–202.

81. Rafter, "Prisons for Women," 140.

82. See Angela Y. Davis, *The Meaning of Freedom and Other Difficult Dialogues* (San Francisco: City Lights Books, 2012); Beth Ritchie, *Arrested Justice: Black Women, Violence, and America's Prison Nation* (New York: New York University Press, 2012); and Jill A. McCorkel, *Breaking Women: Gender, Race, and the New Politics of Imprisonment* (New York: New York University Press, 2013).

83. Talitha LeFlouria, "'The Hand That Rocks the Cradle Cuts Cordwood': Exploring Black Women's Lives and Labor in Georgia's Convict Camps, 1865–1917," *Labor: Studies in Working-Class History of the Americas* 8, no. 3 (2011): 61; LeFlouria, *Chained in Silence*.

84. "'Not Part of My Sentence': Violations of the Human Rights of Women in Custody," Amnesty International, February 28, 1999, www.amnestyusa.org/node/57783; Michelle VanNatta, "Conceptualizing and Stopping State Sexual Violence against Incarcerated Women," *Social Justice* 37, no. 1 (2010–11): 27–52; Angela Y. Davis and Cassandra Shaylor, "Race, Gender, and the Prison Industrial Complex California and Beyond," *Meridians: Feminism, Race, Transnationalism* 2, no. 1 (2001): 1–25.

85. This argument has been popularized by the organization *Critical Resistance* (criticalresistance.org).

"Anarchist Beauties" in Late Meiji Japan

Media Narratives of Police Violence
in the Red Flag Incident

Tomoko Seto

On June 22, 1908, in Tokyo's Kanda area, fourteen socialists were arrested for carrying red flags with anarchist slogans and fighting with police officers in the street outside the Kinkikan meeting hall, where a socialist gathering had been held immediately prior to the arrests.[1] This, the so-called Red Flag Incident, is known today as the beginning of the severe persecution of radicals that later escalated into the 1910 High Treason Incident—the nationwide mass arrest of socialists and anarchists and the subsequent execution of twelve individuals for allegedly plotting to assassinate the Meiji emperor.[2] Immediately after the Red Flag Incident, however, a few major newspapers focused on four young female socialists among those arrested, dramatizing them as "anarchist beauties" who daringly brawled with policemen in the street.[3] Two months later, one article on their trial, titled "Full House, Sold-Out Trial," reported that four hundred spectators had filled the courtroom while another hundred had loitered in the hallway outside the door.[4] During the trial, new reports of their testimony about the severe police brutality highlighted both the women's own physical frailty and their righteous devotion to their political cause. Images of women fighting policemen in the street and dramatic accounts of police violence in the courtroom marked the Red Flag Incident as an unprecedented event, one that caught the attention of bystanders and the media and blurred the boundary between entertainment and politics.

Radical History Review

Issue 126 (October 2016)   DOI 10.1215/01636545-3594333

© 2016 by MARHO: The Radical Historians' Organization, Inc.

This article examines the Red Flag Incident as represented in popular newspapers, with a particular focus on the media's narrative appropriation of police violence inflicted on the female activists. Though the newspapers generally treated these women as criminals, the gendered popular media portrayal of the fight and the subsequent court trials at once helped disseminate these activists' dissident messages and advertise their political activities to a broad range of readers. These media narratives emerged as the result of an accidental entanglement of different assumptions and intentions unwittingly forged by journalists, male and female activists, state authorities, and spectators; no single agent can be identified as the sole instigator of the emergence of such ambiguous representations. By describing the battle between the police and the female socialists with curiosity and amazement, the newspapers became an accomplice to the broad dissemination of socialism. These narratives of police violence also eventually inspired the intensified state persecution of radicals and spurred the political engagement of women with the news media that began in the 1910s.

Historians of modern nation-states have studied the homogenizing functions inherent in newspaper media as one vital force reiterating norms regarding variables such as gender, class, and nationalism. As Lisa Duggan points out, modern cultural narratives, in particular popular newspapers, can profoundly devalue the political meaning of women's struggles and demands for change.[5] In the context of the late Meiji period (1868–1912), scholars of cultural studies in Japan have also discussed the print media's discriminatory nature, which reiterated the norms and boundaries of the imperial nation-state.[6] Indeed, the turbulent years following the media fever of the Russo-Japanese War (1904–5) against the background of the spread of literacy through compulsory education saw a flood of sensational news and scandals in newspapers, simultaneously entertaining and disciplining readers of all classes.[7] In this context, it is indeed possible to view the portrayal of these female socialists as an example of dominant narratives reducing their appearance to a joke and reinforcing gender ideology. As I will demonstrate, however, the end of the war with Russia also inspired the popular media to accuse the government of incompetence in dealing with the social inequalities caused by loss of family members and high taxes for war contributions. The advent of modern media gave rise to not simply a unidirectional dominance between those in power and those subject to power but a constant and contingent series of interactions and ideas involving different actors. Just as the American sporting press helped Victoria Woodhull bring "the idea of sexual hygiene activists into the commercial public sphere" in the late nineteenth century, media coverage of the arrested female anarchists made overtly dissident activists visible in the eyes of the public.[8]

Historians of modern Japan generally examine the Red Flag Incident and police violence within the history of Japanese socialism using police sources and male activists' own accounts. Such studies have often ignored the female activists and have instead stressed police persecution and the unusually harsh sentences given to male leaders.[9] Scholars of women's history in Japan have traced the socialist women's activities and writings to identify them as the "pioneering" feminists but have also overlooked their media portrayal in the Red Flag Incident, presumably judging that it was mere gossip constructed by male writers.[10] Assuming that the movement was mostly limited to a circle of elite activists and their sympathizers, these studies have paid little attention to the popular media narratives in the context of largely shared resentment toward the police, which greatly affected the tone of the news reports. In sum, in treating the popular media as either a disciplining apparatus or gossip entertainment, scholars of both cultural studies and activist history in modern Japan have failed readers.

Popular newspaper depictions of the Red Flag Incident demonstrate that the media did not merely depoliticize the female activists but in fact simultaneously dramatized them and spread their politics, regardless of reporters' intentions. These representations also help us understand perceptions of activism in general—activism that provided one option for late Meiji people to protest against violent authority. By studying the political potential of these seemingly apolitical popular media portrayals, I also challenge the general hierarchical assumption of what counts as "political" content—empirical facts primarily involving famous male activists and "serious" essays written by activists themselves. When assessing the significance of activism, popular media representations of female activists have rarely been included in the realm of the political. But the media plays a role beyond that of a disciplining apparatus, and its widespread influence might inspire collective action. In what follows, I first discuss media depictions of the incident focusing on the female socialists, then analyze the socialists' responses in their own publications, and finally explore the popular media reports on police brutality described in the testimony of the female activists during their trials.

The "Anarchist Beauties" versus Policemen

The Red Flag Incident took place immediately after an "out-of-jail" celebration party at the Kinkikan meeting hall for the socialist activist Yamaguchi Koken (1883–1920).[11] During Yamaguchi's jail term in 1907, an internal conflict had divided leading socialists into the "law-abiding" faction and the "direct-action" faction, led by the radical intellectual Kōtoku Shūsui (1871–1911), which favored syndicalism. From that point on, the debates between the two factions intensified, and police persecution of the direct-action activists became severe. Because Yamaguchi had missed the internal conflict while serving his sentence, his return from jail brought both factions together and resulted in a relatively large socialist gathering. When the attendees dispersed in the late afternoon, some of the direct-action activists left the venue singing revolutionary songs and raising red flags that read "Anarcho-Communism" and "Communism." Policemen at once rushed to stop them, causing a large-scale fight and instantly attracting a crowd of bystanders along the bustling street of Kanda.

Most of the activists who were arrested in the incident had been involved with the socialist press Heiminsha (Commoners' Society, 1903–5), including one of its cofounders, Sakai Toshihiko (1871–1933). Today, the Heiminsha is widely known as the most notable pacifist group opposing the Russo-Japanese War and as Japan's first large-scale nationwide network of socialists advocating equality, socialism, and pacifism.[12] Though the government forced the group's dissolution in 1905 before the end of the war, leading Heiminsha personnel organized the Japan Socialist Party (1906–7) and continued to engage in political activities.

Since their introduction from the West to Japan in the 1890s, the ideas that contemporaries referred to as socialism included various theories, such as Marxism, so-called utopian socialisms, Christian pacifism, syndicalism, and Russian anarchist-style terrorism. Because those who openly identified themselves as socialists likewise held eclectic visions from which they critiqued capitalism and imperialism, socialism in the period can better be described with reference to "socialistic activities and thoughts." Though the term requires detailed contextualization, the media and the police alike at the time of the Red Flag incident usually used *socialist* to refer to an activist involved with the Heiminsha and its successor organizations, and *anarchist* for a member of the direct-action faction. Hereafter I will use the term *socialists* and *anarchists* as the media depicted these activists and as they called themselves.

Initially, journalists' reactions to the Red Flag Incident differed greatly; some depicted those involved as insane and immoral criminals, while others represented them as eccentric yet innocent activists miserably taken into custody by the police. Most notably, newspapers reported on the presence of female socialists, mainly because these women had directly fought the policemen while agitating their male counterparts and the surrounding crowd.[13] Earlier, newspapers had frequently covered street battles between male socialists and policemen due to the proliferation of their activities, ultimately challenging imperialism. Since male socialist leaders had also worked as writers for the major press and published books on political theories and social criticism, they had often appeared in the media as intellectual critics, at times supporting the reformist opinions of major newspapers' editorial writers. In the Red Flag Incident, however, the female socialists unexpectedly entered a scene hitherto dominated by men. Still, these women emerged in the media not as intellectual activists but as astonishing agitators. Images of women's active participation in the street fight were, regardless of their accuracy, newsworthy, and the press used such stories to attract readers.

The most notable initial coverage of the female socialists appeared in the widely circulated *Kokumin shimbun* (*National News*), a newspaper that had been pro-government until the end of the war with Russia but had increasingly turned "vulgar" afterward.[14] Under the headline "A Beauty's Anarchist Speech," *Kokumin* reported the incident using almost one-third of a page in the gossip section.[15] From the tumultuous crowd, according to the article, there emerged

[a] beauty in a purple *hakama* skirt with slight makeup and *hisashi gami* hairdo [a low pompadour style typical for female students], screaming out loud, "Everyone, what a tyranny by policemen!" She grabbed the red flag of anarchism from a man next to her, raised it high, and attempted to attack the policemen while vigorously inculcating anarchism. As she cried out, "True faith," "Revolution," and "Coup d'état," the already excited crowd increasingly behaved suspiciously. . . .

   The big brawl between the socialists and the police lasted about one hour. The beauty with *hisashi gami* hair and three other women resisted most strongly, with their sleeves rolled up unlike women.[16]

The article dramatically depicted the initial appearance of the "beauty," whose outfit implies a female student of higher education. Beginning in the mid-1900s, media images of promiscuous female students were pervasive as objects of erotic curiosity and scorn. Newspapers frequently reported about female students seducing their male counterparts, and novels portrayed female students with mysteriousness or silence in emergent public spaces such as commuter trains and parks in their distinctive clothes and hairstyle.[17] In print media, their appearance acted as a social marker that depicted female students as an anonymous collective without individuality, linking the icon of "anarchist beauty" with the more familiar image of the female student.

   At first glance, the "beauty" implies a temptress quality because she dramatically emerged from a crowd of male socialists. In the *Kokumin* article, however, she confounded readers' expectations by being far more articulate and active than the stereotypical female students in the media. In contradiction to the conventional view of women as bystanders or followers of men, the "beauty" was the one who instigated the quarrel that ended in a fight with the police. Because the 1900 Public Peace Police Law prohibited women's participation in any political event or group, the presence of women in such an overtly political scene likely seemed unprecedented.[18] By contrast, the press generally depicted their male counterparts as rogues fighting against the police and Sakai as an older leader attempting to stop them. In this and other articles describing the Red Flag Incident, it was the "beauties" who engaged in agitating speech and dramatically played a heroic role.

   Popular media depictions of women in the Red Flag Incident stressed both the fear and exotic allure of revolution brought by the "beauties," which could help recruit ordinary men. *Tokyo Asahi shimbun*, another major newspaper, sensationalized the story with a headline reading, "Russification of Japan: Big Fight in Front of Kinkikan; Anarchists Were Arrested; . . . Among Them Were Young Beauties."[19] The report highlighted both the active participation and danger of the "beauty":

Future Dangerous Figure: . . . one of these young beauties is Sugawara Tomoko (age 18), who is currently staying at Mr. Sakai Toshihiko's. She has considered Joan of Arc as her ideal figure and been determined to cause a commotion once there is an opportunity. Needless to say, she is a dangerous figure of the future but astonished gawkers by her unflinching courage based on her self-confidence. One student said, "Japan is gradually becoming like Russia. There will be trouble if more women like her come out." From the rooftop of the nearby schools, [male] students with a twinkle in their eyes saw them [the activists] off to the police station.[20]

The reporter piqued readers' curiosity by indicating the mysteriousness and delinquency of the "beauty" Sugawara, who was likely being confused with Kogure Reiko (1890–1977), Sakai's live-in protégée.[21] This article is one piece of evidence briefly analyzed in literary scholar Naitō Chizuko's study of the media depictions of female activists as a "danger" to the nation-state.[22] As shown by the mention of Sugawara's "unflinching courage" and the students "with a twinkle in their eyes" (Naitō omits these sentences), this report showcased both the woman's serious engagement in the dissident cause and its impression on the male students. The article sensed the "future danger" not simply against the state and gender propriety but also as a means to spread the dissident movement among young men inspired by the valiant "beauty."

The article's reference to Russia also suggests both the perceived danger and heroism of anarchist activity. Since the Freedom and Popular Rights Movement in the 1880s, which had demanded the promulgation of the constitution and the opening of a parliament, political novels and newspapers had typically associated Russian anarchism with assassinations by bombing, particularly at the hands of heroic female anarchists such as Sophia Perovskaya (1853–81).[23] News of the 1905 Russian Revolution and the Bloody Sunday Massacre had not completely faded away by this time, either. Images of anarchists as mysterious figures had reached the realm of popular imagination, as evidenced by an adventure novel published in 1908 that featured an anarchist youth as a righteous outlaw.[24] Linked in popular imagination to their Russian counterparts, the female anarchists' involvement with this event magnified the fear of possible terrorist actions, which could attract the public. The message in this article invoked multiple interpretations: for some readers it was part of the ideological apparatus showing a counterexample, while for others, like the students depicted in the report, it was a spectacular inspiration to be enjoyed and potentially joined as a protest against police violence. It is the latter possibility that the reporter feared as a "danger," because it was not too unrealistic for contemporaries; many male Tokyoites had participated in street fights with policemen during popular protests that had become increasingly common in the city since the 1905 Hibiya Riot.

When covering the Hibiya Riot, many journalists in Tokyo had been particularly critical of police violence. The riot started as a "national rally" on September 5 organized by dissident journalists and politicians, who demanded that the foreign minister more firmly negotiate for the war indemnities from Russia at the conclusion of the Portsmouth Peace Treaty of 1905. The massive crowd at the rally against the treaty took to the streets and rioted throughout the city for three days. During the riot, policemen thrashed rioters with swords, killing seventeen and injuring an additional 528 people.[25] Because the leading opponents of the peace treaty included reporters from major newspapers, the media coverage of police violence against rioting citizens was particularly gruesome and furious.[26] The subsequent government orders temporarily banning the publication of various Tokyo newspapers, including the ones discussed here, further enraged journalists. Immediately after resuming publication, reporters harshly criticized police brutality, and some even organized themselves along with like-minded politicians to propose abolition of the Tokyo Metropolitan Police Department to the Lower House.[27] Against this background of the lingering tension between police and journalists, the Red Flag Incident provided many reporters with another opportunity to use police brutality as a means to criticize the police and, by extension, the Meiji government.

In contrast to the ambivalence expressed in *Kokumin* and *Asahi*, coverage of the Red Flag Incident in *Tokyo Niroku shimbun* sympathized with the male and female socialists as victims of police persecution. Its overt support is perhaps due to the fact that *Niroku* presented itself as a worker- and union-friendly newspaper and employed a Heiminsha socialist as a reporter. As in the other newspapers, its report highlighted the appearance of the female socialists with the headline "Brave Fight of Beauties," stating that they attracted bystanders and implying that it was their alluring beauty that gained their sympathy.[28] Still, these gendered expressions also highlighted the female activists' passionate devotion to their cause. The report continued:

Kicking down a woman: [During the fight] policemen cruelly molested the two women. One of them, some Sugawara, had attended the party despite her illness. [From Kinkikan] she walked toward the nearby Foreign Language College with her comrade and encountered the commotion. As she watched with sympathy, a policeman said, "How dare you, you are just a women. You must be one of them." Immediately, a few policemen sought to capture her. As she resisted, one of them suddenly kicked her down with his shoes.[29]

Similar to those in other newspapers, this report described the woman as resisting the violent policemen. *Niroku's* clear emphasis on police brutality is evident in its reference to "some" Sugawara, likely referring to Kanno Sugako (1881–1911), who was ultimately shown as a frail and innocent activist. By contrast, the report described male activists with concrete names and titles while still provoking the readers' sympathy: Ōsugi Sakae (1885–1923), an "anarchist who is famous as a French scholar and Esperantist . . . repeatedly screamed, 'Long live anarchism,' even as he was being dragged [by the police]."[30]

Niroku also highlighted spectators' participation in the event:

The anarchists firmly held the red flags, but the mighty several dozen
policemen with all their strength forcefully tried to grab the flags. . . . As they
fought, gawkers . . . crowded around like an army of ants and cheered the
anarchists by screaming, "Beat 'em down," "Punch them," and "Don't let the
flags go." As the situation was about to turn into a big event, the policemen who
had grabbed the flags dragged the anarchists in the middle of the grand street
toward the police station. From the crowd, there were many who rushed like a
landslide to help the anarchists.[31]

Unlike the other examples, in this account the spectators emerged as active participants who verbalized their support for the unfairly abused anarchists. The article also mentioned that a few among the crowd assaulted the policemen in an attempt to rescue the activists. According to this report, the socialists themselves were far from belligerent, justifying the spectators' participation in attacking the police to protect them. This participation by the spectators encouraged readers to imagine the event as if it were a theatrical drama. Audience participation in theater and other public events was common among local *shitamachi* ("Low City") residents in Tokyo, or at least the *Niroku* reporter likely imagined this to be so.[32] The reporter's perception of engaged spectators was likely based on the neighborhood of his office in Kanda, one of the central towns of the Shitamachi area of Tokyo typically imagined as the birthplace of "Edo natives" (Edokko), who enjoyed "fires and fights," in commonly used expressions.

Most of the arrested male and female socialists had previously engaged in street demonstrations accompanied by musical instruments and street fights with policemen, particularly in the neighborhood of the socialist headquarters in Shitamachi. On such occasions, a large part of the audience were their immediate neighbors, whose daily lives had been associated with the performing arts and audience participation. The socialists themselves were also aware of the advertising effect of a brawl with the police, as indicated by a 1904 report in the Heiminsha's organ alluding to a speech meeting that was violently terminated by the police, which "turned out to advertise" the next speech meeting, which drew even more spectators.[33] The severity of the police persecution from which the activists suffered cannot be denied, but we also should not ignore the local cultural practices that led to an appreciation of theatrical violence against authority. Likewise, the media's emphasis on the devotion of the "anarchist beauties" to their political cause and their struggle against the police helped maintain the political nature of the incident, potentially fascinating and inspiring readers.

Responses from Socialists

The two socialist factions reacted differently in response to media depictions of the incident. The law-abiding faction defended the arrested men and women of the direct-action faction. By then, the two factions had often quarreled between themselves. However, the law-abiding faction's magazine, *Tokyo Shakai shimbun (Tokyo Social News)*, was one of the only surviving socialist magazines based in Tokyo due to increased state censorship following the 1907 miners' riots in the Ashio Copper Mine, after which the sympathetic *Nikkan (Daily) Heimin shimbun*, the successor of *Shūkan (Weekly) Heimin shimbun*, had been banned. Thus, accounts of the Red Flag Incident in *Social News* did not demonstrate outright hostility toward the arrested activists but rather called for support from their comrades. Claiming "ordinary newspapers' reports [on the Incident] are inaccurate in many cases," *Social News* provided a purportedly accurate report of the incident, which was considerably less dramatic than the newspapers had reported.[34]

By contrast, in *Kumamoto Hyōron (Kumamoto Review)*, in a Kyūshū-based socialist magazine close to the direct-action faction, Takeuchi Zensaku reported that the incident had erupted like a flare-up of urban warfare against the state.[35] The report emphasized the spread of street battle and the courage of the activists, saying, "[The] bourgeoisie was astonished, and the capitalist government was frightened."[36] It also praised the newspapers' accuracy and extensive coverage. Further, in the same issue, Sakamoto Kassui emotionally recounted, "I was surprised and shed tears. But my eyes are filled with the light of hope. This is 'the rebellion of [June] 22nd,' the 'first step toward the revolution.'"[37] Neither Takeuchi nor Sakamoto, however, discussed the female activists besides their names. These sympathetic writers highlighted the male anarchists' "revolutionary" fight as the primary feature of the incident, without detailing the involvement of their female counterparts.

Kumamoto Review further suggested the gendered division within the anarchist faction by emphasizing the anarchist "rebellion" as a masculine act. It also featured comments by Sakai Tameko (1872–1959) and Ōsugi Yasuko (1883–1924), the wives of arrested Sakai Toshihiko and Ōsugi Sakae, respectively. In these comments, Sakai Tameko was presented as a responsible and supportive wife, and Ōsugi Yasuko showed her concern for Kanno Sugako, who was incarcerated in a ward for the sick.[38] The voices of these wives as caretakers and kind comrades reinforced the image of a masculine revolution, emphasizing the virtuousness of female socialists in contrast to the publicized militancy of their male counterparts while reducing the women's role in activism to that of subordination.

Presumably drawing from these and other depictions in socialist publications, historian Vera Mackie assumes that female socialists at this point were primarily limited to roles as "supporters of male activists."[39] After the war with Russia, however, some female activists drew upon socialism as a source of inspiration for their own political engagement. For example, one of the women arrested in the Red Flag Incident, Kamikawa Matsuko (1885–1936), stated her enthusiasm about active engagement with the revolutionary cause, at least at a figurative level. In the issue of *Kumamoto Review* published immediately before the incident, she wrote, "Be loyal to revolution even if you have no friend. Be enthusiastic about revolution even if you have no comrade. Be devout for revolution even if you have no mentor."[40] A student of Russian literature, Kamikawa frequently contributed her poems and essays to socialist magazines.[41] The other arrested women, in particular Kanno, had also written for socialist magazines to express their opinions about activism.

By the time of the Red Flag Incident, female socialists had engaged in a variety of political activities using their own skills and creating their own networks. They had attended and organized women's meetings at the Heiminsha headquarters, taken part in the protest against Tokyo's streetcar fare hike in 1906, and edited socialist magazines catering to women, such as *Sekai Fujin* (*Women of the World*) and *Katei Zasshi* (*Home Magazine*). They engaged in the movement along with their male counterparts while articulating problems relevant to women through writing, public speaking, and networking. Still, the number of female activists was small, and precisely because of their minority status in the socialist movement, their involvement in the Red Flag Incident was novel and notable in the eyes of many newspaper reporters.

Trials of the Red Flag Incident

In August 1908, two months after the Red Flag Incident, newspapers heatedly reported on the court trials of those who had been arrested and relayed the female activists' testimonies of police violence as a form of entertainment. Here, the courtroom emerged as a theater in which socialists performed dramatic roles supported by the policemen and judges, surrounded by curious audience members, including the reporters themselves. The female activists' speeches and actions clearly enlisted the curiosity of some journalists, and the women used these opportunities to further their political agendas, specifically regarding the legitimacy of their actions for gender equality. Journalists' coverage revealed multiple meanings and usages of the symbolic "woman," reflecting different intentions and interpretations. In her study of gendered media, Naitō Chizuko discusses newspaper reports of the Red Flag Incident and the negative depictions of the arrested women as infused with discriminatory language and suggestions of illness, promiscuity, and assassination.[42] Naitō, however, fails to fully examine the dynamics of these contradictions and their meanings. In the newspapers covering the incident, she claims, the "'dangerous' narratives pertaining to 'anarchists' were marked by the sign, 'woman.'"[43] This "symbolic woman," however, did not always carry the same meaning for contemporaries. In what follows, I seek to identify the possible effects of the symbolized women's narrative of police violence that was constructed by newspaper reporters and the female socialists themselves, who were appearing and acting to provoke several audiences, including spectators, reporters, and, by extension, readers.

Newspapers generally captured the theatrical air of the courtroom and particularly highlighted the police brutality in the female socialists' dramatic narratives. Though the contemporary meaning of courtroom spectatorship calls for further study, we can say that media sensationalism of the time had motivated many people to watch trials involving controversial incidents. For example, in June 1908, a famous trial of the so-called Debakame Incident, which involved a purportedly sexually deviant murderer, also attracted a packed courtroom. In that case, according to a *Niroku* report, spectators who could not enter loitered outside expectantly waiting for someone to exit the courtroom, and once it happened, "the crowd rushed into the courtroom ignoring policemen's repression."[44] This article also noted that the spectators later complained about the chief judge, who suddenly closed the trial to the public due to the possible obscene content of testimonies. Frustrated spectators criticized the judge by comparing him with the chief judge who had presided over the case of Noguchi Osaburō, another controversial murder case, evaluating the latter's rank as higher.[45] The spectators reportedly resembled the amateur critics of Kabuki theater and other performing arts. As such cases suggest, courtrooms at this time were considered, or at least depicted, as potential sources of entertainment in the same light as the theater.

Newspaper coverage of the first trial of the Red Flag Incident on August 15, 1908, emphasized the female socialists, and specifically their complaints about inaccurate interrogation documents and inhumane treatment in the police station. Trial coverage was decorated with references to the women as both "eloquent" and "audacious." According to *Yomiuri shimbun*:

> To the [judge's] question to each [of the defendants], "Is your objective anarchism?" most men replied, "The ultimate objective of socialism is anarchism, but we have not publicly mentioned it yet." But Kanno Sugako said, "I am an anarchist rather than a socialist. I feel more strongly so as my thoughts have progressed nowadays." With her stylish (*iki*) outfit of arrow-patterned silk kimono and loosely tied satin purple sash, she said such an audacious thing. Hearing this, even the chief judge was astonished.[46]

Iki refers to a sense of refinement or stylishness, typically appreciated in Shitamachi society. Identifying Kanno's outfit as *iki* stresses the gap between her appearance and the content of her speech. This gap must have provoked some readers to imagine her as dangerous, yet interesting; in order to appear as *iki*, one needs an acquired sense that cannot be easily learned. In other words, she could not be labeled as a mere ignorant woman with no understanding of stylishness or intellect who had simply been dragged along by male activists.

Other newspapers described the same event using different terms while recounting Kanno's claims. *Kokumin* emphasized Kanno's identification with anarchism by noting her characteristic eloquence. At the same time, the description of her eloquence referenced Kanno's own message—that is, the defendants were unjustly subjected to police brutality. The report said, "[After surprising the court officials with her self-identification as an anarchist] she fluently accused the policemen of unlawfulness."[47] It should be noted that the arrested female socialists had experience with public speech from women's high schools and socialist meetings. Christine L. Marran points out that the early Meiji phenomenon of the "poison women" (*dokufu*), or sensationalized female criminals, indicated social anxiety among upper-class men concerning women and lower-class men inappropriately taking advantage of new laws and destabilizing traditional practices.[48] Similarly, when the reporters described Kanno's speaking skills, they were likely hinting at the perceived negative consequences of women's education: the creation of "poisonous" female political criminals, rather than ideally docile women. As newspapers of the time competed to capture any newsworthy part of the story, however, they provided these educated female activists with an opportunity to present themselves as a politically charged spectacle. Thus, the pages of newspapers emerged as the intersection of the multidirectional intentions and assumptions, with both the reporters and the reported unwittingly spreading multiple messages.

Yomiuri mentioned Kanno's remark as also being the source of laughter, again along with the depiction of police violence:

Kanno angrily stated, "Because two policemen came holding the two flags, I pleaded with them to return them, but then they mercilessly pushed me down. When I got up, one of them severely twisted my arm and arrested me. If there were a legitimate reason, I would even accept death sentence. But I had never seen such a violent policeman before." When the judge asked if she recalled the policeman's face, she replied, "I remember his triangular shaped face," causing a burst of laughter.[49]

In order to report the laughter, regardless of the reporter's interest in police violence, he could hardly avoid contextualizing her comment about the policeman's "triangular shaped face." Consequently, he also informed readers about the brutal treatment she had received from the police. In this manner, the narrative of police violence illuminated the female socialists in the readers' imagination with a combination of pity, humor, and righteousness. Though the reporter appropriated Kanno's allusion to the policeman, the layers of dialogue in this and other articles indicate what Mikhail Bakhtin calls a "speech genre," in which any utterance "always responds (in the broad sense of the word) in one form or another to others' utterances that precede it," and is also related to "subsequent links in the chain of speech communion."[50] References to others can be situated as part of both diachronic and synchronic dialogues, which cannot be reduced to the writer's intention. Though a news report is the creation of one writer, he responds to and addresses dialogues using the shared assumption within a speech genre beyond his own capacity as an author.

The arrested women in the courtroom emerged as objects of curiosity, but this did not always involve a negative connotation mainly because of shared antagonism toward the police. *Kokumin* captured Kamikawa's angry statement that she would accept a death sentence but not for a crime that she had not committed.[51] A few days later, *Kokumin* ran an interview with Kamikawa with the headline, "Five Minutes in a Visitation Room: Meeting with a Socialist Woman." The article first described her smile and stylish attire.[52] This benign depiction and her photograph at the top center of the feature page sharply contrasts with the unfeminine remarks that she made in the report, which are all in a larger font: "Since I was in girls' high school, I greatly inclined to manly personality, and my daily behavior rather resembled that of men. . . . Such a manly taste eventually made me who I am today." The portrayal of Kamikawa's stylishness, her higher education, and her unfeminine persona may have been perplexing to readers, but the report ascribed a heroic and stoic quality to her.

The report also included a comment made by her best friend: "Some people say it was out of heartbreak and self-despair that Ms. Kamikawa began to argue for socialism. Particularly to her, however, I have never heard anything about her being involved with a love affair."[53] This also indicates that contemporaries viewed that the reason for a woman to become a socialist was some experience of "heartbreak" or "self-despair," and thus by no means a serious individual pursuit. In reality, however, the four female socialists, like many other male and female activists of the time, became politically engaged by choice. As mentioned above, the four women received education in high school or studied under senior scholars and were familiar with domestic and foreign socialist writings. This gap between general assumptions regarding female socialists and their actual background suggests that the women's activities were virtually unknown outside of their activist circle. During the court trials of the Red Flag Incident, however, the general assumption that female socialists were relatively passive figures proved advantageous. Any seemingly audacious remarks by these women made them seem even more astonishing, thereby piquing the curiosity of reporters and readers alike.

During the next trial on August 22, the scale of theatrical performance in newspapers escalated. A larger courtroom was chosen, and there were reportedly four hundred people in attendance, with another hundred waiting outside the room. Newspapers increasingly stressed the dramatic atmosphere of the trial, comparing the courtroom with a theater. *Kokumin* ran the headline "Full House, Sold-Out Trial"; *Yomiuri* stated "Great Popularity of the Trial since the [Hibiya] Riot."[54] It should also be noted that such theatrical depictions were primarily attached to the female socialists, though their male counterparts were also present at the trial.

Reported laughter was one gauge of audience reactions arising from gendered social expectations. For example, newspapers highlighted the contrast in testimony between a police witness, whose version of events was vague and unclear, and Kamikawa, who harshly attacked his obscure testimony. *Kokumin* stated that the spectators burst into laughter when the policeman could not specify which woman had been present and described how "unwomanly" the strength of the women had been when he had attempted to confiscate the flags.[55] *Asahi* wrote with sympathetic mirth, "Because he seems to have been shocked by such a strong woman as Kamikawa, he only remembered her name. . . . Only the chief judge's permission to leave the courtroom saved him from Kamikawa's harsh offense."[56] Previously, newspaper writers had focused unflattering attention on Kamikawa's "unfeminine" character. On this occasion, however, the police witness became an object of scrutiny, or even prey, as he was emasculated in front of the audience due to his deviation from the expected norms surrounding policemen, namely, physical strength and lucidity.

Theatrical metaphors were also popular, most notably in *Yomiuri*. The reporter explicitly stated his anticipation of something entertaining: "I waited with breathless interest to hear odd replies and unusual speech to shake off drowsiness."[57] In response to a series of remarks made by Kanno, for example, he wrote:

As expected, the former *Mainichi denpō* reporter, the eloquent woman Kanno Sugako, first stood up, and spread out an interrogation document in the manner of *Kanjinchō* [a Kabuki play]. "Chief judge!" she called, "Though I do not think there is any need to testify because all the facts set forth in the interrogation document have almost no traces, I want to clarify a fact, just in case. Because of my tuberculosis, however, I will feel sick even by talking slightly loudly, so please excuse me for not being so clear." By such an imposing condition, she first mystified the chief judge. The chief judge, like Togashi [the guard in *Kanjinchō*], replied, "Then you mean you have a fact to testify to. If it is difficult for you to breathe, come to the front and speak up." She stood up and said: "As I left Kinkikan, I was so sick that comrade Tokunaga suggested that I avoid the crowd because it would be too dangerous. I can never engage in any violent actions." . . . At the end, she obnoxiously exclaimed, "Because I am an anarchist, I am well prepared to be persecuted but would refuse to be incarcerated by such violent policemen, not even for one day." To this, reproved the judge, making a scary facial expression: "We will hear your explanation later. Just tell the facts for now"; thereby she, the female hero though she was, returned to her seat with flushed cheeks.[58]

Kanjinchō (*The Subscription List*) is a renowned Kabuki classic featuring a famous scene involving a loyal retainer, Benkei, who attempts to pass through the Ataka barrier while camouflaging his fugitive lord Yoshitsune in a group pretending to be monks. Relying on his quick wit, Benkei fools the guard, Togashi, by holding a blank sheet of paper and pretending to read aloud a prestigious Buddhist temple's subscription list that serves as a license to pass the gate.[59] The article is thus a parody of the Ataka barrier scene in which Benkei, here played by Kanno herself, solemnly recites from a blank sheet of paper or, in this case, the interrogation document. By using this analogy, the report reemphasized Kanno's assertion that there was no truth to the document.

Through the reference to her tuberculosis, Kanno's status as a dramatic activist was given another twist. At the time, popular conceptions of the disease were imbued with an idealized sense of romanticism, or even heroism, which perhaps derived from existing notions of the disease's indiscriminate nature, because it haunted not only the unhygienic and uneducated poor but also women of respectable upbringing.[60] The incongruity between Kanno's physical fragility as a tuberculosis patient and her masculine declarations delivered with a bravado matching that of Benkei gives rise to the impression of a strangely pitiful and righteous figure.

This theme of self-sacrificial righteousness and pity matched the trend in theater of the time, most notably the rising popularity of the performer of *naniwabushi* narrative chanting Tōchūken Kumoemon (1873–1916), whose repertoires included another classic Kabuki story of self-sacrifice, *Chūshingura* (*The Forty-Seven Ronin*).[61] The reporter created an image of Kanno not merely as an audacious woman condemning the police but also as a tragic hero enduring the pain of a fatal disease. *Asahi* also reported that she "entered the courtroom holding a medicine bottle in her left hand because of pleurisy, and the way she breathed hard looked painful."[62] By simultaneously appearing stylish, eloquent, and sick, Kanno, herself an experienced newspaper reporter, likely manipulated her own image for the purpose of delivering her message—or at least her appearance as a righteous and pitiful anarchist—to readers.

At the extreme ends of these dramatic depictions of the women were those who harshly criticized the socialists and those who were greatly sympathetic to them. *Tokyo Nichinichi shimbun*, a renowned pro-government press, accused the defendants of reviling the policemen during the trial.[63] The worker-friendly *Niroku*, in contrast, provided an overtly sympathetic message: "The painful behavior of Mr. Sakai who cried out, 'Aren't policemen also a kind of workers who live by wage?' was naturally eye-catching."[64] These articles only in passing mentioned the female socialists, thereby providing further layers of different meanings for the trials. Another newspaper, *Yorozu Chōhō*, briefly yet critically reported the incident and the trials. This disapproval is likely due to the personal relationship between *Yorozu*'s editor-in-chief and the Heiminsha leaders; *Yorozu* had once employed Sakai and Kōtoku, but they had resigned in protest to its support of the Russo-Japanese War.

Journalists wrote several versions of the trial proceedings to attract an audience. These articles were not merely the result of the reporters' agency but rather the product of dialogic interactions and assumptions emerging among different actors, including the reporters, socialists, policemen, judge, and audiences. Each of the reporters selectively adapted and modified the participants' presentations. The presence of a large number of spectators, along with the dramatic performances by the defendants, likely inspired reporters to use theatrical metaphors.

In *Kumamoto Review*, the magazine for the direct-action socialist faction, the trials were reported in careful detail, but for a purpose different from that of the popular newspapers. The overall tone of one such article reveals the writer's aim to treat the trial as seriously as possible: the author minimized laughter in parenthetical notes, and the female socialists were depicted as respectably as possible, using the suffix *-joshi*, referring to a female intellectual, after their names.[65] We also find in *Kumamoto Review* the female socialists' own responses to the incident from the police cell. Each of them equally expressed their gratitude to their comrades. Because of heavy censorship, however, they were limited to briefly stating their commitment to activism and solidarity with their comrades. For example, Kanno wrote, "I feel sorry for the authorities because they believe this persecution will stop our great movement."[66] Kamikawa stated, "Before, I was fully determined for revolution . . . but now depressively spend days in the cell without being able to express how I feel inside. . . . I will tell you many stories as a souvenir once I get out."[67] The writers of the *Kumamoto Review*, in response, praised these women and stated that the incident and the related police brutality strengthened their commitment to their political cause.

At the end of the trial, Kamikawa and Kanno were acquitted and Kogure and Ōsuga Satoko (1881–1913) were sentenced to suspended one-year prison terms, whereas the male socialists were given two- to three-year prison sentences. The media depictions of the Red Flag Incident incited readers' curiosity about the female socialists who dramatically criticized police violence. This curiosity worked on the activists' behalf, allowing for both recognition and advertising in the nationally circulating media. Though the ways in which reporters described the trial were ultimately beyond the control of the defendants, this indeterminacy was not disadvantageous for the activists because of the assurance that socialist magazines would always write "accurate" versions.

Conclusion

In September 1909, approximately a year after the trial associated with the Red Flag Incident, *Asahi* featured an interview of Kanno by sympathetic journalist Matsuzaki Tenmin (1878–1934). Though the other three female activists had ceased to be vocal in the movement, Kanno had been imprisoned for illegal publication of socialist magazines coedited by Kōtoku Shūsui and was under continual police surveillance. Matsuzaki favorably introduced her as the once-famous female socialist of the Red Flag Incident and depicted her as an activist who still challenged official notions of ideal womanhood. In the report, Kanno again linked her experience in jail to her own pitifulness and diligence as an activist. She first stated, "Ever since I went to jail, I lost a lot of weight," and "due to my tuberculosis and brain disease, I spent most of my time in a medical prison." She then called for more women's participation, claiming, "With more female socialists, we will be able to discuss women's issues and engage in interesting activities. Socialism is the total opposite of today's good-wife-wise-mother-ism."[68] Her comment indicates lingering expectations that socialist activities were inherently "interesting" (*omoshiroi*), a word that can also be translated as "funny." The interview again depicted Kanno as eye-catching, by including photographs of her face and calligraphy of her own poem.

Regardless of whether the state saw such persistent popular media portrayal of socialist activities as potentially subversive, within a year both Kanno and Kōtoku were arrested in the High Treason Incident, and they were executed in January 1911. As if in punishment for the ephemeral yet grand appeal that Kanno's popular media coverage had for the general public, the state launched a decisive counterattack through nationwide mass arrests of socialists and subsequent executions. At the time of the Red Flag Incident, the media portrayed the female socialists as objects of curiosity, reflecting their potential for social impact. In the High Treason Incident, however, the state unambiguously labeled socialists as impermissible villains—the assassins of the Meiji emperor—and newspapers widely delivered this message. Therefore, to this day, Heiminsha socialists are generally remembered as martyrs who were persecuted by the state. However, popular media coverage of the socialists' narratives of police violence has received little attention.

The female socialists emerged in the media overtly expressing their political views in the form of humorous and dramatic speeches against the police. Not sharing their political agendas and worldviews, journalists depicted these women using further exaggerations, but also unwittingly publicized these activists as an intriguing group worthy of public attention. Such an unpredictable dynamism might have inspired further attempts for control and propaganda from the state, thereby creating the potential for appropriation and transgression to emerge as a new form of spectacle from below. Several months after Kanno's execution, when a new feminist literary movement led by the Bluestockings (Seitōsha) emerged, its members also captured media attention with ambiguous messages mixing gossip and politics. Media portrayals of politically charged women after the Red Flag Incident would continue to serve as a vehicle for political inspiration for subsequent generations of female activists.

Notes

I presented a draft of this article in 2012 at the "Art and Politics of East Asia" workshop at the University of Chicago. I thank the Center for East Asian Studies at the University of Chicago and Yonsei University for supporting the research for this study. I am also grateful to the issue editors and anonymous reviewers for their guidance. To refer to the Japanese names, I follow the conventional order of family name and then first name. All translations, unless otherwise stated, are my own.

1. *Tōhoku hyōron* (*Tohoku Review*) 2, September 1908, 6.

2. Sakai Toshihiko, "Nihon shakaishugi undōshiwa" ("Historical Account of the Japanese Socialist Movement"), *Sakai Toshihiko zenshū* 3 (Tokyo: Chūō kōronsha, 1933): 269–71. For details of the High Treason Incident in English, see Ira L. Plotkin, *Anarchism in Japan: A Study of the Great Treason Affair, 1910–1911* (Lewiston, NY: Mellen, 1991); and Masako Gavin and Ben Middleton, eds., *Japan and the High Treason Incident* (London: Routlege, 2013).

3. *Kokumin shimbun*, June 24, 1908.

4. Ibid., August 24, 1908.

5. Lisa Duggan, *Sapphic Slashers: Sex, Violence, and American Modernity* (Durham, NC: Duke University Press, 2000), 2.

6. Recent studies of late Meiji media include Komori Yōichi, Kōno Kensuke, and Takahashi Osamu, eds., *Media, hyōshō, ideologii: Meiji sanjū nendai no bunka kenkyū* (*Media, Representations, and Ideologies: Cultural Studies of the Meiji Thirties*) (Tokyo: Ozawa shoten, 1997); and Kaneko Akio, Yoshida Morio, and Takahashi Osamu, eds., *Disukūru no teikoku: Meiji sanjū nendai no bunka kenkyū* (*The Empire of Discourse: Cultural Studies of the Meiji Thirties*) (Tokyo: Shinyōsha, 2000).

7. The 1907 circulation of each of the Tokyo newspapers discussed here is as follows: *Kokumin*, 34,000; *Tokyo Asahi*, 82,073; *Niroku*, 60,000; *Yomiuri*, 32,000; *Tokyo Nichinichi*, 24,000; and *Yorozu*, 87,000. James Huffman, *Creating a Public: People and Press in Meiji Japan* (Honolulu: University of Hawai'i Press, 1997), 386–87.

8. Amanda Frisken, *Victoria Woodhull's Sexual Revolution: Political Theater and the Popular Press in Nineteenth-Century America* (Philadelphia: University of Pennsylvania Press, 2011), 15.

9. The arrested male activists included such prominent socialists as Sakai Toshihiko, Yamakawa Hitoshi, and Ōsugi Sakae. For recent studies on these male leaders, see Umemori Naoyuki, ed., *Teikoku wo ute: Heiminsha 100-nen kokusai shinpojūmu* (*Shoot the Empire: International Symposium for the Centennial Anniversary of the Heiminsha*) (Tokyo: Ronsōsha, 2005); and Murata Hirokazu, *Kindai shisōsha to Taisho-ki nashonarizumu no jidai* (*The Modern Thought Society and the Era of Taisho Nationalism*) (Tokyo: Sōbunsha, 2011).

10. For the most representative studies of female socialists, see Suzuki Yūko, ed., *Heiminsha no onna tachi* (*Women of the Heiminsha*) (Tokyo: Fuji shuppan, 1986); and Vera Mackie, *Creating Socialist Women in Japan: Gender, Labour, and Activism, 1900–1937* (Cambridge: Cambridge University Press, 1997).

11. Yamaguchi was a prominent contributor to socialist magazines.

12. The Heiminsha published its organ *Weekly Heinin shimbun* from 1903 to 1905. After being dissolved in October 1905, it was reorganized in 1907 and intermittently continued until the arrest of Kōtoku in 1910. For the Heiminsha's history in English, see John D. Crump, *The Origins of Socialist Thought in Japan* (New York: Palgrave, 1983).

13. The arrested female socialists were Kamikawa Matsuko (1885–1936), a student of Russian literature; Kanno Sugako (1881–1911), a newspaper reporter; Ōsuga Satoko (1881–1913), a former medical student and an Esperantist; and Kogure Reiko (1890–1977), an apprentice of Sakai Toshihiko. Suzuki, *Heiminsha no onna tachi*, 42–48.

14. After the war, *Kokumin's* founder lamented that his paper increasingly featured "vulgarized" news for profit. Huffman, *Creating a Public*, 317.

15. *Kokumin shimbun*, June 24, 1908.

16. Ibid.

17. For instance, *Kokumin* reported a case of "fallen male and female students" being caught by the police for flirting in the train. *Kokumin shimbun*, April 14, 1908. A mysterious female student in Tokyo's commuter train appears in the 1907 novel by Tayama Katai, "The Girl Watcher" (*Shōjo byō*), in *Columbia Anthology of Modern Japanese Literature*, ed. J. Thomas Rimer and Van C. Gessel, trans. Kenneth Henshall (New York: Columbia University Press, 2005), 254–64. For media and literary portrayal of young women in trams, see Alisa Freedman, *Tokyo in Transit: Japanese Culture on the Rails and Road* (Stanford, CA: Stanford University Press, 2011).

18. Suzuki, *Heiminsha no onna tachi*, 294.

19. The term used here is *myōrei no kajin*, "a beautiful young woman." *Tokyo Asahi shimbun*, June 23, 1908.

20. Ibid.

21. Kogure had moved into Sakai Toshihiko's house as an apprentice a few weeks before the incident. Suzuki, *Heiminsha no onna tachi*, 48.

22. Naitō Chizuko, *Teikoku to ansatsu: jendâ kara miru kindai Nihon no media hensei* (*Empire and Assassination: Modern Japanese Media Formation from the Perspective of Gender*) (Tokyo: Shinyōsha, 2005), 285–86.

23. Since the 1880s, Sophia Perovskaya frequently appeared in Japanese political novels. Tanikawa Keiichi, *Rekishi no buntai, shōsetsu no sugata* (*Style of History, Image of Novel*) (Tokyo: Heibonsha, 2008), 314. For Russian influence on Japanese intellectuals, see Sho Konishi, *Anarchist Modernity: Cooperation and Japanese-Russian Intellectual Relations in Modern Japan* (Cambridge, MA: Harvard University Press, 2013).

24. Seitō Shōji, *Bankara kidanji* (*A Bankara Eccentric Man*) (Tokyo: Daigaku kan, 1908).

25. Andrew Gordon, *Labor and Imperial Democracy in Prewar Japan* (Berkeley: University of California Press, 1991), 26–27.

26. For media reports of the riot, see Andrew Gordon, "Social Protest in Imperial Japan: The Hibiya Riot of 1905," *Asia-Pacific Journal* 12, no. 29/3 (2014): n.p, accessed June 6, 2016, http://apjjf.org/2014/12/29/Andrew-Gordon/4150/article.html.

27. *Tokyo Asahi shimbun*, February 23, 1906.

28. *Tokyo Niroku shimbun*, June 23, 1908.

29. Ibid.

30. Ibid.

31. Ibid.

32. For details of the "Low City" culture, see Edward Seidensticker, *Low City, High City: Tokyo from Edo to the Earthquake: How the Shogun's Ancient Capital Became a Great Modern City, 1867–1923* (Cambridge, MA: Harvard University Press, 1991).

33. *Shūkan Heimin shimbun*, June 20, 1904, 5.

34. *Tokyo Shakai shimbun*, July 5, 1908, 2.

35. Takeuchi Zensaku, "Kinkikan mae no katsudō" ("Activities in Front of Kinkikan"), *Kumamoto Hyōron*, July 5, 1908, 2.

36. Ibid.

37. Sakamoto Kassui, "Omoide" ("Memories"), *Kumamoto Hyōron*, July 5, 1908, 6.

38. *Kumamoto Hyōron*, July 5, 1908, 5.

39. Mackie, *Creating Socialist Women in Japan*, 43.

40. Kamikawa Matsuko, "Tomo arazu tomo" ("Even If You Have No Friends"), *Kumamoto Hyōron*, June 20, 1908, 8.

41. Nishikawa [Kamikawa] Matsuko, "25 nen mae wo kaiko shite" ("Remembering Twenty-Five Years Ago"), in Suzuki, *Heiminsha no onna tachi*, 215–16.

42. Naitō, *Teikoku to ansatsu*, 287–88.

43. Ibid., 286.

44. *Tokyo Niroku shimbun*, June 24, 1908.

45. Ibid.

46. *Yomiuri shimbun*, August 16, 1908.

47. *Kokumin shimbun*, August 17, 1908.

48. Christine L. Marran, *Poison Woman: Figuring Female Transgression in Modern Japanese Culture* (Minneapolis: University of Minnesota Press, 2007), 63–64.

49. *Yomiuri shimbun*, August 16, 1908.

50. Mikhail M. Bakhtin, "The Problem of Speech Genres," in *Speech Genres and Other Late Essays*, trans. Vern W. McGee (Austin: University of Texas Press, 2013), 94.

51. *Kokumin shimbun*, August 17, 1908, 3.

52. Ibid., August 21, 1908.

53. Ibid.

54. Ibid., August 24, 1908; *Yomiuri shimbun*, August 23, 1908.

55. *Kokumin shimbun*, August 24, 1908.

56. *Tokyo Asahi shimbun*, August 24, 1908.

57. *Yomiuri shimbun*, August 23, 1908.

58. Ibid.

59. For the latest translation of the play, see Sakurada Jisuke I, "Great Favorite Subscription List: Gohiiki Kanjinchō" in *Kabuki Plays on Stage*: Villainy and Vengeance, ed. James R. Brandon and Samuel L. Leiter, trans. Leonard C. Pronko (Honolulu: University of Hawai'i Press, 2002), 26–47.

60. The most familiar figure of an elite woman with tuberculosis was Namiko in the 1888 novel by Tokutomi Roka, *Nami-ko: A Realistic Novel* (*Hototogisu*), trans. Sakae Shioya and E. F. Edgett (Boston: Herbert and Turner, 1904).

61. Hyōdō Hiromi and Henry D. Smith II, "Singing Tales of the Gishi: Naniwabushi and the Forty-Seven Ronin in Late Meiji Japan," *Monumenta Nipponica* 61, no. 4 (2006): 460.

62. *Asahi shimbun*, August 23, 1908.

63. *Tokyo Nichinichi shimbun*, August 23, 1908.

64. *Tokyo Niroku shimbun*, August 23, 1908.

65. *Kumamoto Hyōron*, August 20, 1908.

66. Ibid., September 5, 1908.

67. Ibid.

68. Matsuzaki Tenmin, "Tokyo no onna" ("Woman of Tokyo"), in *Tokyo Asahi shimbun*, September 13, 1909.

Confronting an Enemy Abroad, Transforming a Nation at Home

Domestic Militarism in the United States, 1990–1996

Josh Cerretti

In a 1991 speech at the end of the Desert Storm operation against Iraq, US president George H. W. Bush told Congress that those who fought "set out to confront an enemy abroad, and in the process, they transformed a nation at home." But what sort of transformation "at home" arose out of this "confrontation abroad"? Here, taking the former president at his word, I ask how this war against Iraq "transformed a nation at home," recognizing *home* as a metaphor for both the land within the borders claimed by the United States and the space occupied by a heteronormative family.[1]

Beginning with the claim of "protecting children" underlying justifications for the Gulf War, I connect the transnational militarism of US intervention abroad to subsequent episodes of militarized violence within the borders of the United States, including the Los Angeles riots, Waco siege, and Oklahoma City bombing. Through a reading of government declarations and documents, print media, and cultural production, I develop the concept of domestic militarism, a term encompassing the double meaning of *domestic* by exploring episodes of state violence exercised both within national borders and to enforce a particular vision of the family. Domestic militarism is an ideology that justifies this state violence through circular

Radical History Review

Issue 126 (October 2016)   DOI 10.1215/01636545-3594345

© 2016 by MARHO: The Radical Historians' Organization, Inc.

logics of heteronormativity and settler nationalism, manufacturing perceptions of sexualized threats and helpless victims while preventing the articulation of connections between violence abroad and violence "at home." Ultimately, the article points towards a series of 1996 laws amending regulations on marriage, public assistance, immigration, and the death penalty in order to trace the concrete effects of this new, post–Cold War militarized heterosexuality, which manifests in spectacular and structural forms of violence ranging from state-sanctioned killing to racial inequity in child malnutrition.

Scholars including Chandan Reddy, Jasbir Puar, and Scott Morgensen have identified the increasingly convivial relationship between militaristic nationalism and certain gay and lesbian constituencies during the 1990s, but few scholars have shown interest in the intertwining of militarism and heterosexuality.[2] Even Lisa Duggan's *Twilight of Equality?*, one of the few works connecting heterosexuality to state violence, remains much more widely cited for the concept of homonormativity than for her analysis of heterosexuality.[3] I expand this work by tracing the reassertion of a reproductive heterosexuality complicit with state violence in the face of epochal change brought on by the end of the Cold War and the gains of feminist and LGBTQ movements. This article historicizes problems emblematic of the age of the War on Terror, such as police brutality, state-sanctioned killings, and reintegrating combat veterans into civilian society, by demonstrating how militarized responses to these issues became normative during the 1990s.

The often-convivial relationship between heterosexuality and militarism, as well as the normalization of heterosexuality in twentieth-century US culture and politics, complicates the project of examining militarized heterosexuality. Such a project must begin from an understanding that the relationships among heterosexuality, the state, and its violences has been constructed through historical struggles and cannot be taken for granted. Jonathan Ned Katz explains that heterosexuality transcends neither history nor culture and, instead, merely "signifies one particular historical arrangement of the sexes and their pleasures."[4] The state has been and remains enormously invested in this arrangement and consequentially works to both regulate these arrangements and simultaneously erase the mark of their influence upon them. As Margot Canaday writes regarding homosexuality, states did not "simply encounter homosexual citizens, fully formed and waiting to be counted classified, administered, or disciplined"; instead the state "was a catalyst in the formation of homosexual identity." She writes, "To uncover those processes is to challenge the law's own tendency to authorize homosexuality as somehow pregiven or even natural in its constitution."[5] Analogously, I dissect the ongoing construction of the heterosexual citizen in order to denaturalize the relationship between heterosexuality and militarism.

The primary dissonance in a specifically heterosexual form of militarism is that war produces death while heterosexuality, through the institutionalization of heteronormativity, claims a monopoly on the production of life.[6] Domestic militarism soothes the tension between these strange bedfellows by justifying the death making of war as a necessary feature of the way in which the nation-state fosters life. This framing functions by characterizing those outside of the "domestic" both as imminent threats to what Judith Butler calls "grievable life" and as ungrievavable should they face death at the hands of the state.[7] More concretely, one need only reflect on the implications of the popular antiwar slogan "Make Love, Not War"—or the more troubling "Girls Say Yes to Boys Who Say No"—to understand the potential for conflict between (hetero)sexual and militaristic imperatives. The potential for raising children in a world free of the threat of nuclear annihilation made possible by end of the Cold War produced a new disconnect between militarism and heterosexual domesticity in the early 1990s.

My central concern in this piece is to demonstrate how proponents of and apologists for state violence increasingly relied on appeals to sexuality in the last decade of the twentieth century. The tireless efforts of feminist and LGBTQ activists and thinkers had already significantly transformed the landscape of US sexualities by the time President Bush and Soviet leader Mikhail Gorbachev met at the 1989 Malta Summit to symbolically end the Cold War. Recognizing that both heterosexuality and militarism faced significant challenges in the late twentieth century that threatened their decentering, I characterize the post–Gulf War transformation of the United States as a cultural and material reinvestment in two institutions in crisis. I argue that as anticommunism and blatant white supremacy became less acceptable justifications for state violence, officials increasingly turned toward justifications for state violence grounded in underexamined assumptions about heterosexuality as natural, normal, and moral. This is not a break with the militarism and heterosexualization of Cold War ideology, but a reformed continuation of it in response to the collapse of its primary justification.

Scholars such as Edward Said, Steven Salaita, and Haunani-Kay Trask have demonstrated how the proponents of this reinvestment cited white supremacist tactics of racializing indigenous, black, and East Asian people to produce evidence of a threat in the form of Arab, Muslim, and "Middle Eastern" people.[8] Recentering the heteronormative nuclear family as the unit for which the state acts, as opposed to individual citizens or the broader public polity, proved equally important to creating the ambiance of peril underlying US policy before, during, and after the Gulf War. Furthermore, the state and media reasserted a commitment to the conventions of heterosexuality in defiance of increasingly louder calls for sexual equity and pluralism. For the purposes of this essay, I rely exclusively on the *New York Times* as the representative example of the media's role in this process. Understanding how this transformation amounted to a militarization of heterosexuality allows for clearer understandings of state violence wielded not only domestically in the 1990s but also transnationally in the 2000s.

Protecting Children in the Persian Gulf

On August 2, 1990, the *New York Times* reported that the Iraqi military had attacked Kuwait and "penetrated deeply into the country." Relations between Iraq and the United States had been declining for months.[9] In July, Senator Nancy Kassebaum argued for sanctions on Iraq, claiming, "I can't believe any farmer in this nation would want to send his products . . . to a country that has used chemical weapons and a country that has tortured and executed its children."[10] Kassebaum did not mention that the United States was the world's largest producer of chemical weapons—technology used against children in Vietnam and shared with Iraq during their war with Iran—and only recently had begun to move some of its chemical weapons stockpile toward destruction.[11] Additionally, Kassebaum's casting of the United States as defender of children belied the government's resistance to ratifying the UN Convention of the Rights of the Child (a resistance arguably related to the fact that the United States continued to execute individuals for crimes committed as juveniles).[12] Children provided justifications for military intervention in three ways: as hostages caught in the middle of the conflict, as the victims of Iraqi brutality, and as the domestic beneficiaries of transnational militarism.

At the outset of war, thousands of foreign oil workers lived in Kuwait. Joseph Treaster's September 8 article about the first US citizens to depart after the invasion staged the story as a gendered drama in which "the American men hoped that some military action would be taken" while "the women burst into tears when they were asked about the husbands they had left behind in hiding."[13] The hostages existed in a clear binary of masculine doers and feminine sobbers. In this same article, the phrase "women and children" appears eight times in ten sentences. According to Cynthia Enloe, news media unselfconsciously use the breathless phrase *womenandchildren* "because in network minds women are family members rather than independent actors, presumed to be almost childlike in their innocence about international *realpolitik*."[14] *New York Times* television critic Walter Goodman's mid-September 1990 article presumed as much in claiming that "the confrontation with Iraq has become a war of the innocents. The screen is dominated not by warriors but by wives, not men but boys, not armor but infants."[15] Thus, even before the United States officially intervened in Kuwait, the media had constructed a dichotomy contrasting the passive role of "womenandchildren" in the conflict with an active militarized masculinity that could not escape gendered tropes, even as many women and young people contributed to both sides. To incite support for that intervention against Iraq, the US government then sought to make this foreign conflict "domestic" through producing evidence of Iraqi violations of heterosexual domesticity in the form of infanticide.

As the occupation of Kuwait stretched into months, many remained unconvinced that distant Iraq posed any sort of threat to the United States.[16] Allegations of murders committed by Iraqi troops ejecting Kuwaiti infants from their incubators provided a vivid rationale for anyone seeking to justify US military action. Beginning in September 1990 with stories in the *Washington Post, New York Times*, and *USA Today*, multiple sources accused Iraqi soldiers of killing 15, 22, 300, or some other number of infants in a variety of fashions, usually completing their alleged crimes by absconding to Iraq with the incubators.[17] The testimony of "Nurse Nayirah" to the Congressional Human Rights Caucus on October 10 increased interest in these stories. The widely broadcasted testimony shows a young Arab woman tearfully claiming, "I volunteered at the al-Addan hospital. . . . While I was there I saw the Iraqi soldiers come into the hospital with guns. They took the babies out of the incubators, took the incubators and left the babies on the cold floor to die."[18]

A month later, President Bush further embellished her story as involving "babies pulled from incubators and scattered like firewood across the floor."[19] In December, Amnesty International issued a report confirming the existence of "300 premature babies who died because incubators were stolen." Anyone who had been reading the news would have understood Bush, on the eve of the US invasion, when he said "innocent children" were "among those maimed and murdered" by Saddam Hussein.[20] The US Senate voted to authorize war by only a five-vote majority, and seven senators cited Nayirah's testimony in their voting statements.[21]

Despite its impact, Nayirah's story was not all it had been made out to be.[22] Not only had the public relations firm Hill & Knowlton written Nayirah's testimony, but the "nurse" was a daughter of the Kuwaiti ambassador and a member of the royal family. Furthermore, no one who was actually at a Kuwaiti hospital corroborated her claims. The truth was unimportant; the US war on Iraq was balanced on a fulcrum of narrative.

Nayirah's story was so compelling in large part because it hinged on the violation of the most valued product of heterosexuality: children. War is the production of death but is best justified as the protection of life, and no symbol appears more useful for making that bait-and-switch than a child in danger. Recent work by Katherine Bond Stockton, Margaret Peacock, and Lee Edelman, all divergent in methods and results, concurs that definitions of childhood trace highly contentious power struggles and that children have been symbolically and rhetorically crucial to disguising oppression as innocence. Stockton demonstrates how adult discourse attempts to confine the messiness of childhood into clear categories that comply with hegemonic power, while Edelman argues that investments in protecting children mask a deeper investment in reproducing heteronormativity, and Peacock shows how Cold War governments used representations of children to starkly differentiate substantially similar militaristic projects.[23] In the case of the Gulf War, imagining that the war's purpose was to defend children served to obscure the war's negative consequences *for* children.

Within a month of the initial US assault, the Iraqi government began negotiating for an end to the conflict. "Iraq lies in ruins," the *New York Times* reported on March 4, and a month later the Iraqi foreign minister took to Baghdad radio to lament "the deliberate destruction of Iraq's infrastructure, including power and water plants, irrigation dams, bridges, telephone exchanges and factories producing infant formula and medicine."[24] The ensuing thirteen years of sanctions, known as the "siege," caused even more harm. "The siege touched every aspect of Iraqi life, causing death, disease, rapid economic decline, and nearly an end to any sort of human development," Haifa Zangana, an Iraqi activist, explains. "By the mid-nineties, half a million children died."[25] As Nadje al-Ali and Nicola Pratt write, the postwar years would prove especially devastating for women as, "aside from the most obvious and devastating effects, related to dramatically increased child mortality rates, widespread malnutrition, deteriorating health care and general infrastructure, unprecedented poverty, and an economic crisis, women were particularly hit by a changing social climate."[26] They detail how women and girls increasingly lost access to the job market and education while being forced to take on increased economic and cultural burdens.

As family life disintegrated in Iraq, President Bush sought to recenter it in the United States. In his 1992 State of the Union Address, Bush connected tales of his own progeny to stories of his wife's charitable work with HIV-positive children and a letter from a grateful Gulf War widow in order to insist that, despite the many challenges they may face, individuals "have responsibilities to the taxpayer . . . to hold their families together and refrain from having children out of wedlock."[27] In this framing, the transnational politics of militarized heterosexuality merge seamlessly with the politics of white supremacy and heteropatriarchy in the domestic context as, whether the problem is geopolitical disorder or blood-borne infection, the only solution remains a reinvestment in the nuclear family. Presented with a diverse range of threats to security and potential solutions, Bush asserted that "we must strengthen the family because it is the family that has the greatest bearing on our future."

What this rhetoric masks is that neither *family* (one kinship group) nor *families* (kinship groups collectively) is homogeneous or identical in interests. Furthermore, the task of "strengthening families" functions without the consent of those least empowered by the culturally specific forms the family takes (in this case, "womenandchildren"). The project of strengthening families implies that they are threatened and in need of the sort of protection the state offers, that is, militarized violence. Whereas Vietnam War–era organizations like Another Mother for Peace were able to use parenthood as a culturally sanctioned perspective from which to make an argument against sending their children to fight in war, the domestic militarism of the 1990s militarized parenthood. Being a "good mother" or a "family man" came to rely increasingly on support for militarized violence; consequently, the rhetoric of *family* became militarized through a perception that state violence is necessary to strengthen families.

The LA Riots and the "Culture of Poverty" Thesis

When making his call for more aggressive military action against Iraq to a joint session of Congress in September 1990, President Bush veered into the topic of how "our ability to function effectively as a great power abroad depends on how we conduct ourselves at home." He further explained that, for the United States, "world leadership and domestic strength are mutual and reinforcing; a woven piece, strongly bound as Old Glory."[28] Rather than dismissing this metaphor as another hackneyed bit of prose, we gain insight into the changing conditions of the 1990s by taking seriously Bush's contention that transnational militarism ("world leadership") structures the conditions of oppression within the borders of the nation ("domestic strength"). Furthermore, this leadership and strength are inextricable from practices of sexuality, or "how we conduct ourselves at home."

Three days after Bush declared "Kuwait is liberated," a Los Angeles man named Rodney King was brutally beaten by group of police officers.[29] That night's events may have lapsed into obscurity like so many other instances of antiblack violence were it not for a nearby resident sharing a videotape of the beating with a local news station. The state's subsequent failure to secure convictions against the offending officers sparked a series of riots centered in Los Angeles during late April and early May 1992. The LA riots were a "coming out" for the new, post–Gulf War domestic militarism that sought to justify the use of state violence within the borders of the United States through appeals to heterosexual normativity, and they set the stage for further militarization of heterosexuality as the decade continued.

Within hours of the "not guilty" verdicts, outrage fanned across the country, and reactions ranged from orderly protests to concerted attempts at property destruction. By April 30, thousands of police officers and the California National Guard had mobilized, soon to be joined by US Army and Marines deployed by President Bush. These forces arrived not to protect the mostly black and Latino neighborhoods of South Central Los Angeles but to wage war on them. Bush's executive order 12804, federalizing the California National Guard and ordering the Marines and Army into the city to suppress "the conditions of domestic violence and disorder," drew its constitutional legitimacy from the chapter 15 of Title 10 of the US Code, which applies only to "insurrection" and "rebellion" against the government. The riots provided an opportunity to display the effectiveness of the Army's newly reorganized Seventh Division light infantry units, which were designed with a post–Cold War mission "to react quickly to emergencies around the world" and to manage "'low spectrum' military crises in remote parts of the world where they would encounter little armored or air opposition."[30] On May 10 most of these troops withdrew, leaving the city with over fifty dead and more than $1 billion in property damage in the largest-scale armed civil conflict in the United States since the 1960s.[31] The persistence of applying a Gulf War metaphor to the urban uprising was made most clear by a reporter who observed "what had been scattered pillars of smoke" on the first day of rioting morphing into "a huge black cloud reminiscent of the burning oil wells of Kuwait during the Persian Gulf war."[32]

In the wake of the uprising, loud criticism of rioters drowned out critiques of the police and National Guard killing ten civilians. The debate after the riots instead focused on the underlying causes, and most prominent commentators endorsed domestic militarism by attributing the uprising to a Moynihanian "culture of poverty." Vice President Dan Quayle stated, "The lawless social anarchy which we saw is directly related to the breakdown of family structure, personal responsibility and social order in too many areas of our society."[33] Quayle located the source of rioters' oppositional actions and politics in their nonnormative sexualities and implied that a militarized response functioned to correct both. President Bush best summarized the intersection of militarized policing and heteronormative orderliness in a speech at the Challengers Boys' and Girls' Club in South Central LA, where he said, "Families can't thrive, children can't learn, jobs can't flourish in a climate of fear, however. And so first is our responsibility to preserve the domestic order."[34] Here, the dual modalities of *domestic* as internal to a household and internal to a nation-state become inseparable as, in Bush's estimation, the acceptable form of both is the same hierarchical order.

The riots revealed a new, post–Cold War terrain in which the external threat of communism receded, to be overtaken by anxieties about internal threats provoked by racial and sexual disorder. Concomitantly, the state abdicated the interventionist promises of the New Deal and Great Society, moving toward a leaner, neoliberal state that militarized by shedding those functions not related to a narrow concept of "national security." Both cultural anxieties and structural adjustments relied upon seemingly neutral descriptive terms like *structure*, *responsibility*, and *order* to mask the raced and gendered components of both policies and their unequal effects. Some of the same soldiers who went to Kuwait to avenge Iraqi depravations against children there would then battle "gangs of armed youths" and supposedly broken families in the streets of urban America to distribute the violence of the state in a way that maintains the inertial security of suburban, white nuclear families.

Long before the riots, hierarchies of sexual shame and the projection of aggression onto the oppressed consistently characterized antiblackness across many historical disjunctures. The poet Sapphire makes as much clear in the 1993 poem "Strange Juice (or the Murder of Latasha Harlins)," which links the 1991 shooting death of black teenager Latasha Harlins, an aggravating factor in the riots often marginalized like the deaths of so many black girls and women, to Billie Holiday's classic song about lynching, the African American Civil Rights struggle, and the colonization of the Americas. Rather than flattening these events into a homogeneous tale of black pain, Sapphire draws these connections to the past to point toward the future. Without infantilizing Harlins as a figure of childhood innocence, Sapphire makes an impassioned case for seeing Harlins as part of a solid intergenerational network "birthed by black people's struggle" in which she *"wasn't* pregnant, but . . . was gonna have a baby, definitely, one day."[35] African American cultural production in response to the riots established a clear precedent that "Black Lives Matter" two decades before Alicia Garza, Patrisse Cullors, and Opal Tometi brilliantly applied the phrase to the movement against another intensification of antiblack violence in 2013.

Although I now turn toward locating the ideological underpinnings of state violence directed against a predominantly white group of people in the United States, the constitutive nature of antiblack violence remains an instructive example in assessing the meaning of domestic militarism in the 1990s. Just as black-majority neighborhoods were used as a laboratory for more militaristic styles of police intervention that later became national phenomena, the United States would continue to visit violence upon its citizens in the name of children and the family throughout the decade.[36] At the same time, the state forged formal connections between transnational militarism and domestic policing through the Defense Logistics Agency Disposition Services, which increasingly distributed surplus military hardware to police forces around the country.

Children in Peril at the Waco Siege

In March and April 1993, the US public focused raptly on the headquarters of the Branch Davidians, just outside of Waco, watching a series of events unfold that would leave eighty-six people dead. Here, I connect the Branch Davidians to the people of Iraq and Los Angeles through their common relationship to domestic militarism without suggesting any equivalence between these communities. I demonstrate the contrast between the state's professed actions "in the interests of children" and the mass immolation of children at Waco.

On the morning of February 28, agents of the Bureau of Alcohol, Tobacco, and Firearms raided the Mount Carmel Center to arrest David Koresh on a weapons charge. Those who saw him as their spiritual leader were known as Branch Davidians, an offshoot of the Davidians, itself a breakaway segment of Seventh-Day Adventism, a Protestant Christian denomination. The exact theology of the group shifted depending on the teachings of successive leaders, but all shared with Adventists a focus on an apocalyptic "second coming" of Jesus.[37] While the siege was ongoing, the *New York Times* had few reservations about referring to the group as a "cult" and characterized members through such a lens.[38]

The Branch Davidians repelled the government raid, initiating a fifty-one-day standoff that provided ample opportunities for news media to speculate on the character of all involved, particularly Koresh. The "big figure in this drama, the mysterious mastermind, in fact the only interesting character" was "an odd mix of religious zealot and frustrated rock performer" comparable to "Jim Jones and Manson" or "Hitler and Stalin" who was "dangerously unstable" and had a "history of learning disabilities."[39] Despite these negative traits, Koresh "proved himself attractive," and "whatever his religious convictions, they did not preclude him from having sex . . . even after he married a 14-year-old girl."[40] Such fascination with Koresh's sexual practices became the primary route through which he was characterized as "deviant" and, consequently, deserving of state violence.

The first quote the *New York Times* provided from Koresh encapsulates much of the ensuing coverage: "I've had a lot of babies these past two years. It's true that I do have a lot of children and I do have a lot of wives." This same article includes reports, by way of hearsay, of "sexually abused girls," as well as rumors that "Mr. Koresh might have abused children of group members and . . . claimed to have at least 15 wives."[41] The number of wives grew to nineteen by the next day alongside reports of his "abusive tendencies, including sexual relations with young girls."[42] He was so thoroughly saturated in nonnormative, excess heterosexuality that even his rise to power was predicated on uncommon sexual relations: Koresh supposedly became a prophet by having sex with his predecessor Lois Roden, five decades his senior.[43] Reporters characterized Koresh as "a madman" and "David Death," but the accusations most instrumental to the standoff all focused on how Koresh related to his presumed dependents, the "womenandchildren" of the Mount Carmel Center.[44]

Domestic militarism assumes a system in which certain men present a sexualized threat and only militarized violence can save innocent children and women from them. Whether the threat rests in the body of an individual like Koresh or Saddam Hussein, or in the faceless "thugs" accused of violating the domestic order in Los Angeles, the state diverts attention from its violence by positioning itself as protector and savior. The raid that sparked the Waco conflict operated on the assumption that the Branch Davidians consisted of dangerous men and helpless "womenandchildren." Stephen Labaton and Sam Howe Verhovek's special report on the raid, explains that the Bureau of Alcohol, Tobacco, and Firearms "timed the raid to take advantage of a period when . . . the cult's routine would separate the men from both the weapons and the women and children."[45] Even though women participated actively on both sides of the raid, reducing them to their supposed helplessness served to cast militarized violence as benevolent protection.

On April 13, Verhovek reported that the FBI had no intention of assaulting the Mount Carmel Center "largely because of fears that such action could harm the 17 children inside."[46] Soon, though, the government began to execute "a plan of slowly stepping up the pressure" through the use of tear gas. US attorney general Janet Reno defended the decision: "We had information that babies were being beaten. . . . I specifically asked, 'You really mean babies' 'Yes, that he's slapping babies around.'"[47] Here, violence against infants, just as in the story of the Kuwaiti incubators, functioned as the ultimate transgression of heterosexual domesticity and an option of last resort to justify militarized violence.

Thus, on April 19, the same Bradley-model tanks used in the Gulf War "pumped tear gas through holes punched in the walls of the compound," smoke appeared in several parts of the complex, and within an hour "David Koresh and more than 80 followers—including at least 17 children—apparently perished . . . when flames engulfed the sprawling wooden complex on the Texas prairie."[48] Immediately following these deaths, government officials asserted that it had been done with the best intentions—that is, for the "womenandchildren." The *New York Times* reported that Reno "described the tear gas attack as an incremental increase in pressure on the cultists designed to encourage women and children to flee." Similarly, a spokesman for the US Department of Justice insisted on the maternal instincts of his boss, saying the factor "that drove her the most was her concern about the children."[49] President Bill Clinton also stuck to the story about ongoing child abuse ("the children who were still inside the compound were being abused significantly"), blamed the deaths on the Branch Davidians ("they made the decision to immolate themselves"), and assured his audience that what mattered most was the children ("I feel awful about the children").[50]

While federal officials insisted on the legitimacy of their conjectures about ongoing child abuse, the Justice Department's October report on the siege conceded, "There was no direct evidence indicating that Koresh engaged in any physical or sexual abuse of children during the standoff."[51] Verhovek's reporting on the children during the siege revealed that "none show any signs of physical abuse, and most seem consumed with a wish to see their parents."[52] Furthermore, "cult members have disputed that there was any child abuse or beatings at the compound, and Texas authorities who had looked into such accusations before the Feb. 28 raid had never found any proof."[53] Although the Justice Department report conceded that Reno "had made an inaccurate statement" regarding the child abuse, it insisted that unsubstantiated innuendo was "sufficient to be relevant to the decision making process."[54] Commentator William Safire was less charitable; he went so far as to claim that "she misled the public after the attack (and probably the President before the attack) by arguing that the children were being 'abused' inside."[55] While questions remain about how children were treated within the Mount Carmel Center, the inferno that killed its residents made such details obscure.

The fire's exact origin also remains a mystery, but both the US government and the *New York Times* settled on the assumption of a mass suicide by the Branch Davidians. What is clearer from accounts of the Waco siege is that the US government sought to solve problems with overwhelming force justified to the public through the logic of domestic militarism. The perception that tanks ramming into a building and spitting noxious gas "represent[s] the best way to resolve the standoff without catastrophic loss of life" concedes significant ground to militarization by imagining this sort of professional administered violence as a life-saving measure. While one reporter claimed that a "confusing swirl of political, practical, and psychological forces inevitably steered officials toward the plan," the most pertinent fact is that "no alternatives were formally presented to Attorney General Janet Reno" besides an assault with tanks and tear gas.[56] Domestic militarism was the driving force that steered officials toward the plan, not inevitably but ideologically. As other standoffs, like the 1994 Justus Township siege in Montana, revealed, loss of life is not an inevitability when citizens clash with their government, but assumptions about the dangers of nonnormative kinship arrangements and the utility of militarized violence make loss of life more likely.

Many surviving Branch Davidians can be found at the ruins of the Mount Carmel Center every April 19 to commemorate the deaths that occurred there. By 1995 the site had become a rallying point for "a political crusade, albeit one that the survivors haven't joined and don't even approve of."[57] The ranks of these crusaders, who "called themselves constitutionalists or patriots or militiamen," grew throughout the early 1990s, rallying around citizen-state conflicts like Waco and Ruby Ridge with their own militaristic fervor, brandishing firearms and peppering federal authorities with bellicose rhetoric.[58] The Branch Davidians, by contrast, stood a skeptical distance from the militiamen, "perplexed, and even offended," wary of the gun-toting militia, and totally unarmed.[59] At the same time, three hundred miles due north of Waco, one of those self-described militiamen turned April 19 into a day that would both eclipse the Waco siege in losses of human life and link the siege into a larger chain of militarized violence.

The "Baby Killer" in Oklahoma City

Just after 9:00 a.m. on April 19, 1995, a bomb made out of ammonium nitrate and fuel oil exploded in front of the Alfred P. Murrah Federal Building in downtown Oklahoma City. Hundreds of millions of dollars of property damage was overshadowed by 168 deaths. Representations of the space of the bombing, its youngest victims, and the bomber's motives for his violent act all demonstrate the historically specific linkages between state violence and heteronormativity, or what I refer to as domestic militarism.

In the aftermath of the bombing, many Oklahomans appeared most disoriented not by the tragedy of bombing itself but, rather, by where it occurred. "One by one they said the same thing," journalist Rick Bragg reported: "this does not happen here."[60] Locals had plenty of ideas about where these things *do* happen: "Beirut," "Bosnia . . . Jerusalem . . . Baghdad . . . Bolivia," and "countries so far away, so different they might as well be on the dark side of the moon."[61] The belief that Oklahoma existed as part of "America's heretofore invulnerable and innocent heartland . . . whose uncorrupted values and innocence were beyond the reach of such violence" required effacing the racialized violence that contours the history of Oklahoma, as well as the transnational exportation of that violence by the United States.[62]

In a defining moment of US-indigenous relations, the federal government began a systematic forcible displacement of the Cherokee, Seminole, Chickasaw,

Creek-Muscogee, Choctaw, and other indigenous nations to contemporary Oklahoma in 1830, causing unknown thousands of deaths on multiple "Trails of Tears."
Furthermore, not only was the state a scene of the quotidian violence of Jim Crow,
but it also was the scene of more spectacular forms of white supremacist violence,
such as the 1921 assault on Tulsa's "Black Wall Street" that left hundreds dead and
thousands more homeless. When those at the scene of the 1995 bombing claimed,
"It's hard to imagine this happening in the heartland," they participated in a collective forgetting of tragedies like the Tulsa race riot that justified ongoing violence
against people of color.[63] Domestic militarism requires effacing the suffering that
was necessary to establish a seemingly benign "domestic order," or as Chandra
Mohanty and Biddy Martin claim in reference to the concept of "being home," it
requires "an illusion of coherence and safety based on the exclusion of specific histories of oppression and resistance."[64]

Histories of transnational militarism were also denied through representations of innocent Okies "newly burdened with an unfortunate sense of connection to
the rest of the world."[65] The normalization of dozens of sudden deaths by explosion
abroad—whether in Beirut, Baghdad, or Bolivia—arises out of the logic of domestic militarism that says the burden of violence should be borne "out there" and not
within the domestic space of the United States. The idea that violence must be suffered in foreign countries existed in a mutually reinforcing relationship with the idea
that violence must also originate from foreign countries, placing immediate scrutiny
upon Arabs and Muslims as the search began for whoever planted the bomb.

A. M. Rosenthal encapsulated the dominant attitude of the moment: "Police
do not know for certain whether the bombing is foreign terrorism or domestic.
Either way . . . whatever we are doing to destroy Mideast terrorism, the chief terrorist threat against Americans, has not been working."[66] This is to say, regardless of
who is responsible for the bombing, Arabs and/or Muslims (it's rarely clear) should
be punished for it. Even after the US government stopped pursuing any Arab suspects and focused on a cadre of white men, Walter Goodman hedged his critique of
how televised news cast "Arab-Americans" as "the suspects of first choice in terrorist
attacks" by adding that this "suspicion is understandable."[67]

While many were immediately occupied with suspicion, the victims of the
bombing transfixed many more, and both government and media represented children at the apex of victimhood in order to promote domestic militarism. Before any
details about the bomb emerged, Rick Bragg would assert that "it was intended to
murder on a grand scale: women, children, old people coming to complain about
their Social Security checks."[68] Little mention was made of the Drug Enforcement Administration, Secret Service, Marine Corps, Army Recruiting Battalion,
or Defense Security Service offices in the same building. Instead, "The enduring
image of this tragedy" was that of bloodied one-year-old Baylee Almon being carried away from the rubble by a firefighter.[69] Photos of Almon "pierced the heart" of

millions who saw the pictures through the Associated Press release and "prompted a flood of calls to newspapers from people concerned about the child's fate."[70] Sadly, Baylee Almon died as a result of the bombing and, like the eighteen other children killed in the blast, became a filter through which to look at domestic terrorism without seeing domestic militarism.

While 168 people died that day, the 19 children became "the focus, the epicenter, of the nation's bereavement over the blast and its rage and loathing at the bomber" because their unquestionable innocence made the bombing appear, as President Clinton put it, like "an attack on innocent children and defenseless civilians" rather than an attack on a centralized node of repressive state power.[71] Furthermore, centering the youngest victims facilitated an image of a "national family" bound together by the strength of fathers and the vulnerability of dependents. The first responders did not just pull Baylee Almon from the wreckage; as the *New York Times* reported, they "called [her] 'my baby,' adopting [her] on the spot, as did the entire nation."[72] The state also rhetorically adopted Almon, using her very real pain as a rhetorical resource to assuage concerns about the very real pain the US government would continue to inflict upon many children.

There was no shortage of familial metaphors in response to the bombing. Todd Purdum claimed "a disaster or security threat transforms the President instantly into a national paterfamilias" and quoted a Harvard historian as calling the attack "against our own family."[73] Clinton, the "national father figure," seemed to relish the role, surrounding himself and First Lady Hillary Clinton with children of federal workers for "a brief national teach-in on anxiety and reassurance" in which he promised that the governmental response would be "putting our children first."[74] With no foreign enemy to punish for provoking this anxiety, the United States turned toward the bombing's primary perpetrator to make sense of the tragedy, but domestic militarism obscured the most important explanations.

Timothy McVeigh, the man charged with and ultimately convicted and executed for bombing the Murrah Building, recalibrated the scale through which negative representations could be judged. Journalists called him a "lunatic," the "most detested of pariahs," "so sick," "Satan," an "evil person," "a demon," and a "monster,"[75] but no invective stuck like "baby killer." McVeigh's widely broadcast "perp walk" in Perry, Oklahoma, featured a crowd screaming, "Baby killer! Burn him!"[76] The *New York Times* fed the image of McVeigh as baby killer, speculating "the Murrah building may have been chosen specifically because its layout insured that a bomb could be placed so close to children" and claiming "McVeigh had displayed no reaction even when he had been shown photographs of maimed and dead children."[77]

In addition to the title "baby killer," a portrait emerged of Timothy McVeigh that emphasized his failed heterosexuality. McVeigh apparently was "a supremely dedicated soldier" who was "well on his way to . . . a brilliant military career" but also a "loner" who "could not imagine settling down, working, marrying, becoming 'domesticated.'"[78] According to some of the men who served with him, McVeigh "embraced the solitude of his pillow night after night" and "never had a date."[79] McVeigh's hyposexuality, his failure to be appropriately "domestic," functioned to pathologize him and mark his militaristic violence as improper and antithetical to the American military ideal. The creation of such a distinction was so important because of the way he blurred the division between his "legitimate" violence as a soldier for the state and his "illegitimate" bombing.

In a letter written a few months before his execution, McVeigh connected his military training to his actions in Oklahoma City: "Bombing the Murrah Federal Building was morally and strategically equivalent to the US hitting a government building in Serbia, Iraq, or other nations." He claimed the bombing was "no different than what Americans rain on the heads of others all the time, and subsequently, my mindset was and is one of clinical detachment."[80] The technical content of McVeigh's actions, from his familiarity with explosives to his composure under pressure, arose out of his training and attachment to militarism. McVeigh's struggle to reckon with his combat experience in Iraq, his revulsion at seeing the sort of tank he manned there used against the Branch Davidians in Texas, and his sense of himself as protecting domestic order, each a highly politicized perception, were completely evacuated before they could even be examined. As Pam Belluck wrote a few weeks after the bombing, "Any argument that Mr. McVeigh had been motivated by political opposition to some drastic Government action or injustice would be very difficult to advance, *since the bombing killed innocent women and children.*"[81] Domestic militarism maintains the cognitive dissonance necessary to disarticulate domestic terrorism from its roots in transnational militarism; it provides a framework for interpreting kinship, nation, and violence in ways that insulate the state from critique. In this way, the connections between McVeigh's combat history in Iraq and the bombing were actively avoided as many of the same people eager to punish McVeigh for the murders he committed in Oklahoma City enthusiastically encouraged the murders he committed in Iraq.

Conclusion

The 104th Congress and President Clinton created a series of laws in 1996 that reflected the changes wrought over the first half of the 1990s and helped to codify a new, post–Gulf War domestic militarism. These four pieces of legislation reflect both the progress and the fragility of militarized heterosexuality in the 1990s, affirming the values of domestic militarism, while also suggesting that the relationship between heterosexuality and militarism did not arise from the nature of either but, rather, was an active construction of the state.

I have argued that representations of and responses to state violence militarized heterosexuality during the early 1990s. I refer to this as domestic militarism, in that these events were both militarized violence used within the borders of the United States and violence used to enforce a particular vision of the family. The US government advanced, and media regularly endorsed, justifications for this violence grounded in binary gender roles, hegemonic whiteness, and genocidal ideas about indigenous people. In this final section, I demonstrate how the imagined "interests of children" provided a convenient excuse for regressive social change that ultimately increased the suffering of many children.

The Antiterrorism and Effective Death Penalty Act of 1996 (AEDPA) went from "a snail into a race horse" due to the "domestic terrorism" of the Oklahoma City bombing but focused its definition of terrorism almost exclusively on what it called "international terrorism."[82] In addition to tightening restrictions on contributions to "foreign organizations" designated as terrorists and opening up foreign governments to suit in US courts, AEDPA created new procedures for deporting immigrants suspected of terrorism through secret trials and limited the ability of people accused of terrorism to seek asylum in the United States.[83] Along with the Illegal Immigration Reform and Immigrant Responsibility Act of 1996 (IIRIA), which increased the authority of Immigration and Naturalization Services to imprison people indefinitely and the speed with which they could deport migrants, the AEDPA reshaped the legal regime governing immigration, separated countless family members from one another, and reflected contemporaneous conceptions of security and national identity.[84] These laws drew upon and reinforced white supremacist conceptions of Euro-Americans as the rightful arbiters of the land within the borders claimed by the United States while projecting the threat of violence regularly committed by the US state—"at home" and "abroad"—onto racialized, "foreign" threats.

IIRIA also sought to eliminate immigrants' access to the limited social safety in the United States,[85] a goal more effectively achieved by the Personal Responsibility and Work Opportunity Reconciliation Act of 1996 (PRWORA). The law begins with two findings: "Marriage is the foundation of a successful society," and "marriage is an essential institution of a successful society which promotes the interests of children."[86] Lest the exact sort of marriage to which this Congress referred be misconstrued, it is worth noting that a week earlier they passed the Defense of Marriage Act, which defined "marriage" as "only a legal union between one man and one woman as husband and wife."[87] This aggressive promotion of heterosexuality evident in PRWORA went hand in hand with the antiblack racism and classism identified by Dorothy Roberts in her work on race and reproduction in the United States. Roberts sees PRWORA as driven by "a set of myths about the connections between family structure, welfare, race, and poverty" toward the goal of "modifying poor people's behavior."[88]

How, then, did this law passed "to promote the interests of children" modify their lives? Quantitatively, fewer than half the number of children receiving Aid to Families with Dependent Children benefits in 1995 were receiving the post-

PRWORA Temporary Assistance for Needy Families benefits by 2000, despite a growing population and a child poverty rate exceeding 17 percent.[89] The Center for Popular Economics reported that the new welfare regime "offers no guarantee that families with young children under the poverty line will receive public assistance" even though children in poverty "are more likely to have behavioral problems . . . are more likely than other children to be overweight and suffer from other chronic health problems . . . [and] are far more vulnerable to neglect and abuse."[90] Clearly, serving children, particularly children of color and working-class children, was not the number one priority of PRWORA. As Roberts claims, "How we interpret child maltreatment is a political issue."[91]

The politics of interpreting what constitutes child maltreatment and the interests of children emerged concurrently with domestic militarism in the 1990s. Heterosexuality, through its claim of producing life, became the mechanism to excuse militarism's destruction of life. The government and media contributed to the structural power and power evasiveness of patriarchal, Euro-American heterosexuality in the way they framed outrage at the alleged maltreatment of children by the Iraqi military and the Branch Davidians. Officials and commentators attempted to excuse deploying military units within the borders of the United States during the Los Angeles riots by proposing it as the only tenable solution to the pathologies of the black family. In the cases of Waco, immigration reform, and welfare reform, the US government positioned itself as operating "in the interests of children," and, in each case, children suffered and died. The Oklahoma City bombing, in which Timothy McVeigh used the training he received abroad from the US military to kill a great number of people within the United States, showed the perverse yet inevitable results of this logic.

The use of symbolic children—bound up in the dynamics of sexuality, gender, race, and other forms of identity—allows for the rhetorical elision of the pain and death experienced by corporeal children. The "transformation at home" heralded by Bush amounted to a militarization of heterosexuality through the ideology of domestic militarism. Critically examining portrayals of state violence allows us to better understand how the representations examined here serve the interests of heteronormativity, settler nationalism, and militarism. Understanding the militarization of sexuality during the 1990s, furthermore, prepares us better to understand the importance of the ideology of domestic militarism in the contemporary War on Terror.

Notes

1. For more on violence, heteronormativity, and "home," see Chandra Mohanty and Biddy Martin, "What's Home Got to Do with It?," in Mohanty, *Feminism without Borders* (Durham, NC: Duke University Press, 2004), 85–105; and Lynda Johnston and Robyn Longhurst, "At Home with Sex," in *Space, Place, and Sex* (Lantham, MD: Rowman and Littlefield, 2010), 41–60. For an examination of the dual meaning of *domestic* in US history,

see Amy Kaplan, "Manifest Domesticity," in *The Anarchy of Empire in the Making of U.S. Culture* (Cambridge, MA: Harvard University Press, 2002), 23–50.

2. Chandan Reddy, *Freedom with Violence: Race, Sexuality, and the US State* (Durham, NC: Duke University Press, 2011); Jasbir Puar, *Terrorist Assemblages: Homonationalism in Queer Times* (Durham, NC: Duke University Press, 2007); Scott Morgensen, *Spaces between Us: Queer Settler Colonialism and Indigenous Decolonization* (Minneapolis: University of Minnesota Press, 2011).

3. Lisa Duggan, *The Twilight of Equality? Neoliberalism, Cultural Politics, and the Attack on Democracy* (Boston: Beacon, 2004).

4. Jonathan Ned Katz, *The Invention of Heterosexuality* (Chicago: University of Chicago Press, 1995), 14.

5. Margot Canaday, *The Straight State: Sexuality and Citizenship in Twentieth Century America* (Princeton, NJ: Princeton University Press, 2009), 4.

6. See Lauren Berlant and Michael Warner, "Sex in Public," *Critical Inquiry* 24, no. 2 (1998): 547–66.

7. See Judith Butler, *Frames of War: When Is Life Grievable?* (London: Verso, 2009).

8. See Edward Said, *Covering Islam* (New York: Vintage Books, 1997); Steven Salaita, *The Holy Land in Transit: Colonialism and the Quest for Canaan* (Syracuse, NY: Syracuse University Press, 2006); Haunani-Kay Trask, "The Color of Violence," in *Color of Violence: The Incite! Anthology*, ed. Incite! Women of Color against Violence (Cambridge, MA: South End, 2006), 81–87.

9. Michael Gordon, "Iraq Army Invades Capital of Kuwait in Fierce Fighting," *New York Times* (hereafter *NYT*), August 2, 1990. Also see Samira Haj, *The Making of Iraq, 1900–1963* (Albany: SUNY Press, 1996); and Albert Hourani, *A History of the Arab People* (Cambridge, MA: Harvard University Press, 1991).

10. Gordon, "US Deploys Air and Sea Forces after Iraq Threatens Two Neighbors," *NYT*, July 25, 1990; Steven Holmes, "Congress Backs Curbs against Iraq" *NYT*, July 28, 1990.

11. "Summary of US-Soviet Agreement on Chemical Arms," *NYT*, June 2, 1990.

12. Bill Bradley, "Rights of the Child," *NYT*, December 16, 1990.

13. Joseph Treaster, "One Hundred Seventy-One Americans Arrive in Jordan from Kuwait," *NYT*, September 8, 1990.

14. Cynthia Enloe, *The Morning After: Sexual Politics at the End of the Cold War* (Berkeley: University of California Press, 1993), 166.

15. Walter Goodman, "The Iraq Conflict on American TV," *NYT*, September 17, 1990.

16. See William Safire, "Not Oil nor Jobs," *NYT*, November 19, 1990; and Jane Gross, "Berkeley; Coffee Is Strong, Opinion Is Split," *NYT*, January 14, 1991.

17. See Glenn Frankel, "Iraq, Kuwait Waging an Old-Fashioned War of Propaganda," *Washington Post*, September 10, 1990; Lisa Leff, "Weary, Wary Evacuees Bring Tales of Horror," *Washington Post*, September 11, 1990; Maureen Dowd, "World Summit for Children: Bush Is in New York for the U.N. Conference," *NYT*, September 30, 1990; and Johanna Neuman, "Kuwait's 'Shell of a Society,'" *USA Today*, October 1, 1990.

18. "Faked Kuwaiti Girl Testimony," YouTube, uploaded June 15, 2010, www.youtube.com /watch?v=LmfVs3WaE9Y (accessed March 11, 2012).

19. "Excerpts from Speech by Bush at Marine Post," *NYT*, November 23, 1990.

20. "Amnesty Report Says Iraqis Tortured and Killed Hundreds," *NYT*, December 20, 1990; George H. W. Bush, "Address to the Nation on the Invasion of Iraq," January 16, 1991, http://millercenter.org/president/bush/speeches/speech-3428.

21. Douglas Walton, *Appeal to Pity: Argumentum ad Misecordium* (Albany: SUNY Press, 1997).

22. "Deception on Capitol Hill," *NYT*, January 15, 1992.

23. Lee Edelman, *No Future: Queer Theory and the Death Drive* (Durham, NC: Duke University Press, 2004); Margaret Peacock, *Innocent Weapons: The Soviet and American Politics of Childhood During the Cold War* (Durham, NC: Duke University Press, 2014); Katherine Bond Stockton, *The Queer Child or Growing Sideways in the Twentieth Century* (Durham, NC: Duke University Press, 2009).

24. "Reparations without Retribution," *NYT*, March 4, 1991; "Excerpts from Letter to U.N.," *NYT*, April 8, 1991.

25. Haifa Zangana, *City of Widows* (London: Seven Stories, 2007), 73.

26. Nadje al-Ali and Nicola Pratt, *What Kind of Liberation?: Women and the War on Iraq* (Berkeley: University of California Press, 2009), 46.

27. Bush, "State of the Union Address," January 28, 1992, http://millercenter.org/president /bush/speeches/speech-5531.

28. Bush, "Address to a Joint Session of Congress," September 11, 1990, http://millercenter.org /president/bush/speeches/speech-3425.

29. Tracy Wood and Faye Fiore, "No Charges Filed against Suspect Beaten by Police," *Los Angeles Times*, March 7, 1991.

30. Jason DeParle, "General and Troops Have Domestic Mission" *NYT*, May 3, 1992; Charles Mohr, "To Modernize, the Army Is Bringing Back Light Infantry," *NYT*, November 25, 1984.

31. See Los Angeles Times, *Understanding the Riots: Los Angeles before and after the Rodney King Case* (Los Angeles: Los Angeles Times, 1992).

32. Seth Mydans, "Twenty-Three Dead after Second Day of Los Angeles Riots," *NYT*, May 1, 1992.

33. Andrew Rosenthal, "Quayle Says Riots Sprang from Lack of Family Values," *NYT*, May 20, 1992.

34. "Excerpts from Speech by Bush in Los Angeles," *NYT*, May 9, 1992.

35. Sapphire, "Strange Juice (or the Murder of Latasha Harlins)," in *American Dreams* (New York: Vintage Books, 1996), 156–57.

36. See Radley Balko, *Rise of the Warrior Cop: The Militarization of America's Police Forces* (New York: Public Affairs Press, 2013).

37. "Sect Arose from Split with Adventists," *NYT*, March 1, 1993.

38. Sam Howe Verhovek, "Four US Agents Killed in Texas Shootout with Cult," *NYT*, March 2, 1993; Sam Howe Verhovek, "Four Hundred Law Agents Are in Standoff with Texas Cult," *NYT*, March 2, 1993; Sam Howe Verhovek, "'Messiah' Fond of Bible, Rock, and Women," *NYT*, March 3, 1993; Stephen Labaton, "Agent's Advice: Attack on a Sunday," *NYT*, March 3, 1993.

39. Walter Goodman, "As Television, Waco Drama Had a Grim Inevitability," *NYT*, April 20, 1993; Peter Applebome, "Bloody Sunday's Roots in Deep Religious Soil," *NYT*, March 2, 1993; Sam Howe Verhovek, "Hardly Mentioned at Cultists' Trial: Their Leader," *NYT*, February 26, 1994; Verhovek, "'Messiah' Fond of Bible."

40. "Apocalypse in Waco," *NYT*, April 20, 1993; Verhovek, "'Messiah' Fond of Bible."

41. Verhovek, "Four US Agents Killed."

42. Verhovek, "Four Hundred Law Agents."

43. Adam Nossiter, "Warning of Violence Was Unheeded after Cult Leader's Gun Battle in '87," *NYT*, March 10, 1993.

44. "The Waco Whitewash," *NYT*, October 12, 1993; Verhovek, "Hardly Mentioned."

45. Stephen Labaton and Sam Howe Verhovek, "Missteps in Waco: A Raid Re-examined," *NYT*, March 28, 1993.
46. Sam Howe Verhovek, "Texas Cult Fortress Is Becoming Prison behind Barbed Wire," *NYT*, April 13, 1993.
47. Peter Labaton, "Reno Sees Error in Move on Cult," *NYT*, April 20, 1993.
48. Peter Labaton, "Confusion Abounds in the Capital on Rationale for Assault on Cult," *NYT*, April 21, 1993; Sam Howe Verhovek, "Death in Waco: The Overview," *NYT*, April 20, 1993.
49. "Apocalypse in Waco"; Labaton, "Confusion Abounds."
50. "Excerpts from Clinton News Conference" *NYT*, April 21, 1993; Labaton, "Confusion Abounds."
51. US Department of Justice, "Report to the Deputy Attorney General on the Events at Waco, Texas, February 28 to April 19, 1993," October 8, 1993, VII-A-2, https://www.justice.gov/publications/waco/report-deputy-attorney-general-events-waco-texas.
52. Sam Howe Verhovek, "In Shadow of Texas Siege, Uncertainty for Innocents," *NYT*, March 8, 1993.
53. Labaton, "Confusion Abounds."
54. US Department of Justice, "Report to the Deputy Attorney General," VII-B-4, VII-A-1.
55. William Safire, "Waco, Reno, Iraqgate," *NYT*, October 14, 1993; see also "Waco Whitewash."
56. David Johnston, "US Saw Waco Assault as Best Option," *NYT*, April 25, 1993.
57. Dick Reavis, "Remembering Waco, and Stealing It," *NYT*, May 13, 1995.
58. See Fred Pfiel, *White Guys: Studies in Postmodern Domination and Difference* (New York: Verso, 1995); and Michael Kimmel, *Manhood in America: A Cultural History* (New York: Oxford University Press, 1996).
59. Reavis, "Remembering Waco."
60. Rick Bragg, "In Shock, Loathing, Denial: 'This Doesn't Happen Here,'" *NYT*, April 20, 1995.
61. Ibid.; "Savagery in Oklahoma City," *NYT*, April 20, 1995; Thomas Friedman, "Beirut, Okla.," *NYT*, April 23, 1995; John Kifner, "At Least Thirty-One Are Dead," *NYT*, April 20, 1995.
62. Serge Schmemann, "New Images of Terror," *NYT*, April 24, 1995.
63. Dirk Johnson, "The Care Center," *NYT*, April 20, 1995; Bragg, "In Shock, Loathing, Denial"; Kifner, "At Least Thirty-One Are Dead."
64. Mohanty and Martin, "What's Home Got to Do with It?," 90.
65. Melinda Henneberger, "Oklahoma City; Where Nothing Ever Happens, Terrorism Did," *NYT*, April 21, 1995.
66. A. M. Rosenthal, "On My Mind; Ending Forgiveness," *NYT*, April 21, 1995.
67. Walter Goodman, "Although Unrestrained in a Crisis, Television Is a Tie That Binds," *NYT*, April 28, 1995.
68. Bragg, "In Shock, Loathing, Denial."
69. "A Twisted Rage," *NYT*, April 24, 1995.
70. "Tiny Victim Shown in Dramatic Photo," *NYT*, April 21, 1995; "Child in Photo Was One-Year-Old Girl," *NYT*, April 22, 1995.
71. Rich Bragg, "Tender Memories of Day-Care Center Are All That Remain after the Bomb," *NYT*, April 20, 1995; Rich Bragg, "Statements by the President and Attorney General," *NYT*, April 20, 1995.
72. "Twisted Rage." Almon's gender was unconfirmed at first, producing pronoun confusion.

73. Todd Purdum, "Undertones of Relevance," *NYT*, April 20, 1995; Linda Greenhouse, "Exposed; Again, Bombs in the Land of the Free," *NYT*, April 23, 1995.

74. Todd Purdum, "Clinton and First Lady Offer Solace to the Young," *NYT*, April 23, 1995.

75. "Twisted Rage"; Peter Applebome, "The Pariah as Client," *NYT*, April 28, 1995; Bragg, "Tender Memories"; Rick Bragg, "Blast Toll Is No Longer in Deaths, but Shattered Lives," *NYT*, April 19, 1996; James Brooke, "All-American Defendant?," *NYT*, June 2, 1996; Jim Yardley, "Execution on TV Brings Little Solace," *NYT*, June 12, 2001; "History and Timothy McVeigh," *NYT*, June 11, 2001; Jo Thomas, "McVeigh Guilty on All Counts in the Oklahoma City Bombing," *NYT*, June 3, 1997.

76. John Kifner, "Authorities Hold a Man of 'Extreme Right-Wing Views," *NYT*, April 22, 1995.

77. Sam Howe Verhovek, "Many Theories about Choice of the Target," *NYT*, April 26, 1995; David Johnston, "Oklahoma Bombing Plotted for Months," *NYT*, April 25, 1995.

78. Robert McFadden, "A Life of Solitude and Obsession," *NYT*, May 4, 1995; Jo Thomas, "Nichols Convicted of Plot and Manslaughter Counts but Not of Actual Bombing," *NYT*, December 24, 1997; "History and Timothy McVeigh."

79. McFadden, "Life of Solitude and Obsession."

80. Rick Bragg, "On the Eve of His Execution, McVeigh's Legacy Remains Death and Pain," *NYT*, June 10, 2001. Full text of the letter is available at "McVeigh's Apr. 26 Letter to Fox News," Fox News, April 26, 2001, foxnews.com/story/0,2933,17500,00.html.

81. Pam Belluck, "McVeigh Said to Play Role in Seeking Holes in Government's Case." My emphasis.

82. Antiterrorism and Effective Death Penalty Act of 1996, S.735, 104th Congress, 1996, Title I, Title II, sec. 233(c), Title III, sec. 324(1); Neil Lewis, "Anti-terrorism Bill: Blast Turns a Snail into a Race Horse," *NYT*, April 21, 1995.

83. Antiterrorism and Effective Death Penalty Act of 1996, Title III, sec. 301, Title II, sec. 221, Title IV, sec. 401, Title IV, sec. 421.

84. Illegal Immigration Reform and Immigrant Responsibility Act of 1996, H.R. 3610, 104th Congress, 1996; Michael Welch, *Detained: Immigration Laws and the Expanding I.N.S. Jail Complex* (Philadelphia: Temple University Press, 2002).

85. Illegal Immigration Reform and Immigrant Responsibility Act of 1996, Title V.

86. Personal Responsibility and Work Opportunity Reconciliation Act, H.R. 3734, 104th Congress, 1996, sec. 101.

87. Defense of Marriage Act, H.R. 3396, 104th Congress, 1996, sec. 3.

88. Dorothy Roberts, *Killing the Black Body: Race, Reproduction, and the Meaning of Liberty* (New York: Vintage, 1999), 217, 202.

89. "Indicators of Welfare Dependence, Annual Report to Congress" (Washington, DC: Department of Health and Human Services, 2008), table TANF 1. Also see "Poverty Status of People, by Age, Race, and Hispanic Origin, 1959–2011," Department of the Census, www.census.gov/hhes/www/poverty/data/historical/hstpov3.xls (accessed October 20, 2012).

90. Jonathan Teller-Elsberg, Nancy Folbre, James Heintz, and the Center for Popular Economics, *Field Guide to the US Economy: A Compact and Irreverent Guide to Economic Life in America* (New York: New Press, 2006), 98–99.

91. Dorothy Roberts, "Feminism, Race, and Adoption Policy," in Incite!, *Color of Violence*, 44.

Fighting Back, Claiming Power

Feminist Rhetoric and Resistance to Rape in the 1970s

Catherine O. Jacquet

In early December 1970, 150 women stormed a Berkeley city council meeting and demanded a public hearing where, they said, "all the raped women of Berkeley can finally speak."[1] Organized as Women of the Free Future, the group had a list of demands, including free, frequent public bus transportation for all women from dusk to dawn; the introduction of self-defense training for all female schoolchildren in Berkeley schools; funding for Women of the Free Future to draw up, print, and circulate a pamphlet on how to prevent rape; and that women be allowed to carry loaded, concealed weapons.[2] One member of the group stood at the council chamber doors, wearing all black and carrying an unloaded Winchester rifle.

The Women of the Free Future organized one of the earliest actions of a burgeoning nationwide feminist antirape movement. This movement came in response to severely inadequate resources and overwhelming hostility toward survivors of sexual assault from the health care system, the criminal legal system, and society at large. In the early 1970s, some emergency rooms refused to admit rape victims, while most others lacked standardized health care protocols to treat survivors of sexual violence. There was little to no state or federal funding for rape prevention or response efforts, rape conviction rates were astronomically low, and women who reported rape were typically doubted, scrutinized, or blamed for their assaults. Feminist activists nationwide demanded change. They stormed city halls and dis-

Radical History Review

Issue 126 (October 2016)   DOI 10.1215/01636545-3594421

© 2016 by MARHO: The Radical Historians' Organization, Inc.

trict attorney's offices; they demonstrated in the streets and held speak-outs, conferences, and workshops; in cities and towns across the country they organized "women
against rape," or WAR, groups; and they created the first rape crisis centers and
hotlines to assist survivors of violence. Some took up arms, claiming their bodies as
their own and angrily declaring they would defend themselves and other women by
any means possible. After a decade of feminist organizing and agitation around rape,
the world looked significantly different. By 1980 rape had become a topic of serious
public debate, widespread social concern, and the target of sustained public policy.

Forty years in the making, the feminist antirape movement continues to this
day. As a result, most scholarship on feminist antirape activism focuses on movement outcomes, analyzing its successes and failures. Largely written by sociologists,
legal scholars, and political scientists, this scholarship typically paints a dismal picture. At best the movement is depicted as misguided and co-opted; at worst, it is
described as a failure.[3] Like the battered women's movement, another innovation
of 1970s feminist organizing, the antirape movement is often framed within a "narrative of decline"—this narrative tells a story of the movement's co-optation by the
state, its depoliticization, and its eventual failure to meet its original, utopic goal to
eradicate violence against women.[4] This interpretation is based largely on studies of
the sweeping rape law reforms that were initiated by feminists in the 1970s and that
took hold in all fifty states by the early 1980s. Many scholars rightly point out that
law reform did not bring about the results that feminists had hoped for.[5] Indeed violence against women remains pervasive in the United States today.[6] Moreover, some
scholars now argue that the reliance on the criminal legal system has both increased
women's vulnerability to violence and had devastating effects on communities of
color.[7] Yet while law reform may not have brought the revolution that feminists had
hoped for, there was more to the 1970s feminist antirape movement than a push for
legal reform alone. Indeed, there were significant currents within feminist organizing that both rejected and fiercely contested state-based solutions to sexual violence.

From antirape squads to self-defense training and vigilante responses, some
feminists in the 1970s became vocal advocates of individual deterrence strategies
rather than focusing on state-based solutions. These critical yet often overlooked
feminist organizing strategies to protect women and avenge victims of sexual violence have an important place in the history of the feminist antiviolence project.
Reductionist narratives that equate feminist antirape activism with law reform alone
neglect these powerful calls for action and obscure what was, and continues to be, a
multifaceted and complex feminist antirape movement.

This article, then, serves to expand the commonly told narrative of 1970s feminist antirape activism. While feminists responded to rape in myriad ways—such as
opening rape crisis centers and creating hotlines to support survivors, holding public
demonstrations, and writing extensive literature—this article focuses specifically
on physical resistance and extrajudicial retaliation. The feminist actions presented

here include both reported instances of resistance and urgent calls for women to fight their assailants. In pursuing and suggesting such methods, feminists created politically meaningful narratives that sought to change how women thought about themselves and the power they had in their own lives. These calls to action also challenged the state's authority by questioning who had the right to protect and defend women. In claiming this right for themselves, feminist activists reimagined women's social roles, disrupted traditional, patriarchal notions of femininity, and demanded their right to self-determination.

"Regaining Our Rights and Depriving the Rapist of His"

One of the earliest strategies of feminist resistance to sexual violence came in the form of antirape squads.[8] In response to a serial violent rapist in East Lansing, Michigan, a group of women from Michigan State University Women's Liberation announced their plan to form antirape squads during the fall of 1970. Writing in their newsletter, *Pissed Off Pink*, the women explained that these squads would be "groups of feminists dedicated to avenging the rape or other kinds of harassment perpetrated on our sisters by male supremacists."[9] By November, readers of *Pissed Off Pink* learned that a group calling itself the Kitty Genevesie (sic) Memorial Anti-Rape Squad had organized in the area. "Any woman who is harassed or attacked by a man" could report the incident to the squad, and "appropriate actions" would be taken.[10] The women of East Lansing were not alone; they announced their plan "in conjunction with our sisters in Berkeley," where one of the first documented anti-rape squads had formed.[11]

In August 1970 the Contra Costa Anti-Rape Squad no. 14 took to the streets.[12] Their first action was picketing the wedding of an alleged rapist. As reported in the Berkeley Women's Liberation newsletter, *It Ain't Me Babe*, the squad learned that the groom had raped a hired dancer who had performed at the bachelor party a week before the wedding. In response, members of the squad showed up at the wedding and reception and left leaflets on the cars of the friends and family of the bride and groom that read: "Women's Liberation thinks that relatives and friends should be the first to know there's a rapist in their midst, not the last. A week ago Saturday a young woman was raped by a man who sits among you today. He's the bridegroom. . . . We tried to warn Nancy [the bride] about the kind of pig she's marrying, but she didn't want to hear. Maybe it's still not too late."[13] Like the members of the Contra Costa squad, many women who joined antirape groups were motivated by a desire to retaliate against violence. The New York Women's Anti-Rape Group, for example, began in early 1972 in part to "go out and 'take care of' the men that rape."[14] Rather than rely on the state for justice, or male "protectors" for revenge, these women sought to take matters into their own hands, organize in their own defense, and fight back on their own behalf.

Stories of antirape squads offered a radical reimagining of the consequences of violence against women. In speeches at the University of Maine and the University of Maryland, New York–based radical feminist Robin Morgan claimed that a Women's Defense League operated a twenty-four-hour hotline in Chicago to protect women. "The most common call," Morgan explained, "comes around 2 or 3 a.m. It's a woman whose husband is drunk again, and who has beaten her up one side and down the other."[15] Following a phone call, black-belt-trained league members would arrive at the abused woman's house and "take care of" the man. Claiming that the incidences of rape in Chicago had dropped since the organization of the league, Morgan announced that antirape squads were putting "rapists in hospitals all over the country. . . . Rapists think twice about committing rape again after six weeks in traction."[16] In 1972, the *Chicago Tribune* and the *Washington Post* reported that the Los Angeles antirape squad had a "special way of dealing with rapists." Squad members would track down an alleged rapist, "jump him, shave his head, pour dye on him, take photographs and use them on a poster saying 'This man rapes women.'"[17] A similar story was told about a New York squad the next year.[18] A 1973 *Time* article reported that in Lansing, Michigan, a group of women spray-painted the word *rapist* across a front porch, scrawled the word on a suspect's car, and "made late-night warning telephone calls." In Los Angeles, an antirape squad adopted a "counterharassing strategy: when a woman called to complain that a neighbor followed her whenever she went out, squad members followed the follower for three days."[19] And the *Chicago Tribune* reported in 1975 that after three women "entered the home of an accused rapist in Daytona Beach, Fla.," one of the women "proceeded to slash the man's shoulders, stomach, and arms."[20]

How numerous or how effective these antirape squads were is not clear. In their 1974 rape survivor's manual, *Against Rape*, Chicago Women Against Rape members Andra Medea and Kathleen Thompson reported that the squads in Detroit had disbanded when the "women decided that this approach was not a very practical one in terms of the time and emotional energy expended."[21] They further reported that on the West Coast all-women street patrols that tried to apprehend rapists who police had failed to arrest also typically abandoned this for other activities. Unlike other forms of feminist action, such as rape crisis lines or legal advocacy services, antirape squads were not a mainstay of the movement. By 1975 there was little mention of squads in either the feminist or mainstream press.

Yet, even if antirape squads largely went out of existence after a few short years, and even if feminists were *not* putting rapists in hospitals all over the country— Morgan's claims do seem somewhat doubtful—calls for violent resistance and retaliatory measures speak to the frustration many women felt and the lack of confidence they had in the state's ability to respond to sexual violence. Additionally, these early voices sought to shape a discourse on rape that at the time largely portrayed women as vulnerable victims. In contrast to this portrayal, narratives of antirape squads offered women a feeling of agency and access to power. By employing or suggesting various retaliatory measures, antirape squads countered the discourse of victims and victimization. With these stories, feminists invoked a scenario where there were serious consequences for male violence, and women were a force to be reckoned with.

"Everyone Has a Tiger Inside of Her"

Unlike antirape squads, self-defense did become a mainstay of the movement.[22] Self-defense strategies ran the gamut from more radical calls for women to take up arms to less controversial measures like learning the martial arts.[23] Yet no matter the form, from its earliest iterations in the late 1960s feminist advocacy for self-defense was always connected to efforts to protect women from male violence. As explained by two women who wrote of their experiences learning karate in 1969: "Women are attacked, beaten and raped every day. By Men. Women are afraid to walk certain streets after dark, and even afraid to walk into buildings where they live. It's about time that we as women got strong in order to defend ourselves."[24] Similar rhetoric accompanied feminist calls for self-defense across the nation. Many feminists understood this prevention effort as a critical piece of women's liberation. If women were to have complete autonomy over their lives, they had to be able to defend themselves. As feminist martial arts activist Dana Densmore explained in a recent interview, "Female liberation is not going to be there as long as this [male violence] is hanging over you."[25] Self-determination was the theory; self-defense was the practice.

Self-defense arrived on the feminist agenda well before a national antirape movement organized. In the summer of 1968, feminist activist Jayne West was nearly abducted by a group of men in Cambridge, Massachusetts. Following her narrow escape, she immediately began martial arts training. Her activist friends, including Dana Densmore and Abby Rockefeller, joined her in intensive training. By the end of the year, these women were giving demonstrations on self-defense at feminist workshops and conferences. Joined by several others, West, Densmore, and Rockefeller organized themselves as Cell 16, a radical feminist group that promoted martial arts training taught to women, by women, as a politically expedient step toward women's liberation.[26] Speaking to this, Densmore explained, "It was serious, and it was feminist. It was intended to be transformative, a political response to the physical assaults on women and [to men's] physical control."[27] Almost two full years before a national antirape movement organized, the women of Cell 16 were at the vanguard of an emerging movement in women's self-defense. They articulated a politics of rape that called for active resistance, focused on prevention, and sought to disrupt the male attacker–female victim paradigm. As Densmore wrote in the November 1969 issue of Cell 16's journal *No More Fun and Games*, "If even a few women, once in a while, stood up and fought back, the rapists would think twice. They are looking for certain sick thrills, and these thrills just aren't available from a woman who breaks out of his hold in one spring and drives an elbow into his solar plexus knocking him cold."[28] While Densmore erroneously suggested that women never fought back against their assailants, her statement was likely not meant to be a condemnation of individual women's behavior but, rather, a comment on women's vulnerability. Densmore suggested an alternative world where, rather than being viewed as easy targets, women could effectively defend themselves.

As the antirape movement gained traction, self-defense became an accepted form of activism and was widely promoted within the movement. By the early 1970s, self-defense permeated feminist antirape discourse and literature and would continue to do so throughout the decade. Indeed, one of the best-known posters from the early years of organizing was radical feminist activist Betsy Warrior's graphic of a woman giving a swift kick to a man in his groin. The man is falling backward, shocked. The words "Smash Sexism, Disarm Rapists" surround the graphic. The poster was circulated nationwide and printed in the July 1971 issue of *No More Fun and Games* (figure 1).[29]

Figure 1. Poster by Betsy Warrior, 1971.

While often illustrated with female figures in karate uniforms, self-defense encompassed a range of activities from basic kicks and punches to the repurposing of keys and cigarettes as weapons. In their handbook on rape, for example, the Detroit Women Against Rape featured a twenty-page section on self-defense with illustrations explaining how to effectively ward off an attacker.[30] This included jabs, punches, stabs, kicks, and instructions on how to use everyday items for defense. "If you smoke, forget what your mother told you about women who smoke on the street," the authors instructed. "You don't have to smoke it anyway; just carry it. It burns." An umbrella should be used "as a bayonet, not a club, and aim for his throat or stomach."[31] Similarly, in their handbook, the Chicago Women Against Rape advised women on basic principles like stance, how to use your hands, breaking a hold, and taking the offensive.[32] The authors included an illustration of a male figure with explanations detailing how to attack various parts of the body:

"Slam heel of hand up under chin or nose . . . wrench little finger; try to break it . . . kick to kneecap."[33] At the root of any method of self-defense was a belief in self-reliance and a challenge to the narrative of women as helpless victims. As New York Radical Feminist member Maryanne Manhart explained to an all-female audience at an April 1971 self-defense workshop, "It's high time we stopped being victims. . . . Since you are living in a jungle and no one may help you, be self-reliant. . . . Everyone has a tiger inside of her."[34]

As a strategy, self-defense reimagined the relationships among embodiment, vulnerability, and gender. Rather than framing women's bodies as inherently rapable, self-defense activists sought to reimagine women's bodies as forces that repelled rapists and stopped rape.[35] Like the stories of antirape squads, retaliation, and revenge, self-defense allowed women to imagine themselves as powerful agents in their own lives.

In a more extreme iteration of self-defense, some feminists advocated that women take up arms. Although not necessarily the most popular method, it is noteworthy that in the era of increasing militancy within social movements, some feminist activists also took up this call.[36] In the early 1970s, for example, the Iowa City women's liberation newsletter *Ain't I a Woman* featured drawings of women holding, aiming, or shooting guns. A September 1970 issue included a series of six drawings that instructed the reader on how to hold and shoot a pistol. A January 1971 issue featured a cartoon of a women confidently pointing and shooting a gun. The word bubble next to her read, "Sisterhood is" with a large blank space following.[37] For the feminists of Iowa City, sisterhood meant protecting themselves and one another from violence by any means necessary.

Perhaps the best example of armed resistance came from a group in Dallas, Texas, who called themselves Women Armed for Self-Protection (WASP). Formed in 1974, WASP advocated both self-defense and violent retaliation against attackers. The group's first leaflet declared, "WE ARE WOMEN. . . . WE ARE ARMED. WE SUPPORT IMMEDIATE AND DRASTIC RETALIATION AGAINST ALL RAPISTS." The group produced provocative posters of women holding rifles—a warning to rapists to beware. One WASP poster featuring a woman holding a rifle read: "Men and women were created equal . . . and Smith & Wesson makes damn sure it stays that way."

While the group faced criticism for their extreme stance, group member Nikki Craft claimed that they received letters of support from women across the country. According to Craft, four women from Chicago even traveled to Dallas to meet with WASP members to share ideas and discuss strategy. "Many women were ready for defiance," Craft explains, "They wanted to channel their anger and were ready to hear what we had to say, even if it was rhetorical and rigid."[38] With the energy and outrage of the antirape movement behind them, some feminists advocated militant means to protect themselves from rape.

"Why Have a Trial—the Criminal Is Dead"

Feminist support for women's self-defense collided head-on with the authority of the state in cases where women were brought up on criminal charges for defending themselves against sexual assault.[39] Many of these cases became feminist causes célèbres, underscoring feminist contentions about the failures of the legal system and its hostility toward women. Perhaps the best-known of these cases was that of Joan Little.[40] On August 27, 1974, twenty-year-old black inmate Joan Little escaped from the Beaufort County Jail in the small town of Washington, North Carolina, after killing Clarence Alligood, a white officer at the facility. Another officer found Alligood dead in Little's cell, naked from the waist down with ejaculate on his thigh. Little was gone. When she turned herself in to the State Bureau of Investigation one week later, Little claimed that she had acted in self-defense, stabbing Alligood eleven times with an ice pick that he had brought into her cell so he could sexually assault her. The state of North Carolina charged Little with first degree murder, a crime that held a mandatory death sentence. With a major outpouring of support from the civil rights, prisoners' rights, and women's liberation movements, the Little case gained national attention over the next eleven months. By the time of the trial in July 1975, nearly every major newspaper in the country was covering it, dozens of demonstrations for Little's innocence had taken place across the country, and the case had garnered international notoriety.[41]

When politicizing the Little case, feminists confronted what they understood as two major failures of the criminal legal system. First, in cases of rape, the legal system criminalized the victim and not the rapist. Second, the law did not support a woman's right to self-defense. As a rape victim on trial for defending her bodily autonomy, Little's case epitomized those failures. The case was equally crucial from the standpoint of racial justice. As a black woman, Little stood at the crossroads of a long history of racial and sexual injustice. Historically, black women had seen virtually no justice in cases of white sexual attack.[42] Her acquittal, therefore, would set a new precedent in particular for black rape victims of white male violence.

"Power to the ice pick!" became a rallying cry for many of Little's supporters. During the trial some of Little's feminist supporters sat in the back of the Wake County Courthouse courtroom wearing T-shirts emblazoned with the slogan. In so doing, they were supporting a woman's right to protect herself from male violence by any means necessary, a right denied by the state.[43] In a *Feminist Alliance Against Rape* newsletter article titled "Killing with Just Cause," author Sue Lenaerts, a self-defense instructor at D.C. Rape Crisis Center, sharply criticized the state's handling of self-defense cases, connecting self-defense with larger feminist goals. "We consider women found guilty of murder in a self-defense case to be political prisoners," Lenaerts wrote. "Supporting women who fight back is politically crucial for feminists. Any time the criminal justice system prosecutes a woman for fighting for her life and dignity, all women stand to lose."[44] Like Lenaerts, many feminists believed that women had a fundamental right to protect themselves. Denying that right kept all women's safety in jeopardy and further increased the levels of violence against them. As one defense committee plainly stated: "In defending themselves, women run the risk of prosecution by the state for a violent crime. As a result women often find themselves facing two violent situations: the first being the physical assault, and the second, a legal assault leading to possible imprisonment."[45] As Little's supporters proclaimed "power to the ice pick!" they rejected the state's interpretation of the crime and supported a woman's right to protect herself.

Outside the Wake County Courthouse, supporters carried picket signs with the slogan "Why have a trial—the criminal is dead."[46] According to this feminist perspective, the only crime committed was the rape, and "the case had no business coming to trial in the first place."[47] The criminal legal system wrongly portrayed Little's killing of Alligood as murder rather than the act of self-defense that it actually was. Justice could only be served, therefore, if the trial was called off. A petition circulated by the Chicago Women's Committee to Free JoAnne Little, which urged the governor of North Carolina to drop all charges, emphasized this viewpoint. The petition stated, "It is abundantly clear that the death [of Alligood] resulted from his own crime of attempted rape. The criminal is already dead."[48] Little, on the other hand, had committed no crime.

On August 15, 1975, the jury for the Joan Little murder trial acquitted the defendant of all charges. According to the jury, the state had not proven its case. This was a major victory for activists of multiple stripes. Little walked out of the Wake County Courthouse that day to the celebration of some one hundred protestors as they cheered "Freedom, freedom, freedom!"[49] National Organization for Women president Karen DeCrow hailed the verdict as the first "legal precedent for a woman's right to self-defense."[50] A significant departure from the past, Little's acquittal held enormous meaning for the movements that rallied around her. For all, the case served as a major milestone in a history of overwhelming injustice.

Self-defense cases like that of Little's sat at a critical crossroads of women's liberation and the criminal legal system. In defending themselves, women like Little claimed the right to protect their own lives and bodies. Their feminist supporters demanded that the state recognize all women's right to self-defense and self-determination. In so doing, these feminists challenged the authority of the state and rejected the notion that the state be the sole arbiter in cases of rape. When confronted with male violence, feminists believed that women had the right to defend and avenge themselves. In denying women this right, the state continued a longstanding pattern of hostility toward all women, and rape victims in particular.

Conclusion

In 1981, Minneapolis's newly founded Cleis Press published *Fight Back! Feminist Resistance to Male Violence*. With over forty contributors, the 392-page volume included accounts of women who retaliated or defended themselves against abusive husbands or rapists, accounts of antirape and battered women's activism, essays on fighting back and the self-defense movement, descriptions of community outreach efforts, and a forty-two-page directory of resource organizations. Like Berkeley's Women of the Free Future who organized over a decade before, the contributors to *Fight Back!* articulated a politics of rape that focused on prevention, advocated women's right to self-determination and self-defense, celebrated resistance, and offered complex reflections on state-based solutions to the problem of sexual violence. Their voices are a reminder that despite the fact that antirape work had turned largely to state-based efforts by the late 1970s, particularly in the form of law reform, some feminists continued to challenge the role of the state and sharply rejected the growing influence of state actors.

Throughout the 1970s, some feminists contested state intervention into antirape work, and many sought alternative means to address sexual violence. In pursuing methods like antirape squads and self-defense, they asserted their right to defend and protect themselves and their sisters, challenging the authority of the state by taking matters into their own hands. These narratives of resistance served as powerful rejections of dominant cultural constructions of women as weak, inferior, or inherently rapable. Even if those who employed combat tactics or engaged in extrajudicial revenge were few, the alternatives they presented challenged women to reconsider the way they thought about themselves and to claim their own power. The narratives of resistance and retaliation that they constructed (and sometimes enacted) did important cultural work—they offered an alternative to women that was based on their own empowerment, and reframed how women saw themselves in relation to men, as well as in relation to a state that largely failed to protect them.

Notes

The author thanks Zevi Gutfreund for his thoughtful feedback on early drafts of this article. Many thanks also to the readers and editors of the *Radical History Review* for their comments.

1. "No More Rape: Berkeley Women Confront City Council," *Liberation News Service*, December 5, 1970, Rape—Newspaper Ephemera folder, Women's Ephemera Collection, McCormick Library of Special Collections, Northwestern University Library, Evanston, IL (hereafter WEF).

2. "No More Rape." See also "The Most Vicious Word," *Wichita Eagle*, March 25, 1971, Rape—Newspaper Ephemera folder, WEF.

3. Kristin Bumiller, *In an Abusive State: How Neoliberalism Appropriated the Feminist Movement against Sexual Violence* (Durham, NC: Duke University Press, 2008); Rose Corrigan, *Up against a Wall: Rape Reform and the Failure of Success* (New York: New York University Press, 2013); Nancy Matthews, *Confronting Rape: The Feminist Anti-Rape Movement and the State* (New York: Routledge, 1994); Janet C. Gornick and David S. Meyer, "Changing Political Opportunity: The Anti-Rape Movement and Public Policy," *Journal of Policy History* 10, no. 4 (1998): 367–98. Gornick and Meyer argue that the feminist antirape movement "was in sharp decline" by 1980—they go so far as to

suggest that as a result of state co-optation of feminist goals, the movement itself actually disappeared.

4.   For a critique of the narrative of decline in the battered women's movement, see Gretchen Arnold and Jami Ake, "Reframing the Narrative of the Battered Women's Movement," *Violence Against Women* 19, no. 5 (2013): 557–78.

5.   See Jeanne C. Marsh, Alison Geist, and Nathan Caplan, *Rape and the Limits of Law Reform* (Boston: Auburn House, 1982); Cassia Spohn and Julie Horney, *Rape Law Reform: A Grassroots Revolution and Its Impact* (New York: Plenum, 1992).

6.   For recent statistics on violence against women in the United States, see Office of Justice Programs, "Full Report on the Prevalence, Incidence, and Consequences of Violence against Women," US Department of Justice, November 2000, www.ncjrs.gov/pdffiles1/nij /183781.pdf. See also the Bureau of Justice Statistics, "Selected Findings: Female Victims of Violence," US Department of Justice, October 23, 2009, www.bjs.gov/content/pub/pdf /fvv.pdf.

7.   See Aya Gruber, "Rape, Feminism, and the War on Crime," *Washington Law Review* 84 (2009): 581–58; Incite! Women of Color against Violence, ed., *Color of Violence: The Incite! Anthology* (Cambridge, MA: South End, 2006); Beth Richie, *Arrested Justice: Black Women, Violence, and America's Prison Nation* (New York: New York University Press, 2012).

8.   The title of this section is from Detroit Women Against Rape, *Stop Rape* (Detroit: Women Against Rape, 1973).

9.   "Jack the Raper," *Pissed Off Pink*, September 1970, Special Collections, Michigan State University Library, Lansing, MI. This announcement was also printed in the October 30, 1970, issue of Iowa City Women's Liberation newsletter, *Ain't I a Woman*.

10. "Anti-Rape Squad," *Pissed Off Pink*, November 1970, Special Collections, Michigan State University Library. It is not clear if the antirape squad was a group of women from Michigan State University or a separate group entirely. It is notable that this group named themselves in memory of Kitty Genovese. In 1964, a male attacker repeatedly stabbed, raped, and eventually killed Genovese in a thirty-two-minute attack outside of her apartment building in New York City. It was reported at the time, although this has since been debunked, that thirty-eight of Genovese's neighbors had either heard or witnessed the attack, yet not a single person intervened or called the police. Antirape activists in the 1970s would take Genovese up as a martyr for the movement.

11. "Jack the Raper."

12. Contra Costa County runs adjacent to Alameda County. Dozens of town and cities sit within the borders of Alameda Country, including Berkeley, Oakland, and San Francisco.

13. "Jack the Raper," *It Ain't Me Babe*, September 4–17, 1970, 5.

14. Notes of National Organization for Women Rape Meeting, May 24, 1973, box 1, New York Women against Rape collection, Schlesinger Library, Radcliffe Institute, Harvard University, Cambridge, MA.

15. Quoted in "Feminist Praises Maine Lib Moves," *Bangor Daily News*, Dec. 10, 1971.

16. Fran Pollner, "Robin: Harbinger of a New Season," *Off Our Backs*, March 31, 1972, 23.

17. Marsha Dubrow, "Women Organize to Combat Rape and Counsel Victims," *Washington Post*, December 21, 1972. See also "Women Join to Combat Rape—the 'Condoned' Crime," *Chicago Tribune*, December 25, 1972.

18. J. Dwyer, "End of the Line for Jack the Ripper?," *Black Belt Magazine*, December 1973.

19. "Women against Rape," *Time*, April 23, 1973.

20. Patricia Anstett, "Defining Defense against Rape," *Chicago Tribune*, September 9, 1975.

Although it is unknown if these women considered themselves a "squad," they used tactics similar to those of antirape squads. Local police described the women as "vigilantes."

21.   Andra Medea and Kathleen Thompson, *Against Rape* (New York: Farrar, Straus, and Giroux, 1974), 126.

22.   The title of this section is taken from Grace Lichtenstein, "Feminists Hold Rape-Defense Workshop," *New York Times*, April 18, 1971.

23.   The scholarship on the feminist self-defense movement is typically focused on martial arts training or street fighting and does not include armed resistance. See Patricia Searles and Ronald Berger, "The Feminist Self-Defense Movement: A Case Study," *Gender and Society* 1, no. 1 (March 1987): 61–84. See also Nadia Telsey, "Karate and the Feminist Resistance Movement," in *Fight Back! Feminist Resistance to Male Violence*, ed. Frédérique Delacoste and Felice Newman (San Francisco: Cleis Press, 1981), 184–96. For an analysis of women's self-defense in the 1990s, see Martha McCaughey, *Real Knockouts: The Physical Feminism of Women's Self-Defense* (New York: New York University Press, 1997).

24.   Susan Pascalé, Rachel Moon, and Leslie B. Tanner, "Self-Defense for Women," in *Sisterhood Is Powerful: An Anthology of Writings from the Women's Liberation Movement*, ed. Robin Morgan (New York: Vintage Books, 1970), 527.

25.   Dana Densmore, interview by the author, June 17, 2015.

26.   Original members of Cell 16 also included Roxanne Dunbar, Betsy Warrior, and Lisa Leghorn. Many others joined the group over the years. Cell 16 was active from 1968 to 1973. They published the feminist journal *No More Fun and Games*.

27.   Densmore interview.

28.   Dana Densmore, "Writing a Leaflet," *No More Fun and Games*, no. 3 (November 1969): 108.

29.   Susan Brownmiller, *In Our Time: Memoir of a Revolution* (New York: Dial Press, 1999), 205; Betsy Warrior, "Disarm Rapists, Smash Sexism," *No More Fun and Games: A Journal of Female Liberation*, no. 5 (July 1971): 19.

30.   The Detroit Women Against Rape published *Stop Rape*, the first feminist handbook on sexual violence, in 1971. *Stop Rape* was distributed to women across the country and, according to Chicago Women Against Rape, inspired antirape activities in many communities.

31.   Detroit Women Against Rape, *Stop Rape*, WEF, 16.

32.   See Medea and Thompson, *Against Rape*, 73–94.

33.   Ibid., 93.

34.   Quoted in Lichtenstein, "Feminists Hold Rape-Defense Workshop." Manhart's self-defense workshop was part of the New York Radical Feminists' Conference on Rape, held in April 1971 in New York City. Two hundred women attended the all-day event, which included workshops on rape and the law, health and medical issues, rape and psychiatrists, incest and child molestation, a speak-out, and a self-defense workshop.

35.   See Sharon Marcus, "Fighting Bodies, Fighting Words: A Theory and Politics of Rape Prevention" in *Feminists Theorize the Political*, ed. Judith Butler and Joan W. Scott (New York: Routledge, 1992), 385–403. In this essay on rape prevention, poststructuralist theorist Marcus defines self-defense as one strategy "which will enable women to sabotage men's power to rape, which will empower women to take the ability to rape completely out of men's hands" (388). Self-defense, she argues, puts the emphasis on "women's will, agency, and capacity for violence," rather than assuming women as subjects of fear and objects of male violence (395). Curiously, with the exception of one academic study published in 1985,

Marcus makes no mention of 1970s feminist calls for self-defense or of the feminist self-defense movement.

36. While there is a significant historiography on the role of violence in movements for social justice (the black freedom struggle being an excellent example), scholars of 1970s feminism have yet to address this discourse in modern feminism. There were indeed currents within 1970s feminism that supported the use of violence, as documented in this article, and there is a literature debating the use and meanings of violence and nonviolence within modern feminism. See, for example, Judith Winthrow, "Should Women Go Armed?," *Feminist Alliance Against Rape*, July/August 1978; Melanie Kaye, "Women and Violence," in Delacoste and Newman, *Fight Back!*, 160–63; D. A. Clarke, "A Woman with a Sword: Some Thoughts on Women, Feminism, and Violence," in *Transforming a Rape Culture*, ed. Emilie Buchwald, Pamela Fletcher, and Martha Roth (Minneapolis, MN: Milkweed Editions, 1993), 393–404; and Pearl Cleage, "What Can I Say," in *Words of Fire: An Anthology of African American Feminist Thought*, ed. Beverly Guy-Sheftall (New York: New Press, 1995), 429–32.

37. "Sisterhood is" cartoon, *Ain't I a Woman*, January 29, 1971.

38. Nikki Craft, "Drifting from the Mainstream: A Chronicle of Early Anti-rape Organizing," in Delacoste and Newman, *Fight Back!*, 112.

39. The title of this section is from Wayne King, "Trial Gives New Twist to Old Racial Issue," *New York Times*, August 12, 1975.

40. Little's first name was spelled differently depending on the source, sometimes Joan, JoAnne, or Joann. I use *Joan* here as that is the spelling used in the legal record. Her name is pronounced "Jo-Anne."

41. For additional scholarship on Joan Little, see Danielle McGuire, "Power to the Ice Pick!," in *At the Dark End of the Street: A New History of the Civil Rights Movement from Rosa Parks to the Rise of Black Power* (New York: Knopf, 2011), 246–78. See also Genna Rae McNeil, "'Joanne Is You and Joanne Is Me': A Consideration of African American Women and the 'Free Joan Little' Movement, 1974–75," in *Sisters in the Struggle: African American Women in the Civil Rights–Black Power Movement*, ed. Bettye Collier-Thomas and V. P. Franklin (New York: New York University Press, 2001), 259–79.

42. For an excellent analysis of white-on-black sexual violence in twentieth-century United States and antirape organizing, see McGuire, *At the Dark End of the Street*.

43. King, "Trial Gives New Twist."

44. Sue Lenaerts, "Killing with Just Cause," *Feminist Alliance Against Rape*, July/August 1976, 8–9.

45. "Free Yvonne Wanrow," box 1, Nkenge Touré papers, Sophia Smith Collection, Smith College, Northampton, MA.

46. King, "Trial Gives New Twist."

47. Karen Lindsey, "Victory for Joanne," *Off Our Backs* 5, no. 8 (1975): 2.

48. "Free JoAnne Little," Rape—Joanne Little folder, WEF.

49. Rick Nichols, "Verdict Comes Quickly," *Raleigh News and Observer*, August 16, 1975.

50. Quoted in Dennis A. Williams, "Trials: It Was the People," *Newsweek*, August 25, 1975, 29.

Protecting the Prestige of the Traditional Family

The Politics of Domestic Violence Discourse

Raphael Ginsberg

Pennies for Change is a thrift shop located in Durham, North Carolina. One of many thrift stores funding victim support services in the state of North Carolina, it donates its proceeds to funding the Durham Crisis Response Center (DCRC). The DCRC provides various forms of socioeconomic support for domestic violence victims, including counseling, emergency housing, and legal advocacy.[1] In addition to thrift store fundraising, PayPal donations are solicited on DCRC's website.

Just thirty-five miles east of Pennies for Change is the headquarters of North Carolina's prison system. Its budget situation is completely different from DCRC's. Its 2012–13 budget of $1.52 billion is funded wholly by tax dollars and requires no thrift shop support or voluntary donations.[2]

This situation is typical in the United States: public resources for prisons are ever available while funding for victims' socioeconomic support remains contingent on uncertain donation and retail revenues. For example, in 2011, the National Network to End Domestic Violence completed a census of 1,726 domestic violence programs across the nation. The census recorded the requests for services each program reported within a twenty-four-hour period, finding that there were 10,581 requests for services that the domestic violence programs could not meet, including over 6,714 requests for housing. The report notes that programs could not meet these requests because "programs did not have the resources to offer these ser-

Radical History Review
Issue 126 (October 2016)   DOI 10.1215/01636545-3594433
© 2016 by MARHO: The Radical Historians' Organization, Inc.

vices."[3] Accordingly, in the 2012 piece "VAWA Is Not Enough: Academics Speak Out about VAWA Reauthorization," leading domestic violence scholars charged that "Congress should focus efforts on economic justice,"[4] shifting its emphasis from the criminal justice system.

This gap between prison funding and victim support services can be traced in part to a series of late twentieth-century federal initiatives. In 1978, a US Civil Rights Commission hearing reflected deep concerns about the relationship between domestic violence and both male authority and female economic subordination. Conservative responses to the nascent battered women's movement in the 1980s, including debates about the 1980 Domestic Violence Prevention Act and the 1984 report of the Task Force on Family Violence,[5] portrayed domestic violence as a matter of aberrant abusers rather than an exercise of patriarchal authority or structural socioeconomic inequality. Congressional debates addressing the 1994 Violence Against Women Act (VAWA), like the task force report, also characterized domestic violence as a problem of aberrant offenders. In the process, criminality displaced gender as the primary framework for understanding domestic violence.

Battered Women: Issues of Public Policy

In the 1970s, domestic violence was treated largely as a private family matter, and arrest rates for domestic violence incidents to which officers responded averaged between 3 percent and 13 percent.[6] Assaultive men were often granted formal and informal immunities from prosecution, to protect the privacy of the family and promote "domestic harmony."[7] In response, feminists formed consciousness-raising groups to condemn domestic violence and publicize its pervasiveness. According to activist and scholar Susan Schechter, by 1977 the term *battered women* reached public prominence.[8] The movement's orientation was feminist and grassroots and articulately critical of traditional gender norms through which males perceive their dominant position as a license to abuse and women, because of their subordination, have difficulty escaping such abuse. Activists contested the lax enforcement of domestic violence laws, advocated for the creation of civil protection orders, established shelters for battered women, and created emotional support systems for victims.

It was in this context that the 1978 US Civil Rights Commission consultation "Battered Women: Issues of Public Policy" was held. The first federal examination of domestic violence, it drew on an array of experts, including law enforcement personnel, scholars, attorneys, and members of the battered women's movement (a precursor to contemporary anti-domestic violence activism). While some participants argued for changing law enforcement responses to domestic violence, many stressed the need for gender equality and socioeconomic support for victims.

The consultation took place over two days and included over thirty presenters. It received scant media attention, with no coverage in either the *New York Times* or the *Washington Post*. Its aims were diverse, including "to identify sound, existing research data, as well as research gaps, and consequently to consider research strategies; to identify necessary state legal and law enforcement reform; to identify needed short- and long-term support services for battered women; to identify, in all of the above, the appropriate Federal role; to facilitate communication among researchers, activists, policymakers, and others; and to inform the public."[9] Law enforcement was only one of many issues the consultation addressed; over two-thirds of the presenters focused on issues of socioeconomic support. The consultation's participants offered feminist, class-conscious analyses of domestic violence, locating the origins of the violence in economic inequality and traditional family roles. In her keynote address, movement activist Del Martin argued, "Marriage is the institutional source and setting in which the violence is carried out. . . . Domestic violence cannot be fully understood without examining the institution of marriage itself as the context in which the violence takes place."[10] She described American gender relations as a "patriarchal structure" in which the "dominant group [men] define acceptable roles of subordinates [women]." Marriage, Martin argued, is the arena in which "women and men are socialized to act out dominant-submissive roles that in and of themselves invite abuse. Husbands/assailants and wife/victims are merely the actors in the script that society has written for them."[11] Lisa Leghorn averred, "That the nuclear family is not working in this culture can no longer be questioned."[12]

Accordingly, participants challenged male dominance within the family. Judge Lisa Richette proposed eliminating the husband as "head of the family" from its "continuing presence in the law, in religion, in administrative procedure, and a taken for granted aspect of family life." She argued, "Full sexual equality is essential for the prevention of wife-beating."[13] Leghorn stressed the need for replacing male domination with female solidarity, hailing support services provided to abused women, which could foster "new ways of living" and the kinds "of transformation in their lives [that] is not only possible, but also necessary."[14]

Participants noted how socioeconomic challenges prevent women from leaving abusive relationships. The consultation's introduction noted that "battered women are limited often in their ability to flee their homes by financial dependence . . . [and] the lack of housing . . . services."[15] The lack of economic resources, housing, and job training constrained victims, Martin noted: "Without a place to go or means of support . . . the wife/victim is often forced to return to her violent husband," and that, in evaluating whether to leave, women are "forced to face the cold, hard fact of the poverty of her existence."[16] The consultation's participants proposed policies responsive to the needs of all women, not just victims. Monica Erler argued, "Abused women don't need treatment programs. They, like other women, need fair income for their labor, decent housing at an affordable price, competent legal advice, dependable child care and other assistance with child rearing. Government policy and funding should take these needs seriously."[17] These resources would ensure independence, which could enable women to leave abusive situations.

It was not only the consultation's battered women's activists who asserted the need for victims' support but the mainstream political figures participating in the consultation as well. Representatives from the Department of Housing and Urban Development, Department of Health, Education, and Welfare, Department of Labor, and the Legal Services Corporation gave extensive presentations about how victims could utilize federal resources to escape abuse, including information about how to find housing, welfare, and legal representation through their respective offices.

Altogether, consultation participants held that the traditional family rests on the exercise of male violence and socioeconomic inequalities that trap women in abusive situations. They proposed mechanisms enabling women to escape abuse, but these mechanisms threatened to undermine the autonomy of the family. Subsequent conservative responses absolved gender norms and socioeconomic inequality of any culpability in domestic violence.

Conservative Opposition to Federal Domestic Violence Assistance

Conservative opposition to the battered women's movement coalesced soon after the consultation took place. According to Elizabeth Pleck, in the late 1970s and early 1980s "the New Right identified domestic violence legislation with feminism, which in turn they associated with an attack on 'motherhood, the family, and Christian Values.'"[18] For example, in 1980, the Moral Majority worked with Republican senators to successfully defeat the Domestic Violence Prevention and Services Act. The proposed act provided $65 million to domestic violence shelters and programs, money that, in contrast to subsequent VAWA legislation, was entirely dedicated to victims' services.

In Senate debates about this bill, Gordon Humphrey argued that the domestic violence shelters poised to receive federal money were "opposed to traditional families"[19] and would function as "indoctrination centers" for "antifamily" ideas.[20] For Humphrey, the matter went "right to heart of the American family, which is the basis of our society."[21] Senator Jesse Helms likewise argued that shelters "encourage the disintegration of thousands of American families." Helms claimed, "This type of social engineering does not command the support of the majority of the American people and I suspect this is the primary reason why these centers have not been able to generate sufficient financial support within their local communities and now seek federal tax dollars." He concluded, "I cannot support legislation which gives every indication of supporting activities which can only further undermine the ability of many families to resolve their problems while preserving their unity."[22]

Senator Strom Thurmond asked, "Who can seriously argue that the Federal Government is better suited than family and friends, churches and community groups to cure this social ill?" He feared that the legislation "would result in dividing the family rather than uniting the family and curing domestic violence."[23] If passed, a Moral Majority lobbyist argued, "radical feminists" will "be coming to the federal trough for a $65 million feed."[24] Another Moral Majority lobbyist said their opposition to the bill was an effort to "counter the federal government's intrusion into the domestic realm."[25] The *Moral Majority Report* complained that the bill would "place undue emphasis on separation as a solution to domestic violence. This would violate a fundamental moral precept and represent a victory for humanism."[26] Howard Phillips, head of the Conservative Caucus, asserted that civil society adequately addressed domestic violence, asking, "How do you suppose the matter has been taken care of the last two hundred years? It's been largely taken care of by private organizations, religious groups, by families."[27]

The conservative defense and absolution of the traditional family took fuller form in the 1983 Final Report of President Ronald Reagan's Task Force on Family Violence.[28] The report marked only a minor moment in domestic violence discourse, as, like the events described above, it received scant media attention and passing mention in subsequent scholarly work. Nonetheless, the document marks an important moment in the growing divide between criminal-justice-based versus victim-support-oriented responses to domestic violence. In contrast to the battered women's movement activists in the 1978 consultation, the Task Force on Family Violence was composed of law enforcement personnel and members of the punishment-oriented wing of the victims' rights movement. The group included the Detroit and Phoenix police chiefs, the Suffolk County, Massachusetts, district attorney, Missouri attorney general John Ashcroft, Ursula Meese (wife of US attorney general Ed Meese), and victims' rights activists Frances Seward, Mareese Duff, and Catherine Milton.

In noting the prevalence of domestic violence, the report is consistent with the consultation. The report also addressed the unique challenges of addressing domestic violence (as opposed to anonymous violence), noting the necessity of specific criminal justice responses. Acknowledging the particular nature of intimate partner violence at all was counter to conservative antipathy for addressing domestic violence at the federal level, and in fact, some conservatives opposed it.[29] However, despite this acknowledgment, the report conformed to conservative orthodoxy concerning the family, hailing the centrality of the traditional family and remaining silent on women's socioeconomic subordination. The report's analysis of domestic violence did not foreground gender and therefore could not address the relationship between gender inequality and victims' inability to leave abusive relationships.

Instead, the report extolled the virtues of the traditional family and the necessity of its promotion and preservation. The report's epigraph quotes President Reagan: "Families stand at the center of society . . . building our future must begin by preserving families."[30] The introduction declares that "the family is the cornerstone of the American community. Preserving valuable traditions and nurturing the country's children, families are the nation's greatest strength and hope for the future" (97). And the report's conclusion reiterates the point: "America derives its strength, purpose and productivity from its commitment to family values" (119). Thus, according to the report, "As important as our families are to us individually and to the health of the nation, it is crucial that public policy support and strengthen family values and family well-being" (119).

The report protects the family's prestige by privileging criminal justice responses and arguing that lax punishment causes domestic violence, not the traditional family's dynamics. The report contains twenty recommendations for the criminal justice system, recommendations geared toward increasing prosecution and conviction rates and toward intensifying criminal sanctions. For example, the report recommends abolishing the requirement that victims testify at preliminary hearings, barring the police from interviewing children multiple times, and promoting prison terms as the appropriate sanction for perpetrators of family violence. The report claims, "Penalties imposed by the court [in domestic violence cases] do not reflect the severity of the injury or the number of prior conviction for the same offense. This under-enforcement of the law tells victims and assailants alike that family violence is not really a serious crime, if a crime at all. It is this widespread perception that has contributed to the perpetuation of violence within the family" (36). Criminal justice concerns permeate the report, including sections of the report that expressly have nothing to do with criminal justice. Recommendations in sections titled "Data Collection" and "Research" aim to increase prosecutions and convictions. For example, in the "Data Collection" section, the report recommends compelling drug and alcohol treatment providers to report when a patient admits to child abuse, a violation of federal privacy laws prohibiting the release of such confidential information.

The task force report's key rhetorical maneuver is to equate domestic violence with stranger crime. It argues, "The legal response to family violence must be guided primarily by the nature of the abusive act, not the relationship between the victim and the abuser" (4). This assertion that "crime is a crime" explicitly denies the unique nature of violence that occurs within, and sometimes as a result of, the traditional family context. Importantly, this argument characterized family violence as aberrant rather than, as the battered women's movement claimed, inherent in the conditions of the traditional family.

The final report further protects the prestige of the family by remaining vague in describing victims' services. This vagueness obscures the larger problems these services were designed to ameliorate, such as gender norms and socioeconomic inequality. For example, the report's "Victim Assistance" chapter names various forms of victims' assistance, such as "family violence prevention and intervention," "victim assistance programs," and "victim assistance services," but does not specify the purpose of such programs or what needs these services fulfill (45–62). Also, the report identifies the need for the coordination between the criminal justice system and service providers, explaining that "law enforcement officers must know where victims can be referred for emergency aid, judges must be familiar with the services that can be employed as alternatives to traditional dispositions, service agencies must know who to call at the police station" (6; see also 21). However, the report fails to define key terms, such as service agencies, emergency aid, and alternatives to traditional dispositions, and therefore does not directly or specifically acknowledge the needs that are addressed by these services and resources.

The report's proposed victims' services include drop-in centers, in-home care, and temporary shelters and childcare. However the report never advocates funding these services or any specific supporting role for the federal government in providing them. More important, such services do not enable permanent separations or enable victims to survive on their own on a permanent basis but give time for unification, perhaps because the task force privileges reunification. The support services were organized around maintaining traditional family formations rather than focusing primarily on victim needs.

The report's specificity about the role of the criminal justice system and vagueness concerning socioeconomic responses frame intimate partner violence as a problem of "bad people" who can be changed by punishment and thereafter reunited with their families. Obscuring solutions obscures the problems those solutions presuppose. The final report's emphasis on prosecuting and punishing offenders frames domestic violence as isolated acts outside of any socioeconomic and gender relationality, thereby preserving the family's autonomy and prestige.

The Violence Against Women Act

The Family Violence Task Force final report's valorization of the family and the criminal justice system reflected the Reagan administration's broader glorification of both. Because Democrats historically avoided family values discourses when supporting a modest welfare state, there was ideological room for domestic violence policy drafted by Democrats to look different. However, the Democratic Party's primary federal response to domestic violence, VAWA, embraced the task force's reliance on criminal justice responses to domestic violence rather than socioeconomic support for victims, while remaining silent on the traditional family.

Feminist scholars contend that "battered women's activists played a major role in crafting VAWA,"[31] despite its limitations as described above and below. The White House declared 1994's original VAWA "landmark" legislation.[32] In contrast to the historical moments discussed above, VAWA received massive media attention and represents a consensus between Republicans and Democrats about the federal government's role in addressing domestic violence.

Introduced by Senator Joe Biden in 1990, VAWA created two federal crimes:

crossing state lines to commit acts of domestic violence and crossing state lines to violate protection orders. It also mandated that any civil protection order receive full faith and credit in every state. VAWA provided funds for socioeconomically supporting victims and changing criminal justice responses to domestic violence. Importantly, however, funding for the criminal justice system dwarfed funding allocated to support victims.

For example, the 2005 version of the act contained $75 million per year for encouraging mandatory domestic violence arrest practices, $55 million per year for rural domestic violence and child abuse enforcement grants, and $225 million per year for Services and Training for Officers and Prosecutors grants. By contrast, VAWA contained no money for temporary shelters, only $40 million per year for transitional housing, and $10 million for grants to develop long-term housing for victims.[33] In the fiscal year 2012, the amount available for transitional housing fell to $25 million, while funding for criminal justice efforts remained constant. While in 2000 over two thousand shelters and transitional housing programs existed, federal funding filled only a tiny portion of shelter and transitional housing program needs.[34] Further, VAWA lacks funds for long-term housing, employment, medical and mental health care, transportation, substance abuse treatment, financial assistance, and child care, all central needs for victims to escape abusive situations.

Democratic rhetoric during congressional VAWA hearings shared the Task Force on Family Violence's focus on criminal justice responses and the "crime is a crime" ethos. For example, Biden argued in the 1990 Senate Judiciary Committee hearing concerning VAWA that the act "uses federal grant money to encourage States to treat domestic violence as a crime and not as a quarrel."[35] In a 1994 statement provided to the House Subcommittee on Crime and Criminal Justice of the Committee on the Judiciary hearing, Biden argued, "For too long, violence in the home has not been treated as seriously as violence in the street . . . while a stranger might serve a lengthy jail term for an assault, a spouse of boyfriend will all too often be neither arrested nor prosecuted for the very same conduct."[36] Similarly, in his speech opening same hearing, Representative Charles Schumer hailed VAWA's criminal justice orientation, declaring, "If there is one message I would like everyone to hear today it is that batterers must be treated like the criminals they are."[37]

Neither Schumer nor Biden discussed patriarchal norms or gender inequality. Like the Task Force on Family Violence, they focused on the criminal justice system's investigation, prosecution, and conviction of abusers, presuming that privileging punishment alone will substantially reduce future victimization and improve abused women's lives. Meanwhile, few of the consultation's ideas about domestic violence are found in VAWA: helping women means little other than enhancing prosecutions and intensifying punishment.

Perhaps unsurprisingly, Republican statements during VAWA hearings mirrored Biden's and the task force "Final Report's" rhetoric, employing the "crime is a crime" ethos and supporting prosecution and criminal sanctions as remedies for domestic violence. For example, in a 1991 hearing, Chuck Grassley said, "We must impose swift, sure, and strict punishment for criminals at least as tough as the crime itself," and "getting tough on the crime means getting tough on the criminal."[38] Strom Thurmond demanded that "vicious acts against women be dealt with by enacting tough crime penalties which harshly punish perpetrators and deter these violent crimes."[39] In the 1994 hearing, Steven Schiff justified treating domestic violence identically to stranger crime by reference to his prosecutorial experience: "I issue[d] instructions to our office and law enforcement agencies in our district that domestic relations violence was violence . . . a charge of assault and battery should be treated like a charge of assault and battery and the relationship between the accused and the victim were [*sic*] not relevant."[40]

Needless to say, not one of them argued for robust socioeconomic support for victims or reformulated gender norms. This approach to domestic violence has continued to leave women vulnerable to abuse. As Donna Coker argues, inadequate resources are a primary reason women do not leave abusive situations. To remedy this, Coker proposes submitting every anti-domestic violence law and policy to a "material resources test," to find if a policy "improves women's access to material resources," thereby reducing victimization.[41] The test shows that criminal justice responses to victimization are ineffective and harmful for victims. For example, requiring that police officers arrest someone at a domestic violence scene risks victims' arrest as well, with severe familial and financial consequences that outweigh the material benefits of the policy (1042–1049).

Instead of costly criminal justice responses, Coker recommends transportation, housing, childcare, and food assistance (1053). She reasons that "inadequate material resources render women's choices more coerced than would otherwise be the case" (1020). Ultimately, "the obvious impact of applying the material resources test is to shift significant monies to direct aid for victims and to target more significant aid to poor women," and away from the criminal justice system (1052). Studies affirming Coker's arguments demonstrate that access to material resources reduces revictimization. For example, employed victims with stable housing are considerably less likely to suffer future victimization by their batterers, because they are materially capable of staying away from them.[42] Very little of this perspective made it into the VAWA policy.

Domestic Violence and Family Values

Instead of the socioeconomic approach, the more conservative "family values" tilt guided VAWA implementation. The state has taken the position that the traditional family cultivates the values necessary for economic success, and members of nontraditional families are doomed to socioeconomic failure and dependence on government support. Martha Fineman argues that "images of the traditional family pervade contemporary discourse" attacking social spending programs and that "it is the intimate unit in policy and legal discussions that is exclusively designated as what is normatively desirable."[43] This discourse includes the 1965 Moynihan Report (which blames black poverty on nontraditional and thus "dysfunctional" families) through President Reagan's treasured *Losing Ground*, written in 1985 by Charles Murray (which holds that welfare causes fathers to leave families, leaving children without proper behavioral models), to welfare reform debates in the 1990s.

Protection of traditional marriage was the cornerstone of these debates. As Senator Phil Gramm argued, "We need to promote marriage. I believe there are only two things that can prevent or eliminate poverty: work and family. No great civilization has ever risen that was not built on strong families."[44] One of the four stated goals of the 1996 welfare reform was to "encourage the formation and main-tenance of two-parent families."[45] This discourse endures today. For example, a 2014 House Budget Committee publication claimed that "poverty is most concentrated among broken families."[46] The Heritage Foundation declared in 2015, "A major rea-son for the nation's lack of success for the last half century has been the collapse of marriage."[47] As 2016 presidential candidate Marco Rubio put it in 2015, "You cannot have a strong country without strong people. You cannot have strong people without strong families."[48]

By absolving the culture of traditional patriarchal family of any responsibil-ity, US policy from Reagan to VAWA treats domestic violence as an aberration, a crime perpetrated solely by individual men. Within this framework, punishment becomes the appropriate response. But when policy makers privilege criminal jus-tice responses, they deemphasize victims' services and starve service providers of the funding needed to provide services preventing victimization and revictimization.[49]

Notes

1. For information on Durham Crisis Response Center, see its website, durhamcrisisresponse .org/ (accessed July 8, 2015).

2. For more information about North Carolina's prison system's budget, see the Office of State Budget and Management's website, osbm.nc.gov/thebudget (accessed July 8, 2015).

3. National Network to End Domestic Violence, "Domestic Violence Counts 2011: A 24-Hour Census of Domestic Violence Shelters and Services," 2012, 1, nnedv.org/downloads/Census /DVCounts2011/DVCounts11_NatlReport_BW.pdf.

4. Caroline Bettinger-Lopez, Donna Coker, Julie Goldscheid, Leigh Goodmark, Valli Kalei Kanuha, James Ptacek, and Deborah Weissman, "Academic Speak Out about VAWA Reauthorization," February 27, 2012, www.feministlawprofessors.com/2012/02/academics -speak-about-vawa-reauthorization/ (accessed December 11, 2015).

5. William L. Hart, John Ashcroft, Ann Burgess, Neman Flanagan, Ursula Meese, Catherine Milton, Clyde Narramore, Ruben Ortega, Frances Seward, *Attorney General's Task Force on Family Violence, Final Report* (Washington DC: Department of Justice, 1984).

6. Barbara Fedder, "Lobbying for Mandatory-Arrest Policies: Race, Class, and the Politics of the Battered Women's Movement," *NYU Review of Law of Social Change*, 23 (1997): 283.

7. Elizabeth Schneider, *Battered Women and Feminist Lawmaking*. (New Haven: Yale University Press, 2002).

8. Susan Schechter, *Women and Male Violence: The Visions and Struggles of the Battered Women's Movement* (Boston: South End, 1982), 3.

9. *Battered Women: Issues of Public Policy: A Consultation Sponsored by the United States Commission on Civil Rights* (Washington, DC: US Civil Rights Commission, 1978), III–IV.

10. Del Martin, "Overview: Scope of the Problem," in *Battered Women*, 11.

11. Ibid., 11.

12. Lisa Leghorn, "Response to Lisa Richette," in *Battered Women*, 140.

13. Lisa Richette, "Support Services: Long-Term Needs for Battered Women—Underpinnings or Foundations for New Structures?," in *Battered Women*, 425.

14. Leghorn, "Response," 459.

15. *Battered Women*, II.

16. Martin, "Overview," 10.

17. Monica Erler, "Response," in *Battered Women*, 113.

18. Elizabeth Pleck, *Domestic Tyranny: The Making of American Social Policy against Family Violence from Colonial Times to the Present* (Urbana: Illinois University Press, 2004), 197.

19. Quoted in Ruth Colker, "Marriage Mimicry: The Law of Domestic Violence," *William and Mary Law Review* 47, no. 2 (2006): 1852.

20. Quoted in Ellen Goodman, "Is a Broken Home Worse than a Broken Wife?," *Boston Globe*, September 30, 1980.

21. Gordon Humphrey, *Congressional Record*, August 25, 1980, S22796.

22. Jesse Helms, *Congressional Record*, September 4, 1980, S24120.

23. Strom Thurmond, *Congressional Record*, September 4, 1980, S24123.

24. L. B. Weiss, "'Moral Majority' Leads Lobby Blitz on Bill," *Congressional Quarterly*, September 13, 1980, 4.

25. "Conservatives Kill Domestic Violence Bill." *CQ Almanac 1980* (Washington, DC: Congressional Quarterly, 1981), 443-45.

26. "Senate Jeopardizes Family Values," *Moral Majority Report*, March 14, 1980.

27. Quoted in Judy Mann, "Help for Battered Women Encounters Opposition," *Washington Post*, May 9, 1980.

28. *President's Task Force on Victims of Crime, Final Report*, December 1982, http://www.ovc .gov/publications/presdntstskforcrprt/87299.pdf.

29. See Mary Thornton, "Task Force Created on Domestic Violence," *Washington Post*, September 20, 1983.

30. *Attorney General's Task Force on Family Violence, Final Report*, i. Further cites to this work in this section appear in parentheses in text.

31. Leigh Goodmark, *A Troubled Marriage: Domestic Violence and the Legal System* (New York: New York University Press, 2012), 19.

32. "Fact Sheet: Violence Against Women Act," www.whitehouse.gov/sites/default/files/docs /vawa_factsheet.pdf (accessed June 14, 2016).

33. National Coalition against Domestic Violence, "Comparison of VAWA 1994, VAWA 2000 and VAWA 2005 Reauthorization Bill," January 16, 2006, talkingback2restrainingorders.files .wordpress.com/2012/08/vawa_94_00_05.pdf (accessed March 20, 2013).

34. Amy Farmer, Amandine Sambira, and Jill Tiefenthaler, "Services and Intimate Partner Violence in the United States: A County-Level Analysis," *Journal of Marriage and Family*, 67 (2005).

35. Joseph Biden, "Opening Statement—Women and Violence," in "Legislation to Reduce the Growing Problem of Violent Crime against Women," hearing before the Committee on the Judiciary, US Senate, 1990, 4.

36. Joseph Biden, "Statement—Domestic Violence: Not Just a Family Matter," in "Domestic Violence: Not Just a Family Matter," hearing before the House Subcommittee on Crime and Criminal Justice of the Committee on the Judiciary, 1994, 35–36.

37. Charles Schumer, "Statement—Domestic Violence: Not Just a Family Matter," in "Domestic Violence," 45.

38. Charles Grassley, "Statement—Violence against Women: Victims of the System," in "Violence against Women: Victims of the System," hearing before the Committee of the Judiciary, US Senate, 1991, 3.

39. Strom Thurmond, "Statement—Violence against Women: Victims of the System," in "Violence against Women," 19.

40. Steven Schiff, "Statement—Domestic Violence: Not Just a Family Matter," in "Domestic Violence," 5.

41. Donna Coker, "Shifting Power for Battered Women: Law, Material Resources and Poor Women of Color," *U.C. Davis Law Review* 33 (2000): 1009-55.

42. See Neil Websdale and Byron Johnson, "Reducing Woman Battering: The Role of Structural Approaches," in *Domestic Violence at the Margins: Readings on Race, Class, Gender, and Culture,* ed. Natalie Sokoloff (New Brunswick, NJ: Rutgers University Press, 2005); and Christina Gibson-Davis, Katherine Magnuson, Lisa Gennetian, and Greg Duncan, "Employment and the Risk of Domestic Abuse among Low-Income Women," *Journal of Marriage and Family* 67, no. 5 (2005): 1149–68.

43. Martha Fineman, "Masking Dependency: The Political Role of Family Rhetoric," *Virginia Law Review* 81 (1995): 2183.

44. Statement of Phil Gramm, in "Family Self-Sufficiency Act," *Congressional Record* 141 (August 7, 1995): S11747.

45. Thomas Gabe, "Welfare, Work, and Poverty Status of Female-Headed Families with Children: 1987–2011," report CRS R41917 (Washington, DC: Congressional Research Service, November 21, 2014).

46. House Budget Committee, "The War on Poverty: 50 Years Later," March 3, 2014, budget .house.gov/uploadedfiles/war_on_poverty.pdf.

47. Robert Rector, "Married to the Welfare State," February 10, 2015, www.heritage.org /research/commentary/2015/2/married-to-the-welfare-state.

48. Chris Adams, "Rubio Makes 2016 Pitch to Evangelicals," McClatchy News Services, June 18, 2015, www.mcclatchydc.com/2015/06/18/270477/rubio-makes-2016-pitch-to-evangelica l.html#storylink=cpy.

49. Rebecca Macy, Mary Giattina, Natalie Johns Montijo, and Dania Ermentrout, "Domestic Violence and Sexual Assault Service Agency Directors' Perspectives on Services That Help Survivors," *Violence against Women* 16, no. 10 (2010): 1138–61.

Which Black Lives Matter?

Gender, State-Sanctioned Violence, and "My Brother's Keeper"

Xhercis Méndez

The death of Trayvon Martin and the subsequent acquittal of his murderer sparked a series of responses across the United States, including an explosion of social media, mass protests, the birth of grassroots movements such as Black Lives Matter (BLM), and state-sponsored initiatives such as My Brother's Keeper (MBK). For many invested in the long struggle for black liberation, the acquittal symbolized the extent to which the American legal system was built on structural injustice and inequality, more often than not providing state support to vigilantes as long as those in the crosshairs were people of color. Martin was seen as yet another casualty in the war on black life and a reminder of the extent to which black lives were deemed disposable, killable, and structurally less worthy within the context of the United States. Indeed, his death, the trial, and acquittal served as yet another reminder of the structural inequalities that introduce violence into communities of color and the urgent need for a radical transformation in a system of legal and state governance that thrives on the demise of black life.

In response to Martin's death and the outrage that followed the acquittal, the nascent BLM movement, spearheaded by three black queer women, Patrisse Cullors, Alicia Garza, and Opal Tometi, proposed a grassroots movement that would broaden the scope of black liberation and address the wide array of struc-

Radical History Review
Issue 126 (October 2016)   DOI 10.1215/01636545-3594445
© 2016 by MARHO: The Radical Historians' Organization, Inc.

tural inequalities that produce violence within black communities. For instance, structural inequalities can best be understood as the sets of conditions (persistent poverty, lack of access to health care, school-to-prison pipeline) and institutions (the legal system, heteropatriarchy) that ensure some communities or group members are systematically denied access to their full rights as citizens and relegated to a lesser humanity. It refers to the conditions that produce some communities or group members as disposable and therefore more available for exploitation. The statement and approach put forth by BLM is noteworthy in that they have foregrounded the concerns of women of color, queer and gender-nonconforming folks of color, trans-folks, and differently abled bodies of color and ultimately centered the voices of those that have been historically marginalized even within the context of liberatory struggle. As a result, BLM seeks to address the diversity of structural inequalities impacting communities of color writ large. These are not limited to the issue of police brutality—they also include prisons, food security, anti-immigrant policy, transphobia, the assault on disabled community members, unequal access to health care and education, wage disparities, and reproductive justice for women of color.

In contrast, President Barack Obama responded to the collective outrage and protest by launching MBK, an initiative whose purpose was to primarily address the challenges facing young men and boys of color. In many ways, overlooking the broader community concerns being put forth by the women of BLM, the initiative was and continues to be an effort to address the *individual* barriers to social mobility for racialized males. These efforts have included providing mentorship and employment opportunities to create a path toward the middle class and creating policies that would work to minimize the disparities for youth of color.[1] Toward these ends, the initiative established a task force and issued a national call to businesses, individuals, nonprofits, and local agencies to come together, bring any and all available resources, and make concrete commitments to change the lives of young men and boys of color throughout the United States.

The response to MBK was and continues to be overwhelming. After only one year, the Obama administration reported raising over $300 million to advance the vision and objectives of MBK. In response to the call, "more than 60 superintendents of the largest urban school districts have pledged to develop aligned strategies. And nearly 200 mayors, county executives, and tribal leaders have accepted [the] challenge to develop locally driven, comprehensive cradle-to-college-and-career strategies aimed at improving the life outcomes [for young men of color]."[2]

As the attention to structural inequality continues to grow, grassroots movements such as BLM and state-sponsored initiatives such as MBK have proposed not only different framings of the problem but also necessarily different approaches to the solution. While throughout this article I reference the BLM movement, I focus primarily on MBK for two reasons. First, many who are wary of grassroots protest have hinged their hopes on MBK as a state-sponsored initiative that seems to be a "step in the right direction." Second, and more important, as a federally sanctioned response MBK has the resources and potential to create necessary change, making it all the more pressing to hold its aims accountable.

For these reasons, this article seeks to consider to what extent MBK misses a real opportunity to improve the lives of youth of color by recycling much of the problematic logic, reasoning, and assumptions of its 1965 predecessor, the Moynihan Report, the controversial government document that aimed to reduce poverty in black communities through an initiative to "reintegrate" the black family.[3] As a matter of accountability for a program with such potential impact, certain key questions must be raised, such as how rehashing central aspects of the Moynihan Report works to derail us from examining the intersectional forms of institutionalized and state-sanctioned racialized gender violence prevalent in the contemporary moment, the very issues that the BLM movement is calling attention to. In other words, to what extent does MBK keep us from examining and altering the structural forms of violence that consistently wreak havoc in the lives of both young women and men of color, regardless of gender identity? To what extent does MBK fall prey to assumptions that reinforce structural inequalities, regardless of intention, thus laying the ground for an oppositional sexual politics by creating yet another set of conditions whereby men and women of color are pitted against each other in a competition for access to resources? And in what ways does MBK serve as strategy to contain and restrict protest and ultimately transformation? Altogether, these concerns carry new significance in the context of continued protests against state-sanctioned violence targeting black lives and black life.

My Brother's Keeper: Moynihan All Over Again?

In an effort to address the "persistent opportunity gaps" that prevent boys and men of color from achieving their full potential, MBK unfortunately recycles key assumptions of the Moynihan Report. In both reports, women of color are presumed to be faring better in terms of education and jobs than their male counterparts.[4] For this reason, women of color have been excluded from the projected program to address racial inequality and structural disparities. Moynihan argued that the United States needed to focus on improving opportunities for African American men because "ours is a society which presumes male leadership in private and public affairs. . . . A subculture, such as that of the Negro American, in which this is not the pattern, is placed at a distinct disadvantage."[5] For Moynihan, the relative success of black women not only hindered the progress of black men but also served as a measure of the pathology of black families. MBK, it seems, is built upon some of the same assumptions.

The claim that women of color are faring better and that they therefore do not need resources directed at improving their lives simply isn't true. The statistics proclaiming the relative success of women of color compared with men of color come at a time when black girls are being suspended from school at six times the rate of white girls and women of color have become the fastest rising prison population.[6] According to a Prison Policy Initiative report, the women's prison population has nearly tripled since the 1990s, the majority of whom are women of color.[7] To assert the relative success of women of color in the contemporary moment is to overlook the series of physical and nonphysical forms of violence that women of color face, including but not limited to being funneled into the prison system at alarming rates, persistent poverty, racialized gender wage gaps, and being marginalized within state institutions such as public schools and health care systems. Indeed, these are the structural inequalities that BLM has identified as hindering the progress of youth and communities of color.

One of the reasons that this misperception persists, as eloquently highlighted by the African American Policy Forum brief "Say Her Name: Resisting Police Brutality against Black Women," is that there are presently no accurate databases collecting accounts of how state institutions also target women of color.[8] The brief's authors contend that the tendency to focus on young men of color leaves us with an incomplete picture of state-sanctioned violence. For example, similar to the cases of young black men who have been murdered with impunity, black women have also been assaulted for "driving while black," being poor, and having mental health issues. The brief brings together cases that illustrate the ways in which black women have also been construed as "dangerous" and "criminal," in addition to more intersectional concerns such as being penalized for defending themselves against domestic violence and having their sexualities policed.[9]

As the brief's authors note, not only are there no readily available databases detailing the particularities of how black women are profiled by police, but there are no databases documenting how black women, as well as nonblack women of color, are vulnerable to other forms of state-sanctioned violence, such as sexual assault and being profiled as sex workers by police.[10] This is not to suggest that men of color are not victims of structural racial inequality; rather, the assumption that they are the *primary* victims allows us to understand only a very small portion of the overall problem. The insistence that women of color on the whole suffer "less" from, or fare better within, structural racial inequality not only keeps us from examining the intersectional forms of institutionalized and state-sanctioned racialized gender violence prevalent in the contemporary moment but also justifies policy initiatives that can only lead to partial solutions.

Moreover, the assumption that women of color are "faring better" creates the conditions for an oppositional sexual politics that undermines collective efforts, such as those of BLM, to improve the conditions of communities of color more broadly. This is a concern in both black and nonblack communities of color. It is also an example of how MBK falls prey to assumptions that reinforce, rather than dismantle, structural inequalities. MBK lays the ground for an oppositional sexual politics by paradoxically putting women of color in the position to argue that they are indeed doing as badly (or perhaps worse) than men of color in order to access state support, resources, and be deemed worthy of investment. Women of color who attempt to correct this misconception are accused of undermining efforts to improve the lives of men of color. *They* become the enemy, not the structural dynamics that pit men and women of color against each other in the battle for resources.

For instance, Roland S. Martin has argued that those pushing to make MBK more inclusive to minority girls "look silly," especially when the Obama administration has established the White House Office on Women and Girls to address the impact of policy on women and girls.[11] And yet, as Kimberlé Williams Crenshaw and others have pointed out, the White House Office on Women and Girls has no initiatives that directly deal with the challenges facing girls and women of color (not to mention queer, gender-nonconforming, or trans folks of color who fall outside of both MBK and any initiatives coming out of the White House Office on Women and Girls), nor do they have nearly the same level of resources, cache, and mobilization as does MBK.[12] On the whole, the myopic focus on men and boys of color in the effort to address structural racial inequalities illustrates the extent to which women of color's lives continue to be marginalized and devalued. Grassroots activists that form part of BLM and the "Say Her Name" brief have consistently identified this as a problem that will only lead us to partial solutions. While I agree that not all initiatives need to be inclusive of everyone, any initiative that claims to address the structural disparities that keep youth of color systemically marginalized needs to also *center* women and girls of color.

It is here that indigenous (Aymara) lesbian feminist Julieta Paredes's argument becomes particularly instructive. In her book *Hilando Fino: Desde el Feminismo Comunitario*, Paredes begins from the assumption that "women are (minimally) half of everything."[13] She stresses this because she and others in her community noticed that when women are being discussed they are treated as though they comprise a minority sector among larger and or more important concerns. An example of this would be to say, "We are going to create policy for the indigenous, for peasants, and for women,"[14] as though women were not also indigenous or peasants. Applying this understanding to MBK, we can argue that if MBK is about telling young people of color that their lives matter, then it is important to remember that women of color do not comprise a smaller or even negligible portion of the people negatively impacted by systemic inequality.

Missing the (Structural) Forest for the (Individual) Trees

In addition to leaving women of color out of the articulated vision to address opportunity gaps and structural inequalities, Obama's promotion of MBK reframed the persistence of poverty in terms of the "absence of fathers" (the breakdown of the black family, in Moynihan's terms) and lack of male role models in communities of color.[15] Implicit in this rhetoric is the idea that the integration of individual men of color into the economy will somehow increase marriage rates for heterosexual African American couples, resolve the issue of "absent fathers," and in the process decrease the level of opportunity gaps for youth of color. Toward these ends, MBK focuses on "fixing" individuals within communities of color. As a result the list of goals primarily focuses on improving the boys themselves, by getting them to read better by the third grade, keeping them from dropping out of high school, and encouraging them to pursue postsecondary education and training.[16] However, the focus on young men of color's individual improvement circumvents the need to address the structural inequalities that introduce both physical and nonphysical forms of violence into their lives or the multiplicity of ways in which black lives are systemically marginalized and targeted for demise throughout the United States.

For instance, MBK fails to address the racialized gender wage gaps that have women of color at the bottom of the global economy and that keep youth of color in conditions of poverty in the first place. In addition, it does little to address the structural dynamics that allow black youth to be assaulted by police while in school (e.g., the teenage girl assaulted at Spring Valley High School in South Carolina by officer Ben Fields) or that have led to the deaths of black children at the hands of police, such as Tamir Rice and Aiyana Jones. It fails to address the fact that the life expectancy for black transwomen is thirty-five years of age. It fails to address the sets of conditions that criminalize black queer, gender-nonconforming, and trans youth of color for carrying condoms, profiling them as sex workers and funneling them into the prison system precisely because they are not "easily" integrated into the heternormative global economy.

Finally, MBK fails to address the fact that even when its stated objectives are met, it is not enough to protect black youth. Certainly, in the case of Trayvon Martin, in whose memory MBK was launched, having an active father and growing up in a middle-class neighborhood were not enough to either prevent his murder or hold his murderer accountable. As Jamelle Bouie notes in his article "The Flaws of My Brother's Keeper," young men like Trayvon Martin and Jordan Davis "didn't die because their parents weren't involved enough; they died because they lived in a country where their lives were feared and devalued."[17]

Rather than proffering a solution for structural inequality, MBK seems to be more about recycling Moynihan's strategies of containment and discipline. Moynihan was particularly concerned with the black liberation struggles of the time that were not opposed to mass militancy and armed self-defense as a means for liberation. He expressed concern that without a resolution to the deep and deepening levels of poverty being experienced by black communities, as well as other communities of color, impoverished communities of color would turn to "more dangerous" alternatives such as the Nation of Islam (what he referred to as the black Muslim doctrines) and Chinese communism.[18] In addition to the social movements taking place within the US, the anticolonial and black liberation struggles taking place on an international scale were also being tracked by Moynihan. With these movements in mind, he wrote that world events would undoubtedly be affected by how successfully African Americans were "peacefully assimilated" into American society, and he urged America to decide if the "Negro [would] be her liability or her opportunity."[19]

In what seems to be a haunting regurgitation of Moynihan's logic and concerns, Obama argues that America's future depends on us caring about the successful integration of men of color into the economy. According to Obama, these men and boys are "our future workforce. . . . [They] are going to be taxpayers. They're going to help build our communities. They will make our communities safer. They aren't part of the problem, they're *potentially part of the solution*."[20] Although seemingly positive, similar to the Moynihan Report, I would argue that MBK is invested in containing and disciplining what are perceived to be "dangerous" protestors and a "criminal" masculinity on the verge of bubbling over. On the one hand, the initiative seeks to contain and appease the outrage of protestors by offering men and boys of color the carrot of future employment and by telling them that "their lives matter," even as these things fail to address the immediate conditions of poverty and violence in their lives. At the same time, although the focus on young men and boys of color may be psychologically satisfying in that it suggests somebody cares, it also serves a disciplinary function. While the funneling of youth of color into postsecondary education carries with it no guarantee of employment, it almost certainly carries with it a guarantee of debt. The current economic crisis is such that fewer and fewer jobs are available to those graduating with postsecondary educations. Without a significant restructuring of the economy, we end up with an initiative that makes youth of color increasingly exploitable by adding new layers of debt to their already precarious circumstances.

Obama claims that MBK is about introducing a new value system that will redefine who we are as a nation and that will transform liberty, justice, and equality for all into more than rhetoric. But ultimately it misses the mark. By recycling many of the problematic assumptions and values of the Moynihan report, MBK sacrifices a very real opportunity and requirement to address the structural inequalities undermining the well-being and future of youth of color, especially as it relates to black life and lives.

Departing from Moynihan's Logic:
Reframing Black Liberation as a Collective and Communal Project

Even in the face of state initiatives that undermine collective struggle, black feminists, gender-nonconforming and queer folks of color, and men of color invested in broader conceptions of black liberation have, since the Moynihan Report, done the work of promoting communal alternatives that are open to and include all black lives. For instance, the open letter widely circulated on the Internet, the "Letter of

Two Hundred Concerned Black Men Calling for the Inclusion of Women and Girls in 'My Brother's Keeper'" respectfully asked Obama for a vision of racial justice that also included black girls and women and that would not express empathy and commitments to "only half of [the black] community."[21] In an inspiring attentiveness to how such initiatives often prioritize one marginalized group at the expense of others, the letter stated,

As African Americans, and as a nation, we have to be as concerned about the experiences of single Black women who raise their kids on sub-poverty wages as we are about the disproportionate number of Black men who are incarcerated. We must care as much about Black women who are the victims of gender violence as we do about Black boys caught up in the drug trade. We must hold up the fact that Black women on average make less money and have less wealth than both White women and Black men in the United States just as we must focus on the ways in which Black men and women are disproportionately excluded from many professions.

The letter went on to suggest that "if the denunciation of male privilege, sexism and rape culture is not at the center of our quest for racial justice, then we have endorsed a position of benign neglect towards the challenges that girls and women face that undermine their well-being and the well-being of the community as a whole." Thus, challenging the long history of state sponsored initiatives purporting to "save" black men at the expense of black women, the letter called for an expansion of the initiative to include the heterogeneity and multiplicity of circumstances negatively impacting black communities as a whole.

In addition to the letter signed by "Two Hundred Concerned Black Men"—arguably one of the more successful efforts to challenge state-sponsored initiatives that pave the way for oppositional sexual politics and undermine collective struggle—is the BLM campaign. The BLM movement has been self-defined as a strategic effort to revitalize the politics of black liberation but in a way that takes up the complexity and diversity of black life. This movement draws from the lessons of the black liberation struggles of the 1960s, as well as from black feminisms and queer of color activism, to promote a much broader vision of black liberation and communal inclusion. According to its founders Cullors, Garza, and Tometi, BLM is a political project that

goes beyond the narrow nationalism that can be prevalent within Black communities, which merely call on Black people to love Black, live Black and buy Black, keeping straight cis Black men in the front of the movement while our sisters, queer and trans and disabled folk take up roles in the background or not at all. Black Lives Matter affirms the lives of Black queer and trans folks, disabled folks, black-undocumented folks, folks with records, women and all Black lives along the gender spectrum. It centers those that have been marginalized within Black liberation movements. It is a tactic to (re)build the Black liberation movement.[22]

Indeed, as they assert, if black lives matter, then *all* black lives matter.

As a result, the BLM movement has pushed the debate on racial inequality to include how systemic poverty, anti-immigrant policies, prison, the assault on black children and families, transphobia, and state-sponsored experimentation on differently abled bodies also constitute forms of state violence targeting black bodies that need to be centered and addressed. BLM, unlike MBK, is clear that any program or initiative that purports to improve the lives of youth of color cannot solely focus on "fixing" individuals but must address the concerns and structural inequalities impacting communities of color as a whole. Challenging the tendency to primarily center males of color in the discussion on racial inequality, their approach takes into account how racialized gender violence manifests differently depending on your body, how you choose to inhabit that body, and how others read your body. More importantly it reframes black liberation as a communal project that refuses to leave anyone behind.

Notes

I extend my sincerest gratitude to my reviewers, Erica Ball, Nikolay Karkov, and Ganessa James, for their thoughtful feedback and reflections on this article.

1.   Arne Duncan and Broderick Johnson, *My Brother's Keeper Task Force: One-Year Progress Report to the President* (Washington, DC: My Brother's Keeper Task Force, 2015), introductory letter, n.p.
2.   Ibid.
3.   See Daniel P. Moynihan, *The Negro Family: The Case for National Action* (Washington, D.C.: Office of Policy Planning and Research, 1965).
4.   Ibid., 31.
5.   Ibid., 29.
6.   Kimberlé Williams Crenshaw, "The Girls Obama Forgot: My Brother's Keeper Ignores Young Black Women," *New York Times*, July 29, 2014.
7.   Aleks Kajstura and Russ Immarigeon, "States of Women's Incarceration: The Global Context," Prison Policy Initiative, www.prisonpolicy.org/global/women/ (accessed December 1, 2015).
8.   Kimberlé Williams Crenshaw and Andrea J. Ritchie, "Say Her Name: Resisting Police Brutality against Black Women" (New York: African American Policy Forum, 2015), 4.
9.   Ibid., 8–24.
10. Ibid., 4.
11. Roland S. Martin, "Black Elites Look Silly over 'My Brother's Keeper' Criticism," *Roland Martin Reports* (blog), June 21, 2014, rolandmartinreports.com/blog/2014/06/roland-s -martin-black-elites-look-silly-over-my-brothers-keeper-criticism/.
12. Crenshaw, "Girls Obama Forgot."
13. Julieta Paredes, *Hilando Fino: Desde el Feminismo Comunitario* (La Paz: CEDEC, 2008).
14. Ibid., n.p.
15. Moynihan, *Negro Family*, 35–38.

16. "The President Speaks at the Launch of the My Brother's Keeper Alliance," YouTube, posted May 4, 2015, www.youtube.com/watch?v=c9_RYZ_54A4.

17. Jamelle Bouie, "The Flaws in My Brother's Keeper," *Daily Beast,* February 27, 2014, http://www.thedailybeast.com/articles/2014/02/27/the-flaw-in-my-brother-s-keeper.html

18. Moynihan, *Negro Family*, 1.

19. Ibid., prelude, n.p.

20. "President Speaks," emphasis added.

21. See "Letter of Two Hundred Concerned Black Men Calling for the Inclusion of Women and Girls in 'My Brother's Keeper,' May 28, 2014," posted at *NewBlackMan (in Exile)* (blog), newblackman.blogspot.com/2014/05/letter-of-200-concerned-black-men.html.

22. Patrisse Cullors, Alicia Garza, and Opal Tometi, "About the Black Lives Matter Network," blacklivesmatter.com/about/ (accessed December 1, 2015).

"Stubborn Masculine Women"

Violence, Slavery, the State, and Constructions

of Gender in Graaff-Reinet, 1830–1834

Carla Tsampiras

In 1832, Lea, a twenty-six-year-old slave from the Camdeboo area of Britain's Cape Colony, complained to the assistant protector of slaves that she had been struck and beaten on the back and other parts of her body by her female owner, Saartjie van der Merwe. Lea claimed that the beating, administered with a piece of wood and a thong, had resulted in her having a miscarriage during the eight days that she walked through the harsh Karoo landscape to the town of Graaff-Reinet to lay a complaint of physical violence against Saartjie.

Lea was able to lay her complaint because of changing colonial legislation in the 1820s and 1830s, framed as ameliorative measures to benefit slaves, that saw, among other amendments, the creation of "protectors" or "guardians" of slaves. One of the protectors' roles was to enforce new restrictions relating to the nature and amount of punishment owners could inflict on slaves. The new legislation regulated how many lashes slaves could receive and—for the first time—distinguished between the types and amounts of punishments that female and male slaves could be subjected to.

The particular experiences and identities that bring these two women to our attention in this instance relate directly to their (gendered) bodies.[1] Lea's pregnant body experienced the pain of a beating but was healthy enough to sustain her through eight days of walking. Saartjie's body was strong enough for her to inflict

Radical History Review

Issue 126 (October 2016)   DOI 10.1215/01636545-3594457

© 2016 by MARHO: The Radical Historians' Organization, Inc.

violence on Lea. It was specifically because the law defined Lea's body as female that Saartjie could be held accountable for inflicting this violence. Inherent in their case are multiple notions of the body and how it is constituted by individuals, societies, laws, and researchers. When examining their cases, we see bodies as sites of political contestation, bodies as legal persons, bodies as violent and violated, bodies as gendered, and bodies as sites of academic research.

Scholars of slavery beyond the borders of the Cape Colony caution that research that does not seriously engage with the gendered experience of slaves and slave owners provides only partial analyses of slaveholding societies. Others have proved the same thing for slaveholding societies in the Cape, while challenging historians to think well beyond existing boundaries (geographic and otherwise) and reimagine various aspects of the historical landscape.[2] These and other works have generated discussions about intimacy in slave societies, evident in household relations, paternalism, patriarchy, violence, and masculinities.[3] Some of the existing literature focuses, appropriately, on the violence of male owners (male owners as perpetrators of violence) and the experiences of violence of female slaves, particularly relating to sexual violence. This work reveals the complex terrains that bodies—both enslaved and free—had to negotiate at various points in the Cape Colony's slave history.

As women, however, Lea and Saartjie complicate this scholarship, as they insist on a different reading of their gendered bodies. Lea emerges as a woman slave who was not just a survivor of violence but also an active, resisting political agent; Saartjie, as a woman slave owner who was neither a passive participant in a violent society nor dependent on a male figurehead to imbue her with authority, but an active perpetrator of violence.[4] The case was not atypical. In at least one district in the colony women slaves used gendered laws to complain about the violence women owners inflicted on them, thus disturbing state efforts to create "feminine" women and threatening to disturb our understanding of state, gender, slavery, and violence.

Using Graaff-Reinet as a case study, this essay explores complaints of violence brought by female slaves against female owners. Social relations evident in the cases reveal ways in which slaveholding households constituted gender and violence and, specifically, women's behaviors relating to violence. Finally, it considers how the disturbances created by Lea, Saartjie, and others might lead to new lines of inquiry into violence, slavery, the state, and gender.

Graaff-Reinet, the Cape Colony, and the Empire: Setting the Scene

One of the eleven districts that made up the Cape Colony in the early 1830s, the District of Graaff-Reinet covered a large area beyond the borders of the town and included the outlying Camdeboo region. It was an important frontier town under the colony's Eastern Division, home to at least two Voortrekker leaders and an important source of sheep and cattle for the rest of the colony.[5] As such, stock farming constituted the region's primary economic activity, alongside tobacco and wheat farming. Khoena people, not slaves, provided most of the labor in the district, but almost 6 percent of the colony's slave population resided in the area, typically in households with fewer than eight slaves each.[6] The dominance of stock farming shaped the experiences of the inhabitants of the town and surrounding areas in ways different from those of urban-based inhabitants or other rural areas with different farming activities. In districts such as Stellenbosch, where wheat farming and vineyards dominated, slaves and workers were subjected to the rigorous demands of planting and harvesting. Work in stock-farming districts, such as Graaff-Reinet and other districts of the Eastern Cape, involved a different type of regime, one that could put some slaves and workers beyond the sight of their owners/employers. Unlike urban areas, farming districts with their isolated farms could also put some slaves beyond the sight and assistance of officials and administrators.

Proximity to the town mediated the ability of people to access services, resources, information, or figures of authority within the district of Graaff-Reinet. In March 1831 a letter from Anthony Berrange, the assistant protector of slaves for Graaff-Reinet, to the Slave Registry Office in Cape Town indicated that 29 percent of the registered slaveholders lived within three hours, on horseback, from the town; 60 percent lived between three and twenty-one hours, and 11 percent from twenty-one to thirty-nine hours from town.[7]

As Lea's determination to lay a complaint shows, these vast distances may have deterred slaves but did not prevent them from making use of new ameliorative legislation to lay their complaints. So what did the new legislation offer slaves, and what did the state-issued orders and proclamations related to state-sanctioned violence have to do with the construction of gender in the Cape Colony?

The early 1830s, both in Graaff-Reinet and throughout the colony, was a period of increased agitation between slaves, slave owners, local officials, and the colonial government, especially in relation to the rights of, or over, slaves. The ameliorative measures, starting in the 1820s and eventually leading to the conditional emancipation of slaves in 1834, challenged the nature of the existing relationships between owners and slaves in ways that fueled resentment against imperial British rule.[8] The amelioration measures of 1823, 1826, 1830, and 1831 (effective in 1832) prompted negative responses from slave owners throughout the colony, ranging from petitions and deputations to government officials, meetings, and even a riot.[9]

Each proclamation or order of the King in Council issued between 1823 and 1834 altered dimensions of slaves' personal, domestic, and working lives and their standing in legal spheres. The legislation regulated the labor they undertook, altered the status of slaves' testimonies in courts of law, allowed for changing interpersonal relationships and family formations, and outlined the type and amount of violent punishment that the state was willing to sanction.[10]

In 1823, punishment of slaves was restricted and meant to be in the form of "mild domestic correction," with a maximum of twenty-five lashes permitted, with a twenty-four-hour respite between punishments. For the first time, in Ordinance 19 of 1826, the punishments permitted for adult slaves were differentiated for female and male slaves. The maximum lashes for male slaves remained twenty-five, but female slaves could no longer be flogged in public and were to be subjected to "moderate," private whipping across the shoulders.[11]

Slave complaints were to be heard by the newly appointed office of the Guardian of Slaves, located in Cape Town, or assistant guardians located in each region. The guardians would examine cases brought to them by slaves, make decisions on whether they were worth pursuing, and either attempt to resolve the conflict themselves through mediation between the slaves and their owners or place the case before the resident magistrate's court.[12] The complaints brought to each guardian were recorded for each district in a standard format and sent to London every six months.

By 1832, the guardians had been renamed "protectors of slaves," slave owners were required to keep punishment record books, and punishment had been further restricted. The maximum number of lashes a male slave could receive was reduced from twenty-five to fifteen, and it became illegal to beat female slaves.[13] Inherent in these restrictions were particular ideas about male and female bodies, their relationship to violence, and their construction as subjects of the state.

Mary Rayner has shown that the amelioration laws themselves were by-products of complex shifts in global economic systems that saw a move from mercantile capitalism to industrial capitalism, with Britain featuring as a major political power.[14] Throughout the empire, slave labor was to be transformed into wage labor, even as the metropole sought to manage and contain tensions between existing and emerging classes. Central strategies for the metropole and colonies drew on notions of moral transformation, an emphasis on the family as a means of social organization and moral regeneration, and changing state methods of disciplining and punishing populations.[15]

Pamela Scully notes that the amelioration programs and associated legislation passed after emancipation "focused on the slave family, women's sexuality, and on the promotion of patriarchal familial structures and gender relations which officials believed conducive to the reproduction of a stable and industrious working class."[16] Throughout this period, then, both colony and metropole governments ascribed and created gender roles and identities along with new relationships among subjects, the state, and the apparatus of state authority.

Amelioration laws framed the physical violence that the state would sanction around ideas about the status and capacity of an imagined and idealized male and female slave body, essentially gendering the type of violence that could be experienced and how often it could be experienced. The language in the laws frames gender and gender roles in particular ways that can be read as echoes of normative ideas of patriarchy, masculinities, and femininities, mediated by conferred status in an imagined hierarchy of state and subjects. For example, Article 13 of Ordinance 19 prohibited flogging, contained the use of solitary confinement, and limited the whipping for female slaves to a manner analogous to that used in "correcting" children in schools.[17] Article 13 moves the spectacle of violence against female slaves out of the public sphere and into the private realm, there to cohabit with (marginally) less publicly sanctioned acts of violence, such as rape.[18] Inscribed in this article is a frailer female requiring greater care than a stronger male and the same protection as a child.

Article 14 of the same ordinance addressed reductions in owners' abilities to undertake violent acts by noting that it would be illegal for anyone other than the owner, employer, or overseer of a slave to punish a slave, "except in cases where the Owners or Employers . . . are Females, or infirm, or suffering under disease, or are upwards of Sixty Years of Age."[19] This article links acts of violent punishment to male owners and, by extension, masculinities while assuming that female owners are unable to inflict violent punishment.

The orders of 1830 and 1831 further (en)gendered violence and constructed "men" and "women" slaves. They reduced the maximum number of lashes for male slaves and made it illegal to beat female slaves at all. Regardless of the existing experiences slaves and slaveholders had of gender and violence, the amelioration laws enforced state-determined understandings of gender roles and held owners accountable to them.

Major George Jackman Rogers, protector of slaves for the Cape Colony, was quick to recognize the implications of the changes in what types of violence could be used against which types of slaves, and his comments reflected ideas of women slaves at odds with the ones imagined by colonial officials in the metropole. In his December 1830 report he observed:

It is certainly highly desirable that the flogging [of] female slaves should be wholly discontinued, but some punishment should be substituted adequate to the degree of the offences which many of these stubborn masculine women commit. The reduction of food and domestic confinement for short periods are insufficient and with Mahomedans [sic] are at particular times no punishment at all, and it is very inconvenient and sometimes not possible to have stocks in private houses. The consequence is that very many Female slaves have become very insolent and most of them highly insubordinate. They will go out at unreasonable hours, and be Guilty of many serious offences, for which there is now no adequate punishment, and they put their Owners therefore at defiance.[20]

In his assessment Rogers straddles a line: he pays lip service to the official position making it illegal to beat female slaves yet articulates what he sees as the realities of the colony. For all the metropole's desire to grant females different protections as a means of entrenching ideas about womanhood or femininity, Rogers maintains that in the Cape Colony female slaves are stubborn, masculine, prone to committing offences, and used to being short of food. For Rogers, removing the threat of physical violence raises the specter of undisciplined, unpunishable women who were becoming increasingly difficult to control instead of turning into compliant, feminine women who could be easily controlled without violence.

A year later Rogers reiterated these ideas in a report that praised the slaveholders for not resorting to greater violence against female slaves. In relation to the lack of cases of "serious" violence committed by owners he observed: "Considering how extremely difficult it is to keep some of the masculine Females in any order since corporal Punishment has been prohibited, it is very satisfactory that so few breaches of the Law are committed by Slave Owners in this respect, when the provocation is so frequent, and often so galling, and the Punishment by putting into stocks or placing them under restraint or low diet, is not felt either as a disgrace, Punishment or Privation."[21] Regardless of the intentions of the laws, Rogers viewed female slaves as too masculine, troublesome, and difficult to control without physical violence. In addition, they failed to evince an "appropriate" sense of feminine shame. He did, however, hold out hope that the next generation of female slaves might be more "susceptible" to shame.[22] Considering the harsh realties of slave life, and slave women's gendered experiences of slavery particularly in relation to notions of family, the domestic sphere, morality, and bodily integrity, it is unsurprising that some slaves continued to resist by not being "well behaved."

Case Studies: Women and Violence in Graaff-Reinet

Far from the chambers in London in which the orders in council were debated and created, and the protectors' office in Cape Town in which the legislation and "masculine" female slaves were critiqued, Lea and others came to the assistant protector to complain. In Graaff-Reinet, between 1830 and 1834, 250 cases of complaint were brought by slaves and recorded by the assistant protector.[23]

Slaves in the district complained about a wide variety of abuses: being made to work when ill, being separated from their families, receiving insufficient food and clothing, being owed money or stock, not being allowed to visit their partners or parents, being overworked, punished, and ill-treated.[24] Most cases included some form of violence—in this context physical acts intended to inflict bodily pain or cause discomfort as a means of retribution or control. These violent acts included beatings with fists, floggings, and whippings with *riemme* (belts or thongs), *sjamboks*, sticks, or other items and, less frequently, sexual violence.[25]

Lea was one of 990 female slaves in Graaff-Reinet who lived alongside 1,257 male slaves and constituted 44 percent of the total slave population in the district. Male slaves complained differently than female slaves and appear to have experienced violence and their owners' discipline differently, too. Of the 134 cases brought by male slaves, the overwhelming majority (128 cases, 96 percent) were against male owners and almost evenly split between complaints of violence and other incidents not related to violence. Only six cases were against female slave owners, and only one of those six cases related to physical violence.

By contrast, of the 116 cases of complaint brought to the assistant protector by female slaves (46 percent of the total 250 cases), 66 cases (57 percent) were complaints against male owners, and the remaining 50 cases (43 percent) were against female owners. Far more of the female slaves' complaints related specifically to violence: 72 percent of those against female slave owners and 45 percent of those against male owners.

The nature of the violence attributed to female slave owners included placing female slaves in stocks, slapping slaves with open hands, beating slaves with fists, and whipping or flogging female slaves. A closer look at the complaints laid by female slaves against female owners reveals complex subjectivities and relationships between these two groups inherent in the maintenance and creation of hierarchical and gendered roles. Rogers made no comments on the masculinity, stubbornness, or inappropriate behaviors of female slave owners in his reports; the cases make clear that neither female slaves nor female slave owners performed the imagined femininities or "womanliness" alluded to in the amelioration acts.

Body Politics: Lea's Story

When Lea laid her complaint against Saartjie van der Merwe on March 24, 1832, the assistant protector noted in his report that she had no marks of violence on her body but nonetheless sent her case on to the resident magistrate.[26] Lea called two witnesses to verify her claims. One denied having seen Lea being beaten. The testimony of a second, Hanna (a Khoena woman), corroborated the beating with the thong and a small twig but not with a piece of wood. Hanna recounted that Lea had been sent to fetch wood and on her return was engaged in cleaning out a pot when Saartjie came in and demanded to know why Lea had stayed away for so long. Lea did not reply, and Saartjie then picked up a twig "no thicker than a quill" and hit Lea. The twig broke on the second blow, and Saartjie then picked up a thong used by Lea to collect the wood and struck Lea "about five blows over her back . . . over her clothes, and apparently not with much violence" (472–73).

In her testimony, Saartjie denied having beaten Lea at all and stated that she had merely threatened to beat her with the thong as "she had stayed away much longer than was necessary when she was sent to fetch some herbs for her Master who was sick" and because she had refused to answer Saartjie's question. Saartjie was fined £10 sterling for being in breach of the order of the King in Council, and the case was closed.

Lea's determination in bringing this complaint becomes evident in the explanatory remarks made by the assistant protector. He notes that when Lea originally lodged her complaint in March she was instructed to return home and told that her case would be prosecuted before the magistrate. On the April 19, however, before the case had reached the magistrate, Lea returned to the assistant protector, informing him that she had been pregnant when she came to lay her complaint and on her way home had "miscarried on the road, and delivered a fetus [*sic*] of about six months old" (474). Lea maintained that the miscarriage was the result of Saartjie having thrown her to the ground and given her a kick during the beating. The kick apparently left a mark, which Lea claimed she had shown her husband, Constant, that same day. She had not, however, mentioned the incident when she laid her complaint or intimated that she was pregnant; when questioned Lea merely stated that she had forgotten to do so. The assistant protector sent the district surgeon, Dr. Perry, to see if Lea's story could be verified. Perry found the fetus "in such a state of putrification that nothing but the bones could be distinguished none of which were broken" (474). Witnesses Hanna and Constant both denied seeing Lea thrown to the ground and indicated that in the week after the beating she had undertaken her work on the farm as usual and without complaint. Constant also insisted that Lea had not shown him any mark on her side or mentioned being kicked (475–76).

The assistant protector noted that from Lea's statement "it appeared that when she came to the place where the abortion [*sic*] took place she had walked 32 hours in eight successive days, carrying all the time a child of hers of about two years old and having little or no food" (474). In light of this he concluded that there was "more reason to attribute the abortion [*sic*] to fatigue and hunger than to any other circumstance" (476).

The case reveals Lea's body as a site of political contestation, resistance, and determination. Lea was resolved to assert her personhood, claim her rights, and seek redress against the violence committed against her even if doing so required walking for days carrying one child and losing a fetus. It is possible that Lea's miscarriage resulted from excessive physical strain on her body during the long walk to the town, compounded by her position as a female slave in a household that may have been affected by droughts, sicknesses, and shortages. Or, perhaps Lea deliberately induced the abortion and then sought to blame it on her owner in an effort to make use of the moral economy of the district under the new amelioration agreements to bring social censure or possible social humiliation to her owners.[27] The case obscures such details and motivations. It reveals, however, that even as Lea and Saartjie participated in a state-sanctioned legal process that sought to construct them as frail women, their behaviors showed them to be active political agents who asserted their own subjectivities.

Further evidence of women asserting their political agency can be found when reading the "substance of complaints" logged in the protector's records. Phrases such as "punished without due cause" or "punished with insufficient reason" indicate that enslaved women made conscious decisions about what constituted infringements against themselves and their persons, even if these were not strictly within the bounds of the ordinances themselves.[28] As Wayne Dooling has observed, "Slaves themselves decided what constituted acceptable treatment . . . and acted in terms of . . . a 'moral economy' [requiring] . . . their actions to be assessed in terms of their perceived rights within the [owner]-slave relationship."[29] These perceptions also extended to notions of personal honor and integrity.[30]

(Un)Suitable Behavior: Malevolence, Insolence, and Indignation

The assistant protectors' reports used words like *insolence*, *insubordination*, and *malevolence* to describe slaves' behavior or speech in ways that judged the attitudes, actions, or tones of voice of slaves' bodies. For example, Rachel, slave of a Graaff-Reinet butcher, sought the assistant protector several times to lay complaints against both her female and male owners, on behalf of herself and her child Francina.[31] In her first complaint, Rachel accused her female owner, Anna Sophia Pienaar, of locking a chain around her leg overnight. In addition, she accused Anna of tying her daughter to a tree and punishing her with a strap over her shoulders. The assistant protector refused to entertain the first case after it transpired that Rachel had a history of deserting and her owner had learned that she was planning to make another attempt and used the chain as a preventative measure. The second case was also unsuccessful as two witnesses, and Francina herself, contradicted the claims Rachel had made. Francina admitted that her mother had instigated the complaint (despite Rachel's denial), and Rachel found herself admonished and cautioned not to make false complaints again.[32]

A month passed, and Rachel returned to lay a complaint against her male owner for putting her in the stocks overnight.[33] Rachel had again threatened to run away, and the magistrate found this sufficient reason for her to have been confined. Her owner was still fined one shilling, however, as he had contravened the law by allowing her to remain in the stocks overnight. The magistrate dismissed Rachel's fourth complaint, again against her male owner for confining her to the stocks. The magistrate judged Rachel guilty of having made "an unfounded complaint with malevolent motive" and had her imprisoned for four days on a diet of rice water.[34]

If the protector or magistrates perceived the slave to be impertinent, insolent, or less obsequious than the officials, owners, or witnesses (including other slaves) deemed "suitable," this could adversely affect the outcome of the case.[35] Eva, for example, brought a complaint against her female owner, listed only as the "widow of the late Barend Jacobus Burger," for confining her in the stocks until after sunset. Both the witnesses Eva called to corroborate the time of her confinement, and the defendant, claimed that Eva had been extremely insolent and obstinate. The magistrate observed that the defendant was completely justified in placing Eva in the stocks but had contravened the law, so he imposed a fine of one farthing.[36] This measly fine could have been intended to show the magistrates' contempt for either the complainant or the amelioration laws—or both.

The case of Amelia, a fifty-five-year-old slave of a widow from Camdeboo River, further highlights the ways that enslaved women and women owners' behavior challenged emerging notions of "ideal" gendered behavior.[37] Amelia claimed her female owner had struck her with a fist in the face and pushed her down in the mud, her bruised and blackened eye being a result of one of the blows. Amelia described how she was washing clothes when her owner scolded her and told her to take them somewhere else, as the water she was using was not clean. Amelia replied that her body was too full of pain to go further and that her owner had better go home as she had already destroyed all the strength of her body and "she was no more able to do anything." Thereafter her owner turned toward her, took hold of her, pushed her into the mud, and struck her several blows on the face with her fist.

According to the testimony of the witness Betje, the defendant verbalized her surprise at Amelia's behavior and indicated that in the sixteen years she had owned Amelia she had been "treated well," receiving punishment only once. The defendant (listed only as the widow of Piet Venter) further claimed she had attempted to pull the clothing Amelia was washing out of her hands to prevent her washing them in dirty water. Amelia let go of the wooden trough the clothes were in, seized her by the petticoat, and pulled her into the water. They both fell into the water, Amelia with her head downward, accounting for bruises and swelling as she had fallen onto some stones. The defendant denied beating her and was acquitted by the magistrate.

Amelia's definition and understanding of what it meant to be treated "well" clearly differed from the defendant's. Perhaps Amelia reached her breaking point after a lifetime of abuse and, indignant at yet another request, simply refused to comply. Or perhaps Amelia was simply tired from the day's work and felt physically incapable of moving the washing. Either way, her "insolence" in telling her owner that her work for the day was done and that she was incapable of any further tasks directly challenged her owner's authority.

Legal Subjectivity

Two additional cases show how some women utilized specific aspects of their gendered subjectivity or expected gender roles as part of their engagement with the court. The unnamed wife of Jan Vorster, for example, pleaded ignorance of the law when Christina brought a charge against her. Christina claimed she had been beaten with a stirrup leather, knocked down, and beaten again. The defendant pleaded guilty to the beating but said she had been unaware of "a law prohibiting punishment on female slaves, nor that it had ever been made known to her."[38] The magistrate did not regard ignorance of the law a sufficient defense and fined her £10.

Elisabeth Hick tried to be more sophisticated in her engagement with the law when Josephina brought a case against her on January 6, 1832.[39] Josephina was the slave of Andries Albertus Venter but was employed by Elisabeth and her husband, Jacobus. She complained to the assistant protector that Elisabeth had struck her two blows that morning with her fists in the face as she had not asked soon enough for some herbs to put with the fowls she was roasting. The case was heard before the resident magistrate on January 10, and two witnesses confirmed that Josephina had received the blows, although with an open hand, not a fist. They described Josephina's conduct as "most provoking" and said she had been frequently spoken to by the defendant but would not return any answer and turned her back toward Elisabeth.

Elisabeth and Josephina had been at loggerheads a month earlier, on December 7, 1831, when Josephina accused Elisabeth of hitting her with a stick, beating her over her shoulders, and striking her in the face with her fists.[40] The district surgeon confirmed that Josephina had recent marks on her shoulders. Elisabeth called a witness to testify that Josephina had been very disobedient and obstinate during the last month and so deployed Josephina's inappropriate behavior as one strand of her defense.

For the second strand she used a gendered reading of the law. Elisabeth claimed that she did not have the management of her husband's slaves and therefore could only be prosecuted for common assault and not for breach of the order of King in Council of February 2, 1830, as the latter only related to *master* and slave. Her defense failed, and as with the other case, she was found guilty and fined £10.

Elisabeth undoubtedly managed her husband's slaves, regardless of who they were officially registered to, and Josephina and the courts clearly viewed her as the person responsible for breaking the law. Even as Josephina used her status as a female to evoke the protection of the law, Elisabeth used hers, and the gendered language of the law, to protect herself (albeit unsuccessfully) from being held accountable for her violent act.

Disturbances and the Development of Research on Slavery, Gender, Violence, and the State

The cases from Graaff-Reinet illuminate how women slaves and owners negotiated relationships between each other, and between domestic, public, and administrative/legal spheres, that where shaped by the use of, or resistance to, different types of violence. These insights reveal the cocreation of the concepts of violence and gender across different spheres.

Furthermore, the cases reveal gender as a significant vector of power operating differently in a variety of slaveholding households. Rather than becoming compliant, feminine, and unlikely to commit offenses, some women in Graaff-Reinet (slave and owner alike) remained tenacious, active, and disposed to committing transgressions. Conceptions of gender and violence infused both the juridical and administrative management of the colony, and the daily lives of those who lived in it.

Rogers described slave women at the Cape Colony as stubborn, masculine, and prone to committing offenses, in direct contrast to sentimental constructions of female "nature" emanating from the metropole. Ironically, women slaves in the Cape Colony made use of legislation written by the imperial state that produced and prescribed gender norms to challenge the ("unfeminine") violence of women owners, some of whom had apparently embraced their roles as oppressors and "masters." The cases from Graaff-Reinet suggest that we, first, reconsider our normative ideas of patriarchy, masculinities, and femininities and, second, undertake more detailed comparisons of the implementation and manifestations of those normative ideas among embodied beings. Because the embodied beings we will be researching will occupy multiple material and intangible spaces, our work will have to cover physical spaces, like farms, frontiers, and urban areas; abstract spaces like the law, faith, and administration; and oblique spaces like loci of power, emotions, and ideas.

Notes

1. As a political marker of the socially and historically constructed notions of binary sex and the deliberate grouping of people into gendered roles linked to "women" and "men," the author asserts her preference for alternative spellings of *woman/women* such as *womyn* or *womxn*.

2. Barbara Bush, *Slave Women in Caribbean Society, 1650–1838* (Bloomington: Indiana University Press, 1990); Elizabeth Fox-Genovese, *Within the Plantation Household: Black and White Women of the Old South* (Chapel Hill: University of North Carolina Press, 1988); Pamela Scully and Diana Paton, eds., *Gender and Slave Emancipation in the Atlantic World* (Durham, NC: Duke University Press, 2005); Marcia Wright, *Strategies of Slaves and Women: Life-Stories from East/Central Africa* (New York: James Currey, 1993); Patricia Van der Spuy, "Gender and Slavery: Towards a Feminist Revision," *South African Historical Journal* 25 (1991): 184–95; Yvette Abrahams, "Disempowered to Consent: Sara Bartman and Khoisan Slavery in the Nineteenth-Century Cape Colony and Britain," *South African Historical Journal* 35 (1996): 89–114; Helen Bradford, "Women, Gender and Colonialism: Rethinking the History of the British Cape Colony and Its Frontier Zones, c. 1806–1870," *Journal of African History* 37 (1996): 351–70; Jessica Murray, "Gender and Violence in Cape Slave Narratives and Post-narratives," *South African Historical Journal* 62, no. 3 (2010): 444–62; Nicole Ulrich, "Time, Space and the Political Economy of Merchant Colonialism in the Cape of Good Hope and VOC World," *South African Historical Journal* 62, no. 3 (2010): 571–88.

3. See, for example, Clifton Crais, *White Supremacy and Black Resistance in Pre-industrial South Africa* (Cambridge: Cambridge University Press, 1992), 30–52; Wayne Dooling, "The Hegemonic Function of Law," in *Law and Community in a Slave Society: Stellenbosch District, South Africa, c. 1760–1820* (Cape Town: University of Cape Town Press, 1992), 80–82; Robert C. H. Shell, *Children of Bondage: A Social History of the Slave Society at the Cape of Good Hope, 1652–1838* (Hanover, NH: Wesleyan University Press, 1994); John Mason, "Paternalism under Siege: Slavery in Theory and Practice during the Era of Reform, c.1825 through Emancipation," in *Breaking the Chains—Slavery and Its Legacy in the Nineteenth-Century Cape Colony*, ed. Nigel Worden and Clifton Crais (Johannesburg: Witwatersrand University Press, 1994), 45–77; John E. Mason, "'Fit for Freedom': The

Slaves, Slavery, and Emancipation in the Cape Colony, South Africa, 1806 to 1842" (PhD diss., Yale University, 1992); Robert Ross, "Paternalism, Patriarchy and Afrikaans," *South African Historical Journal* 32 (1995): 34–47; and Patricia Van der Spuy, "'Making Himself Master': Galant's Rebellion Revisited," *South African Historical Journal* 34 (1996): 1–28.

4. See Van der Spuy, "'Making Himself Master,'" 7; and Mason, "'Fit for Freedom,'" 196–98.

5. For more on the Eastern Division (or current Eastern Cape area), see Crais, *White Supremacy and Black Resistance.* The two Voortrekker leaders were Gerrit Maritz and Andries Pretorius. More recently (1924) Graaff-Reinet was the birthplace of Mangaliso Robert Sobukwe, founder of the Pan Africanist Congress.

6. See Wayne Dooling, "Slavery and Amelioration in the Graaff-Reinet District, 1823–1830," *South African Historical Journal*, no. 27 (1992): 78–79; "Table submitted by Major Rogers for Return of Number of Slaves Registered at the Cape of Good Hope Colony (by age), August 31, 1833," in General Observations, National Archives (hereafter NA), Colonial Office (hereafter CO), 53/57, 150. Dooling gives the total slave population as 2,836 in 1823 and 2,266 in 1828, with slaves constituting 12 percent of the total population of 19,864 people; people identified as "white" constituted 48 percent of the population, and people classified as "free blacks," 40 percent ("Slavery and Amelioration," 79). In 1830 Rogers estimated that the 32,704 square miles that constituted the District of Graaff-Reinet had 680 slaveholders who possessed 2,630 slaves, with 570 of those slave holders having fewer than 8 slaves. Western Cape Archive, Slave Office (hereafter KAB, SO), 3/6, *Report of the Protector of Slaves of the Colony of the Cape of Good Hope, 25 June–24 December 1830*, 1:625.

7. KAB, SO, 1/22, Slave Registry Office Graaff-Reinet, 1829–1837, "Return of the Number of Slaves Registered at Graaff-Reinet on the 31st December 1830," letter from the Slave Registry Office, Graaff-Reinet, February 9, 1831.

8. See John E. Mason, "Fortunate Slaves and Artful Masters: Labor Relations in the Rural Cape Colony during the Era of Emancipation, ca. 1825 to 1838," in *Slavery in South Africa: Captive Labor on the Dutch Frontier*, ed. Elizabeth Eldredge and Fred Morton (Boulder, CO: Westview Press, 1994): 67–91. Slaves were forced to undergo a four-year "apprenticeship" period before being completely emancipated, so strictly speaking emancipation properly occurred in 1838.

9. The reports by the protectors of slaves mention of increasing tension between owners and slaves and between owners and themselves as government officials. See NA, CO, 53/52, General Observations, 343–61, 409–12; NA, 53/54, General Observations, 507–9; NA, CO, 53/55, General Observations, 132–34; NA, CO, 53/57, General Observations, 129–43 (deals specifically with responses to emancipation) and 341–64 (for owner and slave reactions); and NA, CO, 53/58, General Observations, 144–51. See also Dooling, "Slavery and Amelioration," 83–84; and John E. Mason, "The Slaves and Their Protectors: Reforming Resistance in a Slave Society, the Cape Colony, 1826–1834," *Journal of Southern African Studies* 17, no. 1 (1991): 108–9.

10. For details of contents of each proclamation or order, see Dooling, "Slavery and Amelioration," 76–77; and Mason "Slaves and Their Protectors," 106–9.

11. KAB, SO, Cape Colony Publications 6/3/1/1—Statutes, Acts, Ordinances 1825–1853, Ordinance 19 of June 1826, 4.

12. For more on the protectors of slaves, see John E. Mason, *Social Death and Resurrection—Slavery and Emancipation in South Africa* (Charlottesville: University of Virginia Press, 2003), esp. chap. 2.

13. This was a highly contentious issue among owners, who saw this as an infringement of their property rights, and one that the protector of slaves frequently comments upon. See NA, 53/54–53/58, table A and General Observations relating to table A.

14. Mary Rayner, "Slaves, Slave Owners and the British State: The Cape Colony 1806–1834," *Collected Seminar Papers, Institute of Commonwealth Studies* 28 (1981): 15, sas-space.sas .ac.uk/4111/.

15. Ibid., 15–17.

16. Pamela Scully, *Liberating the Family? Gender and British Slave Emancipation in the Rural Western Cape, South Africa, 1823-1853* (Cape Town: David Philip, 1997), 3.

17. Ordinance 19 of June 1826, 4.

18. For more on rape and slavery in the colony, see Scully, *Liberating the Family?*; and Pamela Scully, "Rape, Race, and Colonial Culture: The Sexual Politics of Identity in the Nineteenth-Century Cape Colony, South Africa," *American Historical Review*, 100, no. 2 (1995): 335–59.

19. Ordinance 19 of June 1826, 4.

20. KAB, SO, 3/6, *Report of the Protector of Slaves . . .* , *25 June–24 December 1830*, 1:619–20.

21. KAB, SO, 3/8, *Report of the Protector of Slaves . . .* , *25 June–24 December 1831*, 3:511–12.

22. Ibid., 512.

23. The actual number of cases recorded was 263, but 13 of these were cases carried over from one annual report to the next, and these have therefore been excluded.

24. For detailed accounts of all cases see NA, 53/50–57, reports of the protectors of slaves of the Cape of Good Hope Colony for 1830–1834.

25. A *sjambok* is a long, stiff whip used throughout South Africa's history to inflict pain on human and other species. That sexual violence is reported less frequently is not to suggest it did not occur or was not common but, rather, that it was more difficult to seek legal recourse for such cases.

26. KAB, SO, 3/9, *Report of the Protector of Slaves . . .* , *24 December 1831–25 June 1832*, case no. 33 for the Graaff-Reinet District, 4:471. Further cites to this work appear in parentheses in text.

27. See Wayne Dooling, "'The Good Opinion of Others': Law, Slavery and Community in the Cape Colony, c. 1760–1830," in Worden and Crais, *Breaking the Chains*, 25–43.

28. Similarly, John Mason observes, "The slaves of the Cape Colony frequently relied not on the law's definition of legal and illegal punishment when deciding whether or not to complain, but on their own notions of just and unjust punishment" ("Slaves and Their Protectors," 122).

29. Dooling, "Slavery and Amelioration," 81.

30. See, for example, the case of Rachel of Sneeuberg, who complained because her female owner accused her of being the cause of death of her own child. NA, 53/51, case 5, 133.

31. NA, 53/54, cases 1 and 2, 193–96.

32. Ibid. As with all the narratives recounted in this article, the accounts recorded in the archive are not taken at face value. The inherent contradictions, counterclaims, and differing versions of events are not only staples of legal proceedings but also are framed by the intentions and desires of those involved in the proceedings and the sociopolitical contexts of the times. The complexity of testimonies have been explored in Van der Spuy, "'Making Himself Master'"; and Nigel Penn, "The Wife, the Farmer and the Farmer's Slaves: Adultery and Murder on a Frontier Farm in the Early Eighteenth Century Cape," *Kronos*, 28 (November 2002): 1–20.

33. NA, 53/54, case 7, 205.

34. Ibid., case 14, 217.

35. See NA, 53/50, case 9, 11; and NA, 53/56, case 18, 211.
36. NA, 53/55, case 7, 48.
37. NA, 53/57, case 25, 261.
38. NA, 53/52, case 7, 302.
39. NA, 53/54, case 13, 215. The defendant's surname may possibly have been Fick.
40. Ibid., case 6, 204.

Torture, the State, and Sexual Violence against Men in Colonial India

Deana Heath

This article aims to broaden the analysis of gendered violence in colonial India by focusing on sexual violence against men. My goal is not to pursue, as Anjali Arondekar terms it, "the additive model of subalternity," which endeavors to fill the gaps of the colonial archive with the voices of those who have been silenced while acknowledging the impossibility of such a project of recovery.[1] I wish to go, in other words, beyond efforts to mine the content of government archives to pay attention to their form and content—to view archives "as both transparencies on which power relations were inscribed and intricate technologies of rule in themselves."[2] Rather than seeking to "recover" the "submerged" history of sexual violence against men, I interrogate the traces of such violence in the colonial archive to consider how and why the sexual violation of Indian men was able to enter the colonial archive. In light, moreover, of the refusal of colonial officials to name such violence as a sex crime, I consider what a nonevent—or, rather, a "recalcitrant event"—reveals about the archive and, by extension, colonial rule.[3] I focus, in particular, on the rape of a man named Rahmat Musalli—not to formulate his subjectivity but to question the sign of rape in the colonial archive. I hope to build, therefore, on existing scholarship on the ways in which both colonialism and colonial archives are gendered.

On January 18, 1915, a theft of grain was committed in the village of Mokhal, in the northern Punjabi district of Sialkot. No police official was available to carry out an investigation, so Sub-Inspector Paras Ram, the officer in charge of the local

Radical History Review
Issue 126 (October 2016)   DOI 10.1215/01636545-3594469
© 2016 by MARHO: The Radical Historians' Organization, Inc.

police station, requested that one Tej Muhammad, who had only that day been appointed the new *zaildar*, or local revenue collector, initiate it.[4] Muhammad, however, clearly did not regard himself in need of such authority, since he had already apprehended a suspect—twenty-six-year-old Rahmat Musalli, *chowkidar* (village watchman) of Mokhal and a former employee of Muhammad.[5] Even though there was no evidence to implicate Musalli in the theft, he was tortured by the zaildar's son and two other relatives to extort a confession from him—torture that two constables, who arrived the following day, joined and in which many others, including another chowkidar, were complicit. The torture included making Musalli "sit with his arms between his legs and hold his ears" while someone sat on his back, and forcing him to stand for long periods of time. But Musalli was also subject to sexual violence, including being "struck on the penis and testicles" and raped.[6]

In the caste system as it operated in colonial India, Musallis, though Muslim, were essentially untouchable, which made Musalli a particularly vulnerable member of his community.[7] As a lower-caste man, the sexual violence that Musalli was subjected to by upper-caste men (primarily Muslim Jats) was far from unique in colonial India. Sexual violence against lower-caste men took many forms, including being stripped naked; having their testicles, penises, and buttocks beaten, burned, or cut; being raped with iron pegs or wooden sticks; having string tied to their penises, hooked over a peg, beam, or branch, and pulled; being emasculated; having chili pepper inserted into their anuses; or being made to strip naked and sit on an ant nest. That men may indeed have become inured to such forms of violence and may even have come to expect them at the hands of men in positions of authority is suggested by the action of a young man who, when brought before a British district magistrate for questioning, simply "mumbled and tried to take off his loin cloth."[8] Such an action is chillingly evocative of Sadat Hasan Manto's Partition story "Khol Do," in which a young woman, who is lying violated and bloodied in a doctor's surgery and presumed dead, hears the doctor say "khol do" ("open it") and, mistaking the doctor's request for someone to open the window as the prelude to yet another rape, starts to fumble feebly at the string of her *salwar*.[9]

Forced to confess that the grain was at his house to escape further torture and sexual violation, upon being taken there Musalli tried to commit suicide by slashing his throat and abdomen with a razor. The constables, instead of sending Musalli to the nearest hospital, sent word of his attempted suicide to Sub-Inspector Paras Ram, who upon eventually arriving in Mokhal recorded Musalli's statement as to what had occurred—in which Musalli declared, in the words of magistrate E. R. Abbott, that "an unnatural offence had been committed on him."[10] Ram then sent Musalli to a local hospital, but he died two days later of peritonitis caused by his injuries and, doubtless, by insufficient medical care.

The Erasure of Sexual Violence against Men

In the past three decades a growing body of scholarship has examined the embodied intimacies of colonialism, including intimacy between men. But the role of violence in shaping such encounters is far from clear, since the focus has primarily been on what Sara Suleri terms the "homoerotic cast assumed by the narrative of colonialism."[11] Yet as Robert Aldrich argues, "Hierarchical relations—master to slave, entrepreneur to employee, officer to subaltern, colonist to houseboy—facilitated sexual expectations and demands" and ensured that sexual encounters between men, while at times consensual, were also "part of the violence perpetrated throughout the colonial world."[12] In his analysis of a scandal in French Central Africa in the 1880s involving the torture and sexual exploitation of African men and boys, Jeremy Rich suggests that such violence was, moreover, tacitly condoned by colonial authorities, since it became a scandal only when it signaled disrespect for colonial authority.[13] The French phrase *faire passer son brevet colonial* (literally, "to give someone an examination for a colonial diploma"), which means to initiate someone into sodomy, may therefore be a particularly telling revelation of the nature of colonial power dynamics.[14]

American slavery offers an example of how hierarchical and racialized relations provided opportunities for sexual violence against vulnerable and exploited male bodies. Since legal ownership conferred control over the enslaved male body, Thomas A. Foster concludes that "no enslaved man would have been safe from the threat of sexual abuse."[15] Such abuse—which ranged from forced penetration or reproduction to sexual coercion and psychic ill treatment—was perpetrated, moreover, not only by white men but also by white women (who could "enact radical fantasies of domination over white men with the knowledge that their victim's body was legally black and enslaved, subject to the women's control").[16] The vulnerability of male bodies to sexual violence in other states of unfreedom, such as detention (as in Musalli's case) and conflict situations, is apparent in contexts ranging from Abu Ghraib to concentration camps in Sarajevo during the Bosnian war, in which as many as 80 percent of male concentration camp inmates were purportedly raped.[17]

Yet while sexual violence against men has been recognized as pervasive, widespread, and unexceptional, it is generally "hidden under [the] rubric terms of 'abuse,' 'torture,' or 'mutilation.'"[18] Three key reasons explain why sexual violence against men in India and other colonial contexts continues to be hidden under such rubrics. First, the sexual abuser is "judged by the moral status of his victim," and in the hierarchy of victimhood men are at the bottom.[19] In nineteenth-century Britain, since sexual acts between men were deemed deviant and aberrant, whether or not the victim consented to such acts, men who were the victims of sexual violence were, in effect, denied the status of victim at all.[20] In fact, since anal intercourse was penalized along with, from 1885, any sexual activity between men, and legislation on sexual abuse was explicitly gendered (which means that the law did not acknowledge rape as something that could happen to men, or sexual violation to boys), sexual violence against men was not deemed a criminal offence and was therefore only prosecutable if it was coded as a different form of embodied violence, such as assault or torture.[21] The same held true in British colonies, including India.[22] When it came to sexual violence against men, colonial law, in denying protection to male victims of sexual violence, thus served to "promote [such] violence and give it impunity."[23]

The lack of legal recourse for male victims of sexual assault helps explain the second key reason that the sexual abuse of men in colonial contexts such as India remains hidden: men rarely speak out about their abuse. Since masculinity defines men as strong, straight, and sexually dominant, "real men" cannot be raped or subject to other forms of sexual assault.[24] For male victims of sexual violence, shame about being sexually assaulted, combined with fears about their loss of masculinity and the risk that they will be blamed (and thus socially ostracized) for their violation, generally ensures their silence.[25] So does the fact that, in contrast to women, men often show no signs of having been violated (such as a ruptured hymen or pregnancy).[26] Because of their difficulty in acknowledging and articulating their experiences, men in colonial contexts have therefore tended, like the legal systems to which they are subject, to frame their violation as abuse or torture.[27]

The third reason that the sexual abuse of men in colonial contexts remains shrouded in silence is that gendered assumptions about power have led to men being framed primarily as perpetrators and women as victims, which not only reifies existing hierarchies of victimhood but also reinforces perceptions of women as inherently violable. Such assumptions therefore normalize sexual violence against women.[28] They also obscure women's sexual agency and the ways in which this is mediated by class and race. The utilization of rape as a trope for the objectification of white women has, moreover, rendered the white woman, to borrow from Jenny Sharpe, as "a category of Other" that keeps the violated bodies of colonized women *and* men "hidden from history."[29] Since acts of sexual violence are directed against individuals on the basis of their gender (not to mention, of course, their race, class, and ethnicity) regardless of the gender of the victim or the perpetrator, sexual violence against men is therefore a gendered practice. It is utilized to effeminize, destroy, and humiliate men and their communities and to delineate between "man" and "other."[30] Rather than being exceptional or aberrant, sexual violence against men is therefore part of an array of institutionalized and socially sanctioned violence that serves to empower certain groups of men as heterosexual, masculine, and dominant.[31]

Colonialism and Sexual Violence

Nowhere is such a power dynamic clearer than in the case of colonialism, in which relationships are inherently gendered and sexualized and the body is a key trope through which difference between the West and non-West is discursively constructed. Not only were "non-Western bodies . . . portrayed as weak, barbarous, unclean, diseased or infantile in comparison with the idealized bodies of the West, which were the opposite, that is strong, ordered, hygienic, healthy and mature," but nonwestern male bodies were categorized largely as effeminate, in contrast to the purported manliness of the bodies of western men.[32] In the case of colonial India, one of the ways in which such effeminacy was produced was through proclaiming British men the saviors of Indian women from patriarchal oppression. Following the Indian Rebellion of 1857 the British also developed an elaborate ethnography of what they termed "martial" and "nonmartial" races, in which certain groups of men, such as Bengalis and Hindu groups from other "settled" regions, were singled out as being effeminate. The response of such groups was to internalize effeminacy and undertake a process of remasculation, a project that unfolded predominantly in the domestic sphere, with the body of the "chaste" and "pure" Hindu woman bearing the burden of marking the difference of the Hindu from the West. While such a project sought to ensure the dominance of a predominantly upper caste, upper class, and Hindu masculinity, it "left unresolved the tensions of traditional patterns of hierarchy across caste, community, class and gender."[33] When such tensions erupted, as they did most dramatically in the Partition of India in 1947, and again in the Bangladesh Liberation War in 1971, sexual violence became a tool for constructing and negotiating power between competing groups. But as sexual violence generally occurs in contexts in which male power is unstable, it is not only to such "exceptional" moments that we should look for evidence of it. As Sarah Solangon and Preeti Patel argue, "In some societies where masculinity is associated with being powerful and being head of the family, some men who feel they have failed to live up to this role, such as unemployed men who are unable to provide for their families, may feel that sexual violence, with its connotations of force and power, allows them to regain some control over their masculinity."[34] Since colonialism is a violation of the world of the colonized, which entails a process of unworlding that includes economic upheaval (and, for many groups, economic breakdown and impoverishment), the undermining of existing social structures, the replacement of traditional law-and-order systems with an alien legal system (in which "difference" is, moreover, enshrined), and—since the British "took over precolonial coercive techniques at the local level and introduced new ones on a global scale"—wide-scale structural violence, we perhaps need, therefore, to start viewing colonialism more as a state of conflict in which violence has been normalized.[35]

What distinguished sexual violence perpetrated against or among the colonized was its sheer brutality. As Sharon Block argues in her study of rape in early America, "Both African American and Native American women were far more likely than white women to be the victims of sadistic and horrific sexual violence that . . . starkly expressed relations of subordination through intentional sexual cruelty."[36] Violence against nonwhite women often took the form of sexual torture because it was carried out by multiple attackers and could involve multiple victims.[37] Such group violence serves to engender compliance, solidarity, and social conformity among the men who participate in it. It is common in war and conflict situations and was the standard means through which sexual violence was perpetrated in colonial India in the many torture cases I have examined. Although the sexual violence that Rahmat Musalli was subjected to was perpetrated by Indian men on an Indian body, this does not make it any less a form of colonial violence. For not only do the psychological effects of colonialism produce self-hatred in the colonized, as Frantz Fanon has argued, that manifests in the form of "collective auto-destruction," but such destruction was enacted by men who arguably felt the most threatened by or had the most to gain from the social and economic upheaval unleashed by colonialism.[38] Acts of sexual violence perpetrated by groups of men also act as a form of resistance to authority.[39] That such resistance is generally directed toward the most vulnerable members of a society rather than the actual source of oppression explains why sexual violence is tacitly condoned by authorities such as the colonial regime in India.

As Andrea Smith observes in her study of the genocidal effect of sexual violence on Native Americans, sexual violence is a tool through which peoples whose bodies are conceived of as inherently degenerate or impure "become marked as inherently 'rapable.'"[40] Although sexual violence obviously predates modern European colonialism, a new form of racism—what Michel Foucault terms "state racism"— began to emerge in the second half of the eighteenth century that was inherently biopolitical in nature.[41] What is particular about this form of racism is its deployment of the concept of the "norm" to single out particular groups within a population and mark them as deviant. Sexuality was central to this process of delineating "abnormal" bodies from normative ones. While the imperative of biopolitics is to optimize life, Foucault argues that such a form of racism, which is modeled on war, made it possible to justify killing "abnormal" segments of the population that are deemed a biological threat in order to purify and strengthen the "race." Racism is therefore "bound up with the workings of a State that is obliged to use race, the elimination of races and the purification of the race, to exercise its sovereign power." Moreover, rather than emerging in Europe and being exported to Europe's colonies, such a form of racism emerged through the process of colonization—or, as Foucault puts it, through "colonizing genocide."[42] It is this biopolitical imperative that explains why not only colonized women but also colonized men have been subjected to what Smith refers to as "reign[s] of sexualized terror," ranging from direct sexual assault to state policies to usurp the land and undermine the welfare of the colonized.[43]

The Sign of Rape

Such an imperative may help explain why Rahmat Musalli's rape was silenced by E. R. Abbott, the magistrate who initially tried his torturers. Abbott disregarded Musalli's claim that "an unnatural offence had been committed on him," since he was convinced that it was "most unlikely that such an offence was committed in the circumstances." For Abbot it was more likely that a stick had been inserted into Musalli's anus—clearly not, for him, an act of sexual violence—and the Sub-Inspector, in the course of translating Musalli's Punjabi into Urdu (the language in which official records in Punjab were kept), used a "wrong translation" for what Musalli had actually said.[44] Furthermore, in light of colonial officials' inherent distrust of Indians' oral evidence, they sought truth in the Indian body, to be unveiled by British medical "experts"—and for Abbott Musalli's body belied the possibility of any such offence having been committed, since the assistant surgeon who examined it did not observe any damage to Musalli's anus (although Abbott admitted that the surgeon may not have actually looked at Musalli's anus, since up to that stage no charge of "torture" had yet been made).[45] Abbott thus sought to deny the truth of sexual violence against Indian bodies.

Because Abbott "sympathise[d]," moreover, "with the accused" (since he felt "it is not improbable that the hurt caused was no more than is frequently employed in burglary investigations when taken up with zest"), the sentences that he imposed were, not surprisingly, nominal, and these were virtually overturned on appeal.[46] But when the government of Punjab appealed against the appeal to the Punjab Chief Court (which was possible to do under Indian law), the judgment of M. Shah Din and W. Chervis broke the conspiracy of silence surrounding Musalli's rape and named it for what it was. In response to opposition from the counsel for the defendants to the introduction of a statement on the cause of Musalli's death, which referred to his violation, the judges noted in their summation that "a statement as to the cause of death, referring to the rape is relevant as against a person tried for the rape when rape and death form parts of the same transaction."[47] Musalli's violators could not be punished for rape since, as Musalli was a man, rape and death did not legally form "parts of the same transaction." Nonetheless, the Chief Court judgment enabled the truth that male bodies could be raped—and that, moreover, state agents were in part responsible for such sexual violation—to enter the colonial archive.

In the numerous Indian police torture cases that I have examined from the nineteenth and early twentieth centuries, Musalli's case is the only one in which an act of sexual violence carried out against a man is explicitly referred to as "rape." Yet what is striking about such cases is not only the sheer ubiquity—and hence banality—of references to sexual violence against male bodies (although these were always coded as "torture") but the detail with which such violence was often delineated. What explains the denial of sexual violence against Indian men in the face of the omnipresence of their violated bodies in the colonial archive? And why was Musalli's rape actually named?

We might begin to answer such questions by considering colonial discourses about rape. Narratives of rape were initially deployed by critics of the East India

Company, such as Edmund Burke, to critique company rule, but with the onset of the Indian Rebellion of 1857 a new rape narrative emerged in which the violence of colonialism was displaced from British to colonized men—from whose lustful desires English women, rather than Indian, now had to be protected.[48] Stories that detailed what rebellious native men purportedly did to English women actually reflect the horrors that British soldiers inflicted on Indian bodies as punishment and retribution for the uprising, and the ways in which spectacular forms of punishment were utilized in the exercise of sovereign power. But since "the binarism of Western civilization and Eastern barbarism is difficult to maintain when the colonizer is an agent of torture and massacre," a discourse of rape that displaced victimhood onto English women rather than Indians made it possible to project counterinsurgency as the restoration of moral order and the articulation of a feudal hierarchy as a relationship of race.[49] As Jenny Sharpe argues, colonial narratives of rape are therefore "so invested with the value of English womanhood that they strategically exclude Indians, *men and women alike*."[50] The sexual violation of Indian men, according to such a reading, is thus unnamed in the colonial archive because colonial officials were unable to "see" such violation.

Not only do such narratives about sexual violence reveal the tremendous insecurity of colonial regimes, particularly in moments of crisis, but they also disclose considerable anxiety about British masculinity. By the second half of the nineteenth century masculinity had become "fused in an especially potent configuration with representations of British imperial identity," which led to the emergence of an aggressive, militaristic, hypermasculinity.[51] But empire also fostered fears of the male body as under threat, weakened by sexual indulgence, enervating climates, and racial intermixing, and of the consequent degeneration of the British "race." In contrast to the fetishistic depictions of English women in "Mutiny" narratives, in which they are stripped naked, sexually violated, and then subjected to a variety of horrific tortures (such as the hacking off of breasts and other body parts), there are notably no detailed descriptions of the slaughter of English male bodies since "such a fragmentation of the male body would allocate British men to the objectified space of the rape victim—a status that would negate colonial power at the precise moment that it needed reinforcing."[52] The focus on sexual crimes against women in narratives of the revolt served, therefore, to shift attention away from the deaths of English men at the hands of the rebels. Acknowledging the rapability of male bodies by according Indian men the status of rape victims would thus threaten the fragile integrity of the bodies of British men.

Since, furthermore, the meaning of masculinity is drawn from the particular power relations that masculinity is employed to replicate in any given historical context, then British masculinity must be seen as something that was not simply transplanted to colonial contexts such as India but shaped by the colonial encounter.[53] Not only was British masculinity forged through "the rupture in the different forms of male interaction, between the strong emotional bonds of the male homosocial world and the strong emotional-sexual bonds of the male homosexual world"—not to mention the "hysteria and cultural terror" generated in the British by their encounter with India—but also the dynamics of a "deferred homosexual decorum" is evident in the script of a racialized gender dynamic in which British men were figured as hypermasculinized and Indian men as effeminate.[54] It is for these reasons that colonial discourse in India relegated both Indian *and* British women to the margins of what was ultimately an exchange between men. Scholars have demonstrated the many ways in which such a homoerotic desire for nonwhite men was configured, from the construction of what Rudi C. Bleys has termed a "geography of perversion" (including, most famously, Richard Francis Burton's "sotadic zone," which encompassed most parts of the "Orient" and in which, he maintained, sodomy was endemic) to the sexual imaginary of the Cannibal Club, an inner circle of the Anthropological Society of London (formed in 1863) whose members published homoerotically charged works that functioned as both science and pornography.[55]

Flagellation featured in much of the writing of Cannibal Club members, as it did in the pornographic literature produced in Britain into the early twentieth century. Although the figure doing the flagellation in such literature is generally depicted as female, she is, according to Stephen Marcus, a surrogate for "the terrible mother, the phallic mother of childhood" whose muscular biceps, hairy arms, and hairy upper lip actually serve to conceal the real perpetrator, the father.[56] Since the figure being beaten is always a boy, Marcus reads such a fantasy as a homosexual one; thus, for Marcus, "the entire immense literature of flagellation produced during the Victorian period, along with the fantasies it embodied and the practises it depicted, represents a kind of last-ditch compromise with and defense against homosexuality."[57] Lisa Z. Sigel observes that, in the case of Cannibal Club flagellation literature, which created "a sexual practice that moved the focus from orgasm to the desire for discipline and control," such writings "worked as a pedagogical technique to teach masculine self-control"; indeed, such prose demonstrates more of a longing for discipline than for intercourse.[58] Such literature therefore reflects the shift in British conceptions of manliness (motivated in large measure by empire) during the nineteenth century from "sexual prowess and maturity" to "sexual restraint and 'cleanness.'"[59]

The displacement of sexuality from desire to discipline mirrors the way in which torture is coded. For although, as Marnia Lazreg remarks in her study of torture as a colonial counterinsurgency tool in Algeria, "the *essence* of torture is sexual," torture is coded as a form of disciplining—or of, in a colonial context, "resocializing" (in order to convince the colonized, ironically, of the justness of colonialism). The sexual violation of colonized men and women was a means, therefore, of making them into obedient colonial subjects.[60] It operates as a form of "calculated" cruelty, which Talal Asad argues was regarded as being necessary to make the colonized "fully human."[61] Torture is thus, as Darius Rejali has demonstrated, a form of physical suffering that is an integral part of a disciplinary society—and hence of the modern state.[62] If public rituals of torture are no longer, per Foucault, necessary for the maintenance of sovereign power, torture persists in secret as an aspect of policing.[63] The sexual and disciplinary nature of torture in colonial India is evident in the ways in which the alien legal regime forced Indians to speak the truth of their sexual violation, or to extract it from them by mining their bodies for hidden truths. Musalli's death prevented him from speaking the truth of his rape in a colonial courtroom, but he was forced to make no less than three confessions before he died.[64] Since magistrates were required to examine the bodies of men who wished to make a confession in order to check for marks of "ill-treatment," had Musalli survived his ordeal he would consequently have been required to submit to a further violation.[65] That violated male bodies litter the colonial archive is therefore emblematic not only of the ways in which torture was utilized to discipline Indian bodies but also of the cultures of desire and disavowal that circulated around such bodies—truths that the Punjab Chief Court judgment on Musalli's torturers served, inadvertently, to reveal.

Notes

1. Anjali Arondekar, "Without a Trace: Sexuality and the Colonial Archive," *Journal of the History of Sexuality* 14, no. 1/2 (2005): 14.

2. Ann Laura Stoler, "The Colonial Archive and the Arts of Governance," *Archival Science* 2 (2002): 87.

3. Arondekar, "Without a Trace," 22.

4. In addition to being revenue collectors, *zaildars* were also responsible for village policing.

5. *The Crown v. Faiz*, IOR/L/PJ/6/3554, British Library, London.

6. Ibid.

7. H. A. Rose, *A Glossary of the Tribes and Castes of the Punjab and North-west Frontier Province*, 3 vols. (Lahore: Civil and Military Gazette Press, 1911), 2:182.

8. *King Emperor v. Muhammad Ismail Khan*, Home, Police, B Proceedings, January 1911, no. 145–46, National Archives of India, New Delhi.

9. A salwar is a pair of loose, pleated and tapered trousers that are tied at the waist with string. Sadat Hasan Manto, "Khol Do," in *Manto: Selected Stories*, trans. Aatish Tasheer (Gurgaon, Haryana: Random House India, 2008), n.p.

10. *Crown v. Faiz*.

11. Sara Suleri, *The Rhetoric of English India* (Chicago: University of Chicago Press, 1992), 16.

12. Robert Aldrich, *Colonialism and Homosexuality* (New York: Routledge, 2003), 4, 1.

13. Jeremy Rich, "Torture, Homosexuality, and Masculinities in French Central Africa: The Faucher-d'Alexis Affair of 1884," *Historical Reflections* 36, no. 2 (2010): 19.

14. Aldrich, *Colonialism and Homosexuality*, 1.

15. Thomas A. Foster, "The Sexual Abuse of Black Men under American Slavery," *Journal of the History of Sexuality* 20, no. 3 (2011): 448.

16. Ibid., 450.

17. Sarah Solangon and Preeti Patel, "Sexual Violence against Men in Countries Affected by Armed Conflict," *Conflict, Security, and Development* 12, no. 4 (2012): 419.

18. Ibid.

19. Joanna Bourke, *Rape: A History from 1860 to the Present Day* (London: Virago Press, 2007), 48.

20. Human Rights Watch, "This Alien Legacy: The Origin of 'Sodomy' Laws in British Colonialism," 2008, 11, accessed January 18, 2016, https://www.hrw.org/report/2008/12/17/alien-legacy/origins-sodomy-laws-british-colonialism.

21. Ibid., 20. The sexual violation of boys remained largely invisible in Victorian Britain, in spite of knowledge of its existence, because the protection of children from sexual abuse emerged from social purity and rescue organizations' endeavors to protect "fallen" women. Louise Jackson, *Child Sexual Abuse in Victorian England* (New York: Routledge, 2000), 5.

22. While section 377 of the 1860 Indian Penal Code, for example, penalized sodomy (with imprisonment up to life), it made no distinction between homosexual acts committed with or without consent, and section 375, which penalized rape, restricted the crime to the penetration of a woman by a man.

23. Human Rights Watch, "This Alien Legacy," 4. The same held true, of course, for female victims, although both British and colonial law acknowledged that, at least in certain circumstances, women and girls *could* be raped.

24. Valeria Vojdik, "Sexual Violence against Men and Women in War: A Masculinities Approach," *Nevada Law Journal* 14, no. 3 (2014): 940.

25. Solangon and Patel, "Sexual Violence," 422.

26. Bourke, *Rape*, 42.

27. Marnia Lazreg, *Torture and the Twilight of Empire: From Algiers to Baghdad* (Princeton, NJ: Princeton University Press, 2008), 124.

28. Ratna Kapur, "The Tragedy of Victimization Rhetoric: Resurrecting the 'Native' Subject in International/Post-colonial Feminist Legal Politics," *Harvard Human Rights Law Journal* 15, no. 1 (2002): 1–39.

29. Jenny Sharpe, *Allegories of Empire: The Figure of Woman in the Colonial Text* (Minneapolis: University of Minnesota Press, 1993), 130.

30. Solangon and Patel, "Sexual Violence," 427.

31. Vojdik, "Sexual Violence," 927.

32. James H. Mills and Satadru Sen, introduction to *Confronting the Body: The Politics of Physicality in Colonial and Post-colonial India*, ed. James H. Mills and Satadru Sen (London: Anthem Press, 2002), 1.

33. Indira Chowdhury, *The Frail Hero and Virile History: Gender and the Politics of Culture in Colonial Bengal* (Oxford: Oxford University Press, 2001), 3.

34. Solangon and Patel, "Sexual Violence," 426.

35. Sharpe, *Allegories of Empire*, 80.

36. Sharon Block, *Rape and Sexual Power in Early America* (Chapel Hill: University of North Carolina Press, 2006), 80.

37. Ibid., 83.

38. Frantz Fanon, *Concerning Violence*, trans. Constance Farrington (London: Penguin, 2008), 23.

39. Bourke, *Rape*, 343.

40. Andrea Smith, *Conquest: Sexual Violence and American Indian Genocide* (Cambridge, MA: South End Press, 2005), 3.

41. Michel Foucault, *"Society Must Be Defended": Lectures at the Collège de France, 1975–76*, ed. Maurio Bertani and Alessandro Fontana, trans. David Macey (New York: Picador, 1997), 257.

42. Ibid., 256, 258, 257. See also Ann Laura Stoler, *Race and the Education of Desire: Foucault's "History of Sexuality" and the Colonial Order of Things* (Durham, NC: Duke University Press, 1995).

43. Smith, *Conquest*, 8.

44. *Crown v. Faiz.*

45. Ibid. Torture was penalized in the 1860 Indian Penal Code.

46. The convictions that Abbott imposed on Musalli's torturers were reduced to a fine or imprisonment in default.

47. "Judgement in the Chief Court of the Punjab, Appellate Side, Criminal," case no. 922 of 1915, IOR/L/PJ/6/3554, British Library.

48. Nicholas Dirks, *The Scandal of Empire: India and the Creation of Imperial Britain* (Cambridge, MA: Harvard University Press, 2006); Nancy L. Paxton, "Mobilizing Chivalry: Rape in British Novels about the Indian Uprising of 1857," *Victorian Studies* 36, no. 1 (1992): 5.

49. Sharpe, *Allegories of Empire*, 6.

50. Ibid., 129; emphasis mine.

51. Graham Dawson, *Soldier Heroes: British Adventure, Empire, and the Imagining of Masculinities* (New York: Routledge, 1994), 1.

52. Sharpe, *Allegories of Empire*, 67.

53. Mrinalini Sinha, "Giving Masculinity a History: Some Contributions from the Historiography of Colonial India," *Gender and History* 11, no. 3 (1999): 454.

54. Mrinalini Sinha, "Gender and Imperialism: Colonial Policy and the Ideology of Moral Imperialism in Late Nineteenth-Century Bengal," in *Changing Men: New Directions in Research on Men and Masculinity*, ed. Michael S. Kimmel (Newbury Park, CA: Sage, 1987), 228; Suleri, *Rhetoric of English India*, 17.

55. Rudi C. Bleys, *The Geography of Perversion: Male-to-Male Sexual Behaviour outside the West and the Ethnographic Imagination 1750–1918* (London: Cassell, 1996); Lisa Z. Sigel, *Governing Pleasures: Pornography and Social Change in England, 1815–1914* (New Brunswick, NJ: Rutgers University Press), 54.

56. Stephen Marcus, *The Other Victorians: A Study of Sexuality and Pornography in Mid-Nineteenth-Century England*, 3rd ed. (London: Corgi Books, 1970), 261.

57. Ibid., 263.

58. Sigel, *Governing Pleasures*, 77.

59. Ronald Hyam, *Empire and Sexuality: The British Experience* (Manchester: Manchester University Press, 1990), 71.

60. Lazreg, *Torture and the Twilight*, 143, 120, 134; emphasis mine.

61. Talal Asad, "On Torture, or Cruel, Inhuman, and Degrading Treatment," in *Social Suffering*, ed. Arthur Kleinman, Veena Das, and Margaret Lock (Berkeley: University of California Press, 1997), 294.

62. Darius Rejali, *Torture and Democracy* (Princeton, NJ: Princeton University Press, 2007).

63. Michel Foucault, *Discipline and Punish: The Birth of the Prison*, trans. Alan Sheridan (London: Lane, 1977).

64. The criminal justice system as it emerged in India was virtually dependent on confessions to ensure convictions. Douglas Peers, "Torture, the Police, and the Colonial State in the Madras Presidency, 1816–55," *Criminal Justice History: An International Annual* 12 (1991): 48.

65. This requirement was introduced in the Indian Evidence Act of 1872.

Gendered Violence and Cultural Forgetting

The Case of the Irish Magdalenes

Jennifer Yeager and Jonathan Culleton

Irish narratives of femininity facilitate a persistent gendered violence toward women formerly incarcerated in Magdalene Laundries and continue to affect Magdalene survivors today. The case of the Magdalene Laundries illustrates how the Irish state has shaped cultural narratives of gender. Further, it demonstrates the vital role played by cultural memory in constructing these gendered identities. As Anthony Smith argues, memory "by definition is integral to identity, and the cultivation of shared memories is essential to the survival . . . of such collective identities."[1] We argue that memory and dominant national narratives are powerful cultural constructions with broad repercussions in Ireland's past and present.[2]

To understand collective memory, it is necessary to take note of "collective amnesia."[3] "Forgetting becomes part of the process of national identity formation" as "a new set of memories are accompanied by a set of tacitly shared silences."[4] The women who inhabited Magdalene Laundries are subject to this shared silence, as they are omitted from Ireland's dominant historical narrative. Not everyone is equally powerful in their ability to claim and define the past.[5] What becomes defined as the official memory reflects the power of certain groups.[6] The result is that different groups claim the same past in sometimes contradictory ways; hence, "memory can be a potential oppressor as well as a potential liberator."[7]

Restriction of archival material related to the Magdalene Laundries contributes to the invisibility of these survivors. The lack of access to the archives points to the role of the Irish state and religious orders as gatekeepers of information and key

Radical History Review
Issue 126 (October 2016)   DOI 10.1215/01636545-3594481
© 2016 by MARHO: The Radical Historians' Organization, Inc.

participants in gendered violence toward survivors. Integral to historical scholarship is the notion that knowledge of the past can inform future behaviors.[8] Political forces constrain knowledge of the past, restructuring events so that "society better remembers."[9] Championing one version of events (in this case, one that silences Magdalene women) has implications for survivors. Trauma experiences are social; recovery is a *collective* process, necessitating social support.[10] We argue that survivor oral histories (for example, those gathered as part of the Waterford Memories Project) provide a way both to understand the meaning of what happened to the Magdalene women and to provide a record of these narratives.[11] As a method, oral history is particularly appropriate for examining "subjective experiences of shifting historical periods" as it emphasizes processes of meaning making.[12]

Women in Postindependence Ireland and the Magdalene Laundries

From the 1920s, "the Irish State conceived its national identity in terms of a predominantly Gaelic and Catholic cultural ethos."[13] In particular, the Catholic Church sought control of socialization processes by "establishing a firm grip on education as well as by the doctrine of familism."[14] This meant enforcing a moral control over women, which encompassed domestic life, education, health, the arts, welfare entitlements, and religious participation.[15]

Historical discourse surrounding the sexuality of the Irish has rarely challenged the self-proclaimed belief in Irish moral superiority.[16] Evidently, those guilty of such crimes as extramarital sex contradicted the prescribed national narrative that emphasized conformity, valued community over the individual, and esteemed conservative Catholic moral values.[17] The control of sexuality (or that of Irish women, at least)—as a practice and a discourse—became one of the strategies by which the Catholic Church maintained power.[18] The interaction between notions of female sexual purity and the nation is critical. As Claudia Lenz notes, women are constructed as biological and moral bearers of the nation, responsible for its future existence, yet regarded as neither capable of coping with the challenges of public affairs nor reliable in political matters.[19] Postindependence Ireland contained what it perceived as sexual immorality by locking it away. Ireland's "architecture of containment" (after James Smith's formulation) encompassed an assortment of interconnected institutions, including mother and baby homes, industrial and reformatory schools, mental asylums, adoption agencies, and Magdalene Laundries.[20] In effect, Magdalene women were hidden from society and written out of Irish history.

With a decline in prostitution after independence (1922), Irish Magdalene asylums began to alter their orientation, and the population of inmates became increasingly diverse; "hopeless cases," "mental defectives," infanticide cases, those on remand from courts, transfers from industrial and reformatory schools, and some "voluntary" committals increasingly formed cohorts of inmates.[21] They accommodated fewer voluntary entrants, and increasing numbers were detained for longer periods (many for life). These institutions increasingly served a punitive function, containing unmarried mothers, victims of sexual assault, and girls who were "sexually aware" or "demonstrating . . . tendencies towards sexual immorality."[22] The laundries became places where those who did not fit the model of Irish morality were effectively "excluded, silenced or punished."[23]

Ten Magdalene Laundries operated in Ireland between 1922 and 1996, with the stated mission to "protect, reform, and rehabilitate."[24] According to James Smith, many of these institutions shared overriding characteristics, including "regimes of prayer, silence, work in a laundry and a preference for permanent inmates."[25] The longevity of Irish Magdalene Laundries is also noteworthy; women were still entering Irish laundries in the 1980s.[26] The Sean McDermott Street laundry was the final laundry to close in 1996.

Magdalene Laundries provided a powerful mechanism for patriarchal control by the Irish state and religious orders, which deemed sexuality the principal cause for the downfall of morality.[27] Hence, the laundries formed part of a system of moral regulation and social control.[28] Moral reformation took place through industrial discipline, which had the additional benefit of being profitable through unpaid labor.[29] Society sought to render invisible the challenges these women embodied: they were sexually active when Irish women were expected to be morally pure; they were unmarried mothers when the constitution rendered marriage and motherhood inseparable; they were the victims of abuse under a legal double standard that evaded male culpability and condemned victims.[30]

The Carrigan Report (1931), as James Smith demonstrates, was particularly important in the inauguration of a state attitude toward sexual immorality through its hegemonic discourse, which in turn encouraged public consent.[31] The report established a state-sanctioned precedent for church-state advocacy of moral purity by criminalizing sex outside marriage. The report further ensured Irish women's ignorance about biological reproduction and their rights, while simultaneously stigmatizing young women (and exculpating young men) for sexual immorality.[32] So controversial were its revelations at the time that the Department of Justice advised against its publication, believing "it might not be wise to give currency to the damaging allegations made in Carrigan regarding the standard of morality in the country."[33]

The penalty for sex outside marriage was exorbitant. If a working-class woman became pregnant outside marriage, the common practice was for her to leave home (in disgrace) and go to a Magdalene Laundry; parents who tried to stand by their daughters had the priest hammering at the door, telling them it was their Christian duty to turn their back on their child.[34] The state's responses to sexual immorality also suppressed and concealed child sexual abuse in the 1930s; this concealment continued for decades. As James Smith notes, "The precedent established between 1930 and 1935 . . . legitimized secrecy and silence as a response to child abuse and pedophilia."[35]

Survivor oral histories provide a powerful challenge to this official silencing.[36] As one survivor of the Magdalene Laundries describes her experiences:

Soon after [my mother] got married, the abuse started with my stepfather. . . . I was taken away by the [Irish Society for Prevention of Cruelty to Children]. . . . Instead of taking the abuser out of the home, which was a man, they took an innocent child out of the home. And, of course, you had the church still continuing with my mother years later when she left him, to go back to her husband, even though he had abused me, her only, her first child, so I'm kind of confused about the Catholic teaching.

Concealment retraumatized abused children and punished already vulnerable citizens. Additionally, girls deemed to be in danger of engaging in sexual activity were incarcerated, as were girls referred through the criminal justice system. Disposing of vulnerable women in Magdalene Laundries ensured their personal silence, while creating a larger silence that safeguarded Ireland's identity as a morally pure society.[37]

Life in the laundries was characterized by silence, prayer, and hard labor.[38] Women worked with containers of boiling water for laundering and steam from the irons while washing soiled sheets from hospitals, hotels, and other businesses.[39] The girls were kept in a constant state of emotional and psychological turmoil, often unaware of why they were there, how long they would remain, or whether they would be transferred elsewhere. For example, one survivor of the laundries describes being moved from the industrial school in Tralee to the Peacock Lane laundry in Cork: "We went in, and a nun came in and then as she was leaving she said 'be a good girl now.' . . . I wanted to run over and say to her please, please don't let me stay here, please take me away, I'll be so good, I'll be very good for you. Even though it was all abuse and starvation, and whipping and beating. But I didn't, I don't know what held me back, but I had this, such a strong urge to do it." Transferal of girls from industrial schools to the laundries was common, typically with no warning or explanation.[40] Survivors reported to the McAleese Committee that, despite conditions, they were heartbroken to leave the only place they could call home.[41] At the laundries they were under constant surveillance and deprived of privacy, education, leisure, and rest; deprived of their identity, they were assigned new names, their hair was cut, and they were provided with uniforms.[42] As one survivor recalls,

She cut my hair, bitch, she changed my name, she cut my hair, and we had to wear a uniform. . . . I've got my name changed, I got my hair cut, and I've got my name changed. I'm wearing this glorified sack kind of thing, from the Bible, I call it biblical uniform. . . . It was just constant work, work, work, work, work.

Funnily enough, we didn't have a lot of prayers. When I look back, it was all
about money, it was all about raking in this bloody money.

As this reflection suggests, the laundries' economic value conflicted with its moral
project.[43] In the 1990s, shocking revelations began to crack the conspiracy of silence
about the Magdalene Laundries. In 1993 High Park Convent in Dublin was sold to
developers,[44] who discovered the unmarked graves of 133 women who had previously been in the Magdalene Laundry. The bodies of the women from High Park
were exhumed, cremated, and interred in Glasnevin Cemetery before any attempt
was made to determine their identities. More disconcerting has been the limited
public outrage regarding the treatment of these women.[45]

The following decade witnessed a series of high-profile criminal cases and
state inquiries into the abuse of children by families, in state care, and by priests.
While it is outside the scope of this article to discuss this abuse in detail, the main
inquiries are summarized in the Ferns, Ryan, Murphy, and Cloyne Reports,[46] which
document evidence of abuse. In another act of complicity between church and state,
the government signed an indemnity deal with the religious congregations in 2002,
in return for the congregations making a contribution of €128 million to the redress
scheme toward compensating those abused in institutions.[47] In a damning response
to the Ferns, Ryan, Murphy, and Cloyne Reports, Amnesty International Ireland
found "the Catholic Church was the dominant service provider for the majority of
people in the State, and remains a significant service provider. . . . The State failed
to ensure . . . proper systems of regulation and accountability. . . . In the absence of
such systems, abuse was endemic."[48]

Survivor testimony forces a reconsideration of the civic impact of the laundries, despite the indemnity deal. As one survivor reflects, "About us Irish, we love
to think we are loved around the world. We give a false impression about ourselves.
We can't accept that we are corrupt, that we are immoral, that we are . . . so wrong
about human rights." By characterizing Ireland as "wrong on human rights," survivor testimony invokes international conventions.

Such framing by survivors and advocates has power to enlist international
support. In response to reports submitted by the Justice for Magdalenes advocacy
group, in 2011 the UN Committee against Torture requested the Irish government
launch an investigation into human rights violations in the Magdalene Laundries
and consider redress for survivors. The UN recommended that

the State party should institute prompt, independent, and thorough
investigations into all allegations of torture, and other cruel, inhuman or
degrading treatment or punishment that were allegedly committed in the
Magdalene Laundries, and, in appropriate cases, prosecute and punish the
perpetrators with penalties commensurate with the gravity of the offences

committed, and ensure that all victims obtain redress and have an enforceable right to compensation.[49]

International scrutiny had some impact on internal Irish recognition of survivors. The government's response was the *Report of the Inter-departmental Committee to Establish the Facts of State Involvement with the Magdalene Laundries.* The report is limited: it attempted only to establish the facts surrounding the extent of the state's involvement. While the report includes testimony from survivors (chapter 19), "the Committee did not make specific findings in relation to [the living and working conditions in the Magdalene Laundries], in light of the small sample of women available."[50] Justice for Magdalenes and other survivor groups roundly criticized the report. Solicitors, academics, and activists responded that the evidence demonstrates that the state colluded with the laundries, provided the religious orders with support, and failed to supervise the running of the laundries.[51]

Tellingly, the Department of Justice's report placed little significance on survivor testimony. By contrast, Justice for Magdalenes' efforts to collate its own archive of survivor testimony in the form of oral histories established a clear (and oppositional) focus on understanding how survivors experienced Magdalene Laundries.[52] The group's faith in oral history as a method for exploring how people make sense of their past by contextualizing their memories in the present allows us to reflect on how participants can make both micro- and macrolevel connections between their individual memories and collective experiences (within families, cultures, nations, etc.). Similarly, oral histories collated in the Waterford Memories Project demonstrate how many of the women draw connections between their personal experiences and the mechanisms of the state and religious orders. As Paul Thompson maintains, "Once the life experience of people of all kinds can be used as its raw material, a new dimension is given to history."[53]

Impact on Survivors

Our knowledge of the Magdalene women's experiences is constrained by societal forces, restructuring events so that "society better remembers."[54] Championing one version of events (which silences Magdalene women) makes it harder for survivors to integrate their experiences into personal narratives. If trauma experiences are social, like all historical events, recovery is similarly a collective process, necessitating acknowledgment and support.[55] Further, recognizing the cultural invisibility of these survivors makes plain their reduced ability to define their own past.

While the Department of Justice report was interested in establishing "the facts" of what happened, the oral histories recorded as part of the Waterford Memories Project allow us to know how these women survived and how they lived with long-silenced trauma. Their stories reflect the very current trauma of women actively processing the meaning of their experiences. For them, this is not history per se, given its continuing impact. As one survivor insists:

> They never even saw to our education . . . they made sure we were not educated because it was all part of the plan for the Magdalene laundries. That's all. It's as simple as that. What other ulterior motive would they have not to educate us? And how long were they doing this in Irish society? How long were they doing it to children in Irish society, training them for the Magdalene laundries so Senator McAleese, as nice as he may be and all that, his work was very narrow in the sense he could have found out how far back it went the pattern. How many industrial schools there were, how many children each year came out from the industrial schools went into the Magdalene laundries. Forced in there I should say because the religious had control with their support of the government paying them for our keep in in the industrial schools, and then the payment continued because they were paying the laundries, for us anyway, 'til we were eighteen and so on.

For this survivor, the trauma of the past affects her life today; she laments not just its impact on her life but the continuing intergenerational effects. The women do not simply describe the past; they testify to its ongoing relevance.

In this sense, oral history refuses to comply with the silence surrounding these women's lives. By sharing the survivors' stories, the Waterford Memories Project makes them available inside and outside of Ireland. Videotaping (rather than audio recording) further captures the emotion inherent in the stories. Thus, we witness how the survivors construct meaning from past events in order to make sense of their current situation. For the survivor above, confronting her past involved providing testimony for the first time, recognizing her trauma, and engaging in dialogue through oral history. Where this is problematic, as in the previous quote, we see how many survivors have difficulty in making sense of the past in the absence of information about what happened; silence hinders coping.

It is the public purpose of oral history that is important in the Waterford Memories Project and other oral history projects. Collecting and displaying survivors' stories enable the women to take some control over the history of the laundries. The narration alone becomes "a subversive act, especially in light of powerful . . . forces working against it."[56] Hence, the dissemination of oral histories is an act of resistance against collective forgetting as humiliated silence; this is particularly true where broad-scale silence around an event is unacknowledged, resulting in collusive silence (as a desire to forget) and collective shame. When we consider the Magdalene institutions' presence, in conjunction with decades of silence on the subject, we are faced with "the tacit imposition of a taboo."[57] Eviatar Zerubavel notes how "washing one's community's 'dirty laundry' in public" is taboo, resulting from informal codes of silence prohibiting this act.[58] This statement works literally and metaphorically for Magdalene history: survivors literally scrubbed the community's dirty laundry while metaphorically representing what Irish society wanted hidden. Such "conspiracies of silence" often emerge after a major traumatic experience, comprising an individual's decision to remain silent, an imposed silence, and a collusion of silence between survivors and society.[59]

Reducing a person's *choice* to speak comprises meaning making, which is, like trauma, a collective process, "particularly when the shared experience is a historic event."[60] For Zerubavel, such "silent witnessing" highlights a core tension between knowledge (personal awareness) and acknowledgment (public discourse) in mutual denial.[61] Maria Ritter notes that traumatic silences in therapy can reflect both the initial disconnect with trauma and "a silencing identification with the original silencer."[62] In this way, silence around trauma is both an individual and collective experience. Survivors of trauma will often report feeling sworn to silence as "bearers of a secret" that is transferred to the next generation in a collective act of remaining silenced.[63]

Further, if the process of recovery from trauma is collective, social interaction and support are necessary for "ending" the silence.[64] Silence here must be understood at a personal, cognitive level (as a form of survival) and in terms of broader social processes. A survivor explains how she felt constrained in her ability to be heard: "The Irish government has failed in their duties. . . . Governments are not and never were thinking of any violence perpetrated against Irish women. Sadly this is in the mindset of the Irish governments. . . . Irish society is so enshrined in their negative attitudes towards women collectively . . . this mind set has . . . instilled their Catholic indoctrination, and the men in power are on a macho trip." This quote underscores how gendered violence and silencing of Irish women inherently intertwine with the patriarchal government and societal norms. This has implications for how we approach understanding collective memory. We cannot ignore the importance of social interaction and context on an individual level in understanding how public silence can promote collective forgetting. If we acknowledge the import of social contact in dealing with trauma memories, the restriction of the archives related to the laundries can be viewed as inflicting ongoing distress. Oral histories therefore constitute an organized effort to bring "meaningful history to a public audience"[65] to begin addressing the lacuna of survivor testimony in official histories of the laundries.

How Do We Remember the Magdalenes?

The modest public engagement with the history of the Magdalene laundry points to the lack of a "common historical consciousness" on the subject.[66] Analyses of the laundries are constrained by the lack of access to the records of the religious orders,[67] resulting in an absence of intervention, as well as a failure to remember officially.[68] It is also the case that the "quality and quantity of the material held in various archives varies to a great extent."[69] Thus, public engagement with Magdalene history remains, in James Smith's formulation, at the level of "story," rather than at the level of history, supported by official documentation.[70] Religious orders did submit documentation to the government as part of the compilation of the 2013 report but required that the records submitted be returned and copies destroyed. A Residential Institutions Redress Board was established after the release of the report to compensate women incarcerated in the laundries, but survivors are legally prohibited from publicly communicating their experiences of either the institutions or redress scheme; the archive collated during the report remains vulnerable and inaccessible. State and religious orders thus remain gatekeepers of information about, and participants in, the continued gendered silencing of survivors.

The statements of Magdalene survivors throughout this article reveal previously obscured relationships between gender and the state. A survivor highlights such collusion in her own reflections:

Ireland [still hasn't asked] people like me, not just me you know, collectively, to give our versions of, of how we feel and how it should be changed. Well first all what I would like to see is if some horrible disaster struck Ireland again do not let the church get involved, nope . . . no matter how good they say they are. Do not let one specific organization be in control. Let them work side by side in honesty and in partnership and to be honest with people.

This quote emphasizes how the state, despite attempts to position itself as less culpable than the church, emerges in survivors' conviction that these "previous partners in hegemony—state and familial institutions—evaded all intimations of culpability."[71] Stephen Sloan argues that, "for the oral historian, moments of crises . . . can offer an environment when the larger weaknesses or strengths of a society are quite visible."[72] Oral histories provide a means for survivors to document emotion, thus providing insight into their experiences.[73]

Further, recording the personal accounts of these women facilitates our understanding of the meaning of these events. Only when the voices of these women enter collective memory will the nation be able to confront its gendered violence. T. W. Moody argues that history is a matter of "facing the facts of the Irish past, however painful some of them may be. . . . The study of history . . . enlarges truth about our past . . . [and] opens the mind."[74] Remembering the Magdalene women accurately necessitates a willingness to revisit our national narrative and to include that which we have forgotten through a collective "therapeutic voluntary amnesia."[75]

As their reflections make clear, Magdalene survivors actively embrace their role in realigning our collective memories by breaking the collective silence. Gathering and sharing their stories thus encourages us to focus on recording the "essential purpose of history": to "give to people who experienced history, through their own words, a central place."[76] As Mark Cave highlights, collecting oral histories validates survivors' experiences through the process of recording the story as the researcher becomes an agent of the community's collective memory.[77] This is a salient point: at the heart of oral history is empathy, on the part of both the story-teller and the researcher.

Notes

1. Anthony Smith, *Myths and Memories of the Nation* (Oxford: Oxford University Press, 1999), 10.
2. Eviatar Zerubavel, *The Elephant in the Room: Silence and Denial in Everyday Life* (Oxford: Oxford University Press), 289.
3. Charles Mills, "White Ignorance and Hermenuetical Injustice," *Social Epistemology Review and Reply Collective* 3, no. 1 (2007): 28–29.
4. Paul Connerton, "Seven Types of Forgetting," *Memory Studies* 1, no. 1 (2008): 63.
5. Brian Conway, "Active Remembering, Selective Forgetting, and Collective Identity: The Case of Bloody Sunday," *Identity: An International Journal of Theory and Research* 3, no. 4 (2003): 319.
6. Rudolf De Cillia, Martin Reisigl, and Ruth Wodak, "The Discursive Construction of National Identities," *Discourse and Society* 10, no. 2 (1999): 169.
7. Michael Kammen, "Review of Frames of Remembrance: The Dynamics of Collective Memory, by Iwona Irwin-Zarecka," *History and Theory* 34, no. 3 (1995): 253.
8. James Pennebaker and Amy Gonzales, "Making History: Social and Psychological Processes underlying Collective Memory," in *Collective Memory*, ed. James Wertsch Pascal Boyer (New York: Cambridge University Press, 2008), 110–29.
9. Alin Coman, Adam Brown, Jonathan Koppel, and William Hirst, "Collective Memory from a Psychological Perspective," *International Journal of Politics, Culture and Society* 22 (2009): 128.
10. Pennebaker and Gonzales, "Making History."
11. Oral history is a method of qualitative, in-depth interview that emphasizes the participant's narrative of personal experiences and memories of events.
12. Patricia Leavy, *Oral History: Understanding Qualitative Research* (Oxford: Oxford University Press, 2011), 23.
13. John Marsden, *Redemption in Irish History* (Dublin: Dominican, 2005), 92.
14. Patrick O'Mahony and Gerard Delanty, *Rethinking Irish History: Nationalism, Identity and Ideology* (London: Palgrave Macmillan, 2001), 66–67.
15. Ibid. See also Maryann Valiulis, "Power, Gender, and Identity in the Irish Free State," *Journal of Women's History* 6, no. 4 (1995): 117–36.
16. Maria Luddy, *Prostitution and Irish Society* (Cambridge: Cambridge University Press, 2007).
17. James Smith, *Ireland's Magdalen Laundries* (Notre Dame, IN: University of Notre Dame Press, 2007).
18. Tom Inglis, *Moral Monopoly* (Dublin: UCD Press, 1998), 157.
19. Claudia Lenz, "The Silenced Memories of the Sexualised Other in Post-war Norway," in *Minority Narratives and National Memory*, ed. Cora Doving and Nicolas Schwaller (Oslo: Unipub, 2010), 87. See also Nina Yuval Davis, *Gender and Nation* (London: Sage, 1997).
20. James Smith, *Ireland's Magdalen Laundries*.
21. Luddy, *Prostitution*.
22. Mary Raftery and Eoin O'Sullivan, *Suffer the Little Children: The Inside Story of Ireland's*

Industrial Schools (London: Continuum, 1999), 27–28; Brian Titley, "Heil Mary: Magdalen Asylums and Moral Regulation in Ireland," *History of Education Review* 35, no. 3 (2006): 9.

23. Kathryn Conrad, *Locked in the Family Cell: Gender, Sexuality, and Political Agency in Irish National Discourse* (Madison: University of Wisconsin Press, 2004), 3.

24. James Smith, *Ireland's Magdalene Laundries*, xvi; Frances Finnegan, *Do Penance or Perish* (Oxford: Oxford University Press, 2004).

25. James Smith, *Ireland's Magdalene Laundries*, xv.

26. Raftery and O'Sullivan, *Suffer the Little Children*; Finnegan, *Do Penance or Perish.*

27. Inglis, *Moral Monopoly*; James Smith, "The Politics of Sexual Knowledge: The Origins of Ireland's Containment Culture and the Carrigan Report (1931)," *Journal of the History of Sexuality* 13, no. 2 (2004): 208–33; Titley, "Heil Mary."

28. Diarmaid Ferriter, *Occasions of Sin: Sex and Society in Modern Ireland* (London: Profile Books, 2009); James Smith, *Ireland's Magdalene Laundries*; Titley, "Heil Mary."

29. Titley, "Heil Mary."

30. James Smith, *Ireland's Magdalene Laundries*, xvii.

31. James Smith, "Politics of Sexual Knowledge."

32. Ibid.

33. Finola Kennedy, "The Suppression of the Carrigan Report: A Historical Perspective on Child Abuse," *Studies: An Irish Quarterly Review* 89, no. 356 (2000): 356.

34. Finnegan, *Do Penance or Perish.*

35. James Smith, "Politics of Sexual Knowledge," 224.

36. All of the survivor quotes in this article are taken from interviews conducted by Jennifer Yeager as part of the Waterford Memories Project.

37. James Smith, "Politics of Sexual Knowledge."

38. Katherine O'Donnell, "Justice for Magdalenes" (paper presented at the Irish Human Rights Commission and Law Society of Ireland Ninth Annual Human Rights Conference, Dublin, Ireland, 2011).

39. Department of Justice, *Report of the Interdepartmental Committee to Establish the Facts of State Involvement with the Magdalene Laundries* (Dublin: Department of Justice and Equality, 2013).

40. Raftery and O'Sullivan, *Suffer the Little Children.*

41. The Irish Government established the McAleese Committee in July 2011. The committee consisted of an independent chair (Senator Dr. McAleese) and senior representatives from six centrally relevant government departments: Department of Justice and Equality; Department of Health; Department of Enterprise, Jobs, and Innovation; Department of Education and Skills; Department of Environment, Community and Local Government; and Department of Children and Youth Affairs. The purpose of the interdepartmental committee was to establish if there was state involvement with the Magdalene Laundries and to produce a report on its findings. Department of Justice, *Report of the Interdepartmental Committee.*

42. Maeve O'Rourke, "Ireland's Magdalene Laundries and the State's Duty to Protect," *Hibernian Law Journal* 200, no. 10 (2011): 200–37.

43. The Justice Department report found that the laundries "were operated on a subsistence or close to break-even basis rather than on a commercial or highly profitable basis." Department of Justice, *Report of the Interdepartmental Committee*, 993. However, this conclusion was based on figures submitted from the religious organizations and their accountants, which was not independently audited. Additionally, financial information from the laundries in New Ross, Waterford, Cork, Donnybrook, and Dun Laoghaire

"did not survive" and were not included in the report. The Justice for Magdalenes group has questioned the findings, arguing that the religious orders had an unpaid workforce and lucrative contracts. See James Smith, Maeve O'Rourke, Raymond Hill, and Claire McGettrick, "State Involvement in the Magdalene Laundries: JFM's Principal Submissions to the Inter-departmental Committee to Establish the Facts of State Involvement with the Magdalene Laundries," Justice for Magdalenes, 2013, www.magdalenelaundries.com /State_Involvement_in_the_Magdalene_Laundries_public.pdf. Without open access to the original records, clear conclusions cannot be drawn regarding the economic viability of the laundries.

44. High Park Convent ceased operations in 1991.

45. Eva Urban, "The Condition of Female Laundry Workers in Ireland 1922–1996: A Case of Labour Camps on Trial," *Études Irlandaises* 37, no. 2 (2012): 49–64.

46. Francis D. Murphy, Helen Buckley, and Larain Joyce, *The Ferns Report*, presented to the Minister for Health and Children (Dublin: Government Publications, October 2005), www .bishop-accountability.org/ferns.htm; Ryan Report, *Commission to Inquire into Child Abuse, Report*, vols. 1–4 (Dublin: Government Publications, 2009), http://www .childabusecommission.ie/rpt/pdfs/; Murphy Report, *Commission of Investigation, Report into the Catholic Archdiocese of Dublin* (Dublin: Government Publications, 2009), www .dacoi.ie/, "Dublin Archdiocese Commission of Investigation Report"; Cloyne Report, *Report into the Catholic Diocese of Cloyne* (Dublin: Government Publication, 2010), www .justice.ie/en/JELR/Cloyne_Rpt_Intro.pdf/Files/Cloyne_Rpt_Intro.pdf.

47. Ryan Report.

48. Carole Holohan, *In Plain Sight: Responding to the Ferns, Ryan, Murphy, and Cloyne Reports* (Dublin: Amnesty International Ireland, 2011), 389.

49. UN Committee against Torture, "Concluding Observations of the Committee against Torture," 46th Session, 2011, 6, https://www.magdalenelaundries.com/JFM_UNCAT _Follow%20Up_Complete.pdf.

50. Department of Justice, *Report of the Interdepartmental Committee*, 925.

51. James Smith et al., "State Involvement in the Magdalene Laundries."

52. The Justice for Magdalenes oral history project was a collaborative research project with the University College Dublin, led by Katherine O'Donnell. The project was completed in 2013. The Waterford Memories Project (led by Jennifer Yeager) focuses on collecting narratives associated with the Magdalene institutions in the southeast of Ireland.

53. Paul Thompson, *Voice of the Past: Oral History*, 3rd ed. (Oxford: Oxford University Press, 2000), 6–7.

54. Coman et al., "Collective Memory," 128.

55. Pennebaker and Gonzales, "Making History."

56. Stephen Sloan, "The Fabric of Crisis: Approaching the Heart of Oral History," in *Listening on the Edge: Oral History in the Aftermath of Crisis*, ed. Mark Cave and Stephen Sloan (London: Oxford University Press, 2014), 273.

57. Paul Connerton, "Seven Types of Forgetting," *Memory Studies* 1, no. 1 (2008): 68.

58. Zerubavel, *Elephant in the Room*, 27.

59. Jack Saul, *Collective Trauma, Collective Healing: Promoting Community Resilience in the Aftermath of Disaster* (Sussex, UK: Routledge, 2014).

60. Ibid., 134.

61. Zerubavel, *Elephant in the Room*.

62. Maria Ritter, "Silence as the Voice of Trauma," *American Journal of Psychoanalysis* 74, no. 2 (2014): 176.

63. Clara Mucci, *Beyond Individual and Collective Trauma: Intergenerational Transmission, Psychoanalytic Treatment, and the Dynamics of Forgiveness* (London: Karnac Books, 2013), 79.

64. Judith Herman, *Trauma and Recovery: The Aftermath of Violence—from Domestic Abuse to Political Terror* (New York: Basic Books, 1992); Pennebaker and Gonzales, "Making History."

65. Donald Ritchie, *Doing Oral History*, 3rd ed. (Oxford: Oxford University Press, 2015), 28.

66. Urban, "Condition of Female Laundry Workers," 2.

67. Finnegan, *Do Penance or Perish*; Luddy, *Prostitution*; James Smith, *Ireland's Magdalene Laundries.*

68. Emilie Pine, *The Politics of Irish Memory* (Basingstoke, UK: Palgrave Macmillan, 2010).

69. Luddy, *Prostitution*, 107.

70. James Smith, *Ireland's Magdalene Laundries.*

71. Ibid., 434.

72. Sloan, "Fabric of Crisis," 265.

73. Mark Cave, "Introduction: What Remains: Reflections on Crisis Oral History," in Cave and Sloan, *Listening on the Edge*, 273.

74. T. W. Moody, "Irish History and Irish Mythology," *Hermethena* 124 (Summer 1978): 18.

75. Roy Foster, *The Irish Story: Telling Tales and Making It Up in Ireland* (Oxford: Oxford University Press, 2001), 58.

76. Thompson, *Voice of the Past*, 3. See also Robert Perks and Alistair Thomson, *The Oral History Reader* (London: Routledge, 2006).

77. Cave, "Introduction," 2.

Looking beyond the Frame

Snapshot Photography, Imperial Archives, and the US Military's Violent Embrace of East Asia

Jessie Kindig

Nestled within a fairly innocuous collection of US soldiers' Brownie camera snapshots from the Korean War, most of which show everyday life in camps and bases in Korea, is a series of more than one hundred and twenty photographs of Asian women—in clubs, in bars, in bed, on the street. Taken by US Army Sergeant Richard H. Rohrbach, on "Rest & Relaxation" leave (R&R) in US-occupied Japan with his buddy Whimp, the snapshot series documents Rohrbach and Whimp's pleasure at their vacation from the war: the skies are sunny, and the anonymous women the two embrace in almost every photo usually smile for the camera when their skirts are pulled up or their breasts grabbed playfully by one of the soldiers. The series features dozens of women, some in western fashions and some in traditional Japanese dress, some embraced by one of the soldiers and some, it seems, captured for the camera as they walked down the street. The anonymous women function as interchangeable props to illustrate the soldiers' enjoyment—here are the two friends with smiling beauties at a bar, outside a restaurant, just emerged from the bedroom. Rohrbach and Whimp smile and make silly faces for the camera, and as a testament to their good time, the archival records note that Rohrbach referred to the women in these snapshots as "good pieces."

Some of these snapshots, though, reveal darker meanings of this phrase *good pieces*: the women sit uncomfortably under the camera's gaze, implicitly challenging

Radical History Review

Issue 126 (October 2016)   DOI 10.1215/01636545-3594493

© 2016 by MARHO: The Radical Historians' Organization, Inc.

Figure 1 Photograph courtesy of the Center for the Study of the Korean War, Richard Rohrbach photograph collection, PP.901

their designation as either cooperatively "good" or objectified "pieces" to be enjoyed. In one snapshot, Rohrbach embraces a woman by binding her arms behind her (figure 1). She stands primly with her legs together, her body held apart from his. Her black bangs frame her face as she purses her lips and looks away from the camera, pivoting toward the crowd to her left. Rohrbach, perhaps sensing her discomfort, gives a tight half smile and keeps his body angled toward the camera, attempting to direct the woman's attention there too. The woman neither resists, it seems, nor cooperates, and in this refusal she might not qualify as a "good piece."[1]

One woman in the snapshot series did qualify as "good" in the men's determinations. Dressed in a checkered skirt, white blouse, and sandals, with a fashionable modern bob, she embraces Rohrbach in front of a house with a white picket fence, using her left hand to secure his arm at her waist. Unlike the other woman, her body leans into his, and she smiles at the camera. On the back of this snapshot, Rohrbach has scrawled in uneven cursive "This was good fucking" (figure 2). She appears again in another snapshot, this time enveloped in a bear hug by Whimp, with another caption, "How about that?"[2]

How about that. These snapshots, and their captions, implore us to reconsider the historical landscape of the US military presence in East Asia during the post–World War II and Korean War period. Rohrbach and Whimp appear in nearly every photo, taking turns groping or embracing each woman, documenting the realization of their sexual fantasy of R&R. The women, many of whom are likely sex workers, are visible in the photographs because the soldiers hold them in place, sometimes willingly and sometimes less so. The snapshots prompt an interrogation of the character of this embrace, its varied shadings into coercion, and the soldiers' belief that these "good pieces" were just features of their good time. Attending to what is outside the snapshots' frames—what is not seen—helps clarify the connection between gender violence and archival silence and requires new research methodologies. If Rohr-

Figure 2 The handwritten caption on the back of this snapshot reads "This was good fucking." Photograph courtesy of the Center for the Study of the Korean War, Richard Rohrbach photograph collection, PP.957.

bach and Whimp framed the series as wartime fun, what other framings can be constructed to attend to the dissonances, the subtle coercions, the sexualized landscape, and the prurient gaze of their camera?[3] What sexualized terrain were these women negotiating?

The Violent Embrace of US Empire

Since their first introduction to the peninsula, Americans had relied on gendered metaphors to figure their relationship with Korea. In 1868, US Navy Commodore Robert W. Shufeldt described the Pacific as "the ocean bride of America" and imperialism as sexual consummation: "Let us as Americans—see to it that the 'bridegroom cometh.' . . . It is on this ocean that the East & the West have thus come together, reaching the point where search for Empire ceases & human power attains its climax."[4] In 1882, Shufeldt would be the chief American architect of the treaty "opening" Korea to American and western trade, a relationship he once described as "amicable intercourse."[5]

Since the late nineteenth century, a gendered language of sexual embrace helped naturalize the belligerent US presence in East Asia as a benevolent, guiding, and welcomed presence. Rohrbach and Whimp's snapshots can thus be read as a synecdoche of US empire. As Koreans and Japanese were embraced by an often violent US partner during the simultaneous military occupations of South Korea (1945–48) and Japan (1945–52) and the war for communist containment on the Korean peninsula (1950–53), US imperial ambitions took on intimate, sexual, or familial connotations. Historian Naoko Shibusawa has described how Japan's relationship to the United States was figured as that of a feminized, immature "geisha ally," and South Korea was understood by the US military government in Korea as the junior partner in a "big-little brother relationship."[6] Both countries, in this imperial mindset, needed to be guided on the path toward western development, wrought through their union with US empire.

Rohrbach and Whimp were typical of the many thousands of American soldiers who experienced and produced the occupations of Korea and Japan and the war in Korea through the sexualized embrace of Asian women. Soldiers moved through occupied Japan en route to and from Korea and took part as consumers in the thriving economy of sex work in Japan's geisha houses and Korea's camptowns. During their tours of duty, American soldiers learned to expect Asian women's sexual embrace as part of their mission—this was, after all, what they were told R&R was all about. Soldiers' expectations of East Asia as an erotic paradise combined with the US military's institutional policies to legitimate and normalize sexual access to Asian women. This in turn produced an unequal climate of gendered power, one in which dating and sex work became means of financial support for many women facing wartime devastation, but also one in which soldiers' expectations of sexual access to Asian women frequently led to rape.

As an imperial structure of feeling, the violent embrace combined sexual expectations and benevolent arrogance with military coercion, structuring US policy and shaping the landscape in which Asian women encountered American soldiers. Captured in Rohrbach and Whimp's photo series, this structure of feeling shaped historical narratives of US power in East Asia, obscuring both imperial power and systemic sexual violence in state archives and later historians' accounts. Archival sources, like these snapshot photographs, frame this wartime landscape as a kind of pleasure, fun, or benevolence and only hint at the scale of coercion and violence that lies outside the photograph's borders. A full accounting of the violent embrace must ask critical questions of these sources, and must look outside the frame for what isn't shown, what remains unseen or only hinted at, what is only partially divulged, and what isn't being seen at all.

"Babysan Will Be Coy and Shy about Having Her Picture Taken . . . but She Loves It"

Like many American servicemen in East Asia, Rohrbach and Whimp likely looked through a copy of Navy petty officer Bill Hume's immensely popular cartoon book, *Babysan*, to help them envision their wartime vacation. A particular favorite of troops in occupied Japan and during the Korean War, *Babysan* billed itself as a sexualized travelogue, introducing the naive and bumbling GI to "the land of the cherry blossoms" by instructing them on how to acquaint themselves with the flirtatious "Babysan"—how to be, as Hume put it, "occupied while occupying."[7] Thumbing through the pages, American soldiers could consult the pidgin Japanese glossary to figure out how to refer to parts of Babysan's body or how to greet her family respectfully. Through pseudo-pornographic cartoons, *Babysan* cheekily instructed soldiers to understand Japanese/American interaction as a sexual embrace, teaching soldiers about Japanese customs they might not understand in order to better win Babysan's affections. With her carefree charm, her exotic racial difference, and her pinup girl figure, Hume's *Babysan* introduced Americans to military duty in East Asia as first and foremost a sexual adventure.

Advances in camera technology after 1945 allowed soldiers to document this erotic adventure. Servicemen purchased Kodak's new affordable "Brownie" camera at PX stations, and one contemporary observer noted that the occupation forces in Japan shot so many photographs that a camera seemed to be a part of every American's uniform.[8] In one of Hume's cartoons, he explained "Babysan will be coy and shy about having her picture taken—at first—but she loves it."[9] Whimp and Rohrbach seemed to agree, and the roving eye of their camera, which seemed to focus on any woman or girl walking down the street, illustrates the effort to find Babysan in any woman, no matter how young, unsmiling, or unposed she might be.

Rohrbach and Whimp's search for Babysan was encouraged and sanctioned by the institutionalization of military prostitution in Japan and Korea. In US-occupied Japan, new economies emerged based around soldiers' desires and catering to their fantasies about the erotic Orient. Of the $185 million spent by American troops there, roughly half went toward the sexual procurement of Japanese sex workers.[10] Despite its illegality, prostitution in occupied Japan was tolerated by the US military, who saw it as a necessary service.[11] In South Korea, R&R facilities were built for American occupying forces starting in 1947, alongside shopping centers full of American products. Both the newly independent Republic of Korea and US military leaders encouraged the development of these camptowns outside US military installations, viewing them as a "release" for troops that improved morale and as a way to protect "virtuous" Korean women from the possibility of rape by sexually frustrated American soldiers.[12]

For soldiers like Rohrbach and Whimp, led to believe that Babysan "loved it," the culture of the violent embrace cloaked women's post–World War II dislocation and economic need in the language of romance and seduction. Sex workers in Japan emphasized not romance and pleasure but economic necessity: as Otoki, a leader of sex workers from Tokyo's Yūrakuchō district, explained in a 1947 Japanese radio broadcast, "Of course it's hard to be a hooker. But without relatives or jobs due to the war disaster, how are we supposed to live? . . . There aren't many of us who do this because we like it."[13] As the war began in Korea in 1950, dislocating and impoverishing millions of Koreans, some women found that selling sex or finding a live-in American boyfriend offered a viable form of employment, as well as access to luxury goods, gifts, and a steady stream of income from American clients, boyfriends, and husbands.[14] For others, entering the camptowns was not even a question of their own limited agency: some of the first camptown women were kidnapped or sold by poor families into prostitution or could find no other employment after being enslaved as a Japanese "comfort woman."[15]

The violent embrace transformed a landscape of dislocation and war into one of pleasure and necessity by casting servicemen's sexual "need" as natural and laudable and all Asian women as welcoming and seductive as Babysan.[16] As Brig. Gen. Bryan Milburn remarked in September 1950, it was "a problem which cannot be solved by discipline of the soldier alone," whose "comparatively new and strong sex awakening" made it "difficult for the soldier to cope" with the "abundant opportunity of attractive and submissive girls."[17]

As GIs came to see Japan as an erotic playground, sex and dating shaded easily into sexual violence. In the US military's lexicon of pleasures, R&R leave, in Korean War–era GI alliterative slang, took on variations that included "Rape & Restitution," "Rape & Ruin," "Intercourse & Intoxication," or "Booze & Broads," attempts at humor that blurred the line between consensual and coercive embrace and normalized sexual assault.[18] Japanese women, for example, reported being abducted and raped by servicemen while walking home at night, on empty buses, or in their homes.[19] Gang rape was a particularly common and brutal practice of soldiers in Japan, as it would be in Korea—in Yokohama, an eleven-year-old Japanese boy witnessed four or five US Marines rape a twenty-six-year-old woman and then take a photograph of her vagina.[20]

The US Army's small number of recorded cases is historically misleading. Between 1947 and 1949, the army received reports of 455 rapes of women in Japan by US personnel, leading to 306 arrests and 44 total convictions.[21] One Japanese estimate, however, recorded 330 sexual assaults and rapes per day during the US occupation.[22] The discrepancy may reflect the difficulty Japanese women experienced in reporting their cases: at least one Japanese woman who reported her rape said she was then treated like a prostitute and put in a guarded venereal disease hospital.[23]

In keeping with the language of the violent embrace, American officials lauded the "complete camaraderie" between Japanese and Americans.[24] Japanese women and men, however, saw the occupation differently and complained, protested, and organized against their treatment. Victims of assault lodged their cases with the Japanese police and the Supreme Commander for the Allied Powers (SCAP). Japanese citizens wrote constantly to MacArthur, SCAP, or US military officers about injustices directed toward them and asked for redress.[25] And despite SCAP's press censorship that forbade discussion of social issues criticizing the US occupation, the Japanese press reported consistently on crimes by US forces and published articles about rapes by US servicemen.[26]

With the start of the Korean War, rapes of civilian Korean women by American, South Korean, and United Nations forces also became commonplace. American troops were said to entice Korean refugee girls across the Naktong (Nakdong) River to rape them, and informal accounts describe families either hiding their daughters or trading time with their daughters to American soldiers in exchange for cigarettes or gum.[27] American Lieutenant Colonel Charles Bussey remembered overhearing his troops discussing how best to "rape a woman."[28] One US Army chaplain complained to American general Matthew Ridgway that early in the war, the murder and rape of Korean civilians was widespread because of the lax army attitude toward crimes against civilians; the chaplain reported one case of seven American soldiers caught raping Korean women in Pyongyang who were released unpunished. By winter of 1951 this violence, including rape, had increased, particularly in UN-occupied Seoul.[29] Postwar truth and reconciliation commissions in Korea have found that "sexual punishment" of suspected communist women by right-wing youth groups and US-allied South Korean military and police forces was routine during the war.[30]

Many army commanders decried American soldiers' crimes against Korean civilians, including rape, but understood these crimes as exceptions to an otherwise amicable relationship. On March 9, 1951, General Ridgway sent a letter to all subordinate commands warning that such "misconduct" and "molestation" fueled communist propaganda and debased "the honorable record of military achievement of our and other United Nations forces in Korea."[31] The idea that assault was an anomaly committed by a few lawless soldiers in an otherwise benevolent war is borne out only if the story is framed by using the army's official crime statistics. The most complete data specific to US forces in Korea is for April through August 1951, in which the provost marshal reported sixty-two rape cases over a five-month period.[32] Yet these statistics are misleadingly small: for a report to make it into military files, it would have to be a formal complaint lodged by the Korean woman or her family, an undertaking that would have been difficult at best in the midst of active combat fighting, language barriers, and mutual distrust.

Looking outside the Frame

Because of this archival record, sexual violence during the Korean War appears only sporadically, partially, or tangentially in English-language archives; the US military's own reports of investigations make it impossible to determine whether sexual violence by US soldiers in occupied Japan and Korea was rare or frequent. In fact, I doubt that an institutional history of rape cases will ever give a full accounting; as feminist legal scholars, analysts, historians, and activists have argued for decades, writing the history of gender violence demands an archive beyond state and military institutional records.[33]

Glimpses of the US military's violent embrace of East Asia appear in a traditional historical archive most often not as criminal reports or military police cases but as captions on soldiers' snapshots, in wartime slang and jokes, and as offhand references from war correspondents and in soldiers' memoirs. The violent embrace rested on just this occlusion, resolving the tension between romance and coercion, benevolence and occupation, love and war, by coding it as a kind of "good" fun or the securing of western democracy. If military occupation was "camaraderie," then assault could be pleasurable, "Rape & Restitution" could be "Rest & Relaxation," and fighting a brutal war could be, in President Truman's words, "fighting for peace."[34]

Further, this occlusion formed the way Korean War stories were and are told in the United States. War correspondents, historians, and scholars have detailed the Korean War's military violence by outlining the US and allied forces' devastating use of napalm, search-and-destroy tactics, the designation of "free-fire" zones that included rural villages, and racial violence against any Korean deemed to be a "gook."[35] Surprisingly, though, few contemporaneous American and British accounts, so intent on describing the use of napalm, guerrilla warfare, and Americans' anti-Asian racism, describe the rape of Korean women.[36] English-language histories of the war, from military histories to revisionist and contemporary ones, make only scant mention of sexual violence (or camptown prostitution, for that matter).[37] For example, sociologist and criminologist J. Robert Lilly, whose 2007 book documents incidences of GI rape in World War II's European theater, scoffed at the idea of widespread GI rape in Korea because of the lack of "verifiable sources."[38]

At times, the US government actively suppressed accounts of sexual violence during the war. In May 1951, the Women's International Democratic Federation (WIDF), a UN-affiliated network of antifascist and leftist women's organizations centered in Europe, sent a twenty-member fact-finding delegation to North Korea to investigate war crimes against Korean civilians. The delegates found evidence of the systematic use of torture and sexual torture, the destruction of food supplies and stores, targeted destruction of towns, hospitals, and schools, and the use of banned weapons—all forms of violence suppressed or sidelined in broader public discourse. The WIDF asked that their report, *We Accuse!*, be circulated to all governments, and they sent it themselves to the United Nations in June 1951, where its circulation was blocked by US representatives.[39]

Tellingly, only two rape cases reached mainstream American news, perhaps because one involved the culpability of other UN allies, not US soldiers, and the second was a racially charged case in which African American Navy steward Paul Crosslin was convicted by military court-martial for the alleged rape of a US Navy nurse, not a Korean woman. Crosslin's defense was taken up by the National Association for the Advancement of Colored People (NAACP), which recognized the case as a part of a longer American tradition of falsely accusing black men of raping white women.[40]

The silence in American accounts belies the memories of Korean women and men during the war, for whom rape forms one of the most enduring memories of the war.[41] Some women explicitly remember US soldiers calling out "saekssi, saekssi" as they looked for Korean women, using the Korean word that meant "maiden" but sounded to American ears like "sexy" and to Koreans as an intention of violation.[42] Rape and sexual exploitation of Korean women by American soldiers has become a trope in contemporary Korean fiction and film about the Korean War and postwar camptown life.[43] We might see the unnamed woman in Rohrbach and Whimp's snapshot not just embraced by the smiling GI but enfolded within a longer history of the violent embrace. This might allow space for her story to be much more than that of a "good piece" and different from my story of American militarization in East Asia. Rather, she might tell her own, complicated story.

Accommodating these new stories requires examining the silences, partial references, and traces left in the archive: it means interrogating the qualities of the embrace seen in the snapshots, asking what lies outside their frames, and theorizing what cannot be seen. Disavowal and elision were at the heart of the violent embrace, for the same framing of Whimp and Rohrbach's R&R leave as fun with "good pieces" made rape ubiquitous to US military culture, and the women who experienced it silent figures for the retrenchment of a story of American benevolence. Accommodating these new stories also calls for a recognition of the work war narratives do to reinscribe and naturalize gendered power relationships in which female bodies—particularly those already made precarious by racial and national differentiations—are made potentially violable.

In the absence of full accounts of US empire's gendered violence, Rohrbach and Whimp's photographs urge us to reconsider the framing of US power in the Pacific as benevolent or equitable. The sometimes fraught embraces in the snapshots, and Rohrbach's characterization of the women as "good pieces," bring into focus how the assertion of American democracy in Korea and Japan depended on both structural gender violence and its attendant disavowal. We need new epistemologies, new frames of vision that attend to the silences by outlining them, constructing histories that show the shape of what is lost.

Notes

I thank Moon-Ho Jung, Ellen Wu, the Histories of Violence Collective, and the History Department Colloquium at Indiana University for their comments on this piece.

1. Richard Rohrbach Photograph Collection, PP.901, Center for the Study of the Korean War, Independence, Missouri.
2. Ibid., PP.904 and PP.957.
3. Judith Butler's discussion of "frames of war" is central to my thinking: Butler, *Frames of War: When Is Life Grievable?* (New York: Verso, 2010).
4. Shufeldt's lecture quoted in Frederick C. Drake, *The Empire of the Seas: A Biography of Rear Admiral Robert Wilson Shufeldt, USN* (Honolulu: University of Hawai'i Press, 1984), 115–16.
5. Gordon Chang, "Whose 'Barbarism'? Whose 'Treachery'? Race and Civilization in the Unknown United States–Korea War of 1871," *Journal of American History* 89, no. 4 (2003): 1362.
6. Naoko Shibusawa, *America's Geisha Ally: Reimagining the Japanese Enemy* (Cambridge, MA: Harvard University Press, 2006); Korean Military Advisory Group Public Information Office, *The United States Military Advisory Group to the Republic of Korea, 1945–1955* (Tokyo: Daito Art Printing, 1956), viii, 60.

7.   Bill Hume, *Babysan: A Private Look at the Japanese Occupation* (Tokyo: Kasuga Boeki K.K., 1953), dedication and 6–7. The popularity of the text is discussed in Shibusawa, *America's Geisha Ally*, 36.

8.   Shibusawa, *America's Geisha Ally*, 17.

9.   Hume, *Babysan*, 76–77.

10.   Shibusawa, *America's Geisha Ally*, 38.

11.   A state-run system of sex work was closed after one year by US occupation authorities. John Dower, *Embracing Defeat: Japan in the Wake of World War II* (New York: Norton, 1999), 123–32; Sarah Kovner, *Occupying Power: Sex Workers and Servicemen in Postwar Japan* (Stanford, CA: Stanford University Press, 2012), chap. 1.

12.   Whitney Taejin Hwang, "Borderland Intimacies: GIs, Koreans, and American Military Landscapes in Cold War Korea" (PhD diss., University of California, Berkeley, 2010), 26–28, 89–90; Ji-Yeon Yuh, *Beyond the Shadow of Camptown: Korean Military Brides in America* (New York: New York University, 2002), 25; Seungsook Moon, "Regulating Desire, Managing the Empire: US Military Prostitution in South Korea, 1945–1970," in *Over There: Living with the US Military Empire from World War Two to the Present*, eds. Maria Höhn and Seungsook Moon (Durham, NC: Duke University Press, 2010), 41.

13.   Dower, *Embracing Defeat*, 123–24.

14.   Hwang, "Borderland Intimacies," chap. 1, esp. 38–40.

15.   Yuh, *Beyond the Shadow*, 31; Hwang, "Borderland Intimacies," 89.

16.   Hwang, "Borderland Intimacies," 25–27; Kovner, *Occupying Power*, 30–33; Susan Zeiger, *Entangling Alliances: Foreign War Brides and American Soldiers in the Twentieth Century* (New York: New York University Press, 2010), chap. 3, esp. 75.

17.   Control of Solicitors and Streetwalkers, 1950, folder 250.1 and 2, box 199, General Correspondence (GC) 1950, Adjutant General (AG), Far East Command (FEC), Record Group (RG) 554, US National Archives, College Park, MD (NACP).

18.   E. J. Kahn, *The Peculiar War: Impressions of a Reporter in Korea* (New York: Random House, 1951), 12–13; Paul Dickson, *War Slang: American Fighting Words and Phrases since the Civil War*, 2nd ed. (Dulles, VA: Brassey's, 2004), 236, 246, 253.

19.   See the complaints filed by named and unnamed Japanese women, reported in folder 250.1, "(Jan Dec) 1946 (OCC)," box 909, Official File, AG, Eighth Army, RG 338, NACP; folder 250.1, "Morals and Conduct," box 32, GC 1946–48, G-2, Eighth Army, RG 338, NACP; folder 250.1, "Alleged Misconduct of Occupation Troops against Japanese Nationals," box 199, GC 1950, AG, FEC, RG 554, NACP; folder 250.1 no. 1, box 884, Secret General Correspondence 1952, AG, FEC, RG 554, NACP.

20.   Kovner, *Occupying Power*, 50–51.

21.   The figures were tallied by the Provost Marshal Office between March 8 and 10, 1950, at the specific request of the Army Staff Branch G-1, compiled from detailed monthly crime reports prepared for each command within the entire Far East Command. Numbers of trials and convictions were prepared by the Provost Marshal Office from incomplete files of General Court-Martial orders from the Judge Advocate Section of FEC General Headquarters. Documents held in "Statistics in re: Rape," folder 250.1, "Alleged Misconduct of Occupation Troops."

22.   Charles J. Hanley, Sang-Hun Choe, and Martha Mendoza, *The Bridge at No Gun Ri: A Hidden Nightmare from the Korean War* (New York: Holt, 2001), 28.

23.   Kovner, *Occupying Power*, 54.

24.   General Omar N. Bradley, "Substance of Statements Made at Wake Island Conference on 15 October 1950, Compiled by General of the Army Omar N. Bradley, Chairman of the Joint

Chiefs of Staff, From Notes Kept by the Conferees in Washington," 13, folder 18, "Wake Island—Conference Statements," box 206, Korean War, President's Secretary's Files, Harry S. Truman Papers, Truman Library, Independence, Missouri.

25. "Unfavorable Press in Occupied Japan," November 3, 1952, folder 250.1, box 519, GC 1952, AG, Eighth Army, RG 338, NACP; "Ski Slope Beatings," March 11, 1949, folder 250.1 no. 1, box 575, Secret General Correspondence 1949, AG, FEC, RG 554, NACP; "Japanese Complaint," January 23, 1950, postcard from K. Yukashita, May 17, 1952, and case 2, Mrs. Yasuyo Onishi, folder 250.1, "Alleged Misconduct of Occupation Troops."

26. Dower, *Embracing Defeat*, 211, 410–12.

27. Hanley et al., *Bridge at No Gun Ri*, 103, 189.

28. Lt. Col. Charles M. Bussey, *Firefight at Yechon: Courage and Racism in the Korean War* (Lincoln: University of Nebraska Press, 1991), 238–43, 255.

29. Callum A. MacDonald, *Korea: The War before Vietnam* (New York: Free Press, 1986), 210, 216.

30. Bruce Cumings, *The Origins of the Korean War*, 2 vols. (Princeton, NJ: Princeton University Press, 1990), 2:702; Suzy Kim, *Everyday Life in the North Korean Revolution, 1945–1950* (Ithaca, NY: Cornell University Press, 2013), 234; Masuda Hajimu, *Cold War Crucible: The Korean Conflict and the Postwar World* (Cambridge, MA: Harvard University Press, 2015), chap. 7.

31. "Misconduct of Troops" letter, March 9, 1951, folder 250.1, box 747, Secret General Correspondence 1951, AG, RG 554, NACP.

32. See all Staff Section Report folders in box 2174, Command Reports, December 1950 to December 1952, Provost Marshal Section, Eighth Army, RG 338, NACP.

33. For example, this argument is made in Estelle Freedman, *Redefining Rape: Sexual Violence in the Era of Suffrage and Segregation* (Cambridge, MA: Harvard University Press, 2013); Judith Herman, *Trauma and Recovery: The Aftermath of Violence—from Domestic Abuse to Political Terror*, updated ed. (New York: Basic Books, 1997), 28–32; Kovner, *Occupying Power*, 55.

34. President Harry S. Truman, live television addresses from the White House, CBS network, July 19, 1950, and September 1, 1950, accessed from the Paley Center for Media database, https://www.paleycenter.org/collection/.

35. For example, see Sahr Conway-Lanz, "Beyond No Gun Ri: Refugees and the United States Military in the Korean War," *Diplomatic History* 29, no. 1 (2005): 45–81; Cumings, *Origins of the Korean War*; Réné Cutforth, *Korean Reporter* (London: Wingate, 1952); Max Hastings, *The Korean War* (New York: Simon and Schuster, 1987); Kahn, *Peculiar War*; MacDonald, *Korea*; I. F. Stone, *The Hidden History of the Korean War* (New York: Monthly Review Press, 1952); and Reginald Thompson, *Cry Korea* (London: MacDonald, 1951).

36. For a singular mention of "the bombs and the burning and the raping behind the battle line," see Cutforth, *Korean Reporter*, 189–90.

37. Bruce Cumings's valuable two-volume *Origins of the Korean War* notes that rape was "common" but adds no more (706, 904n120). However, he discusses the issue in later shorter writings: Bruce Cumings, "Silent but Deadly: Sexual Subordination in the US-Korean Relationship," in *Let the Good Times Roll: Prostitution and the US Military in Asia*, ed. Saundra Pollock Sturdevant and Brenda Stoltzfus (New York: New Press, 1993); Bruce Cumings, "Occurrence at Nogun-Ri Bridge: An Inquiry into the History and Memory of a Civil War," *Critical Asian Studies* 33, no. 4 (2001): 520. See also note 41. Several scholarly accounts tabulate rape and sexual violence in occupied Japan and discuss the Korean War as part of that context: Kovner, *Occupying Power*; Yuki Tanaka,

Japan's Comfort Women: Sexual Slavery and Prostitution during World War II and the US Occupation (New York: Routledge, 2002). Susan Brownmiller attempted to account for US Army court-martial convictions for rape, but without access to credible sources: Brownmiller, *Against Our Will: Men, Women, and Rape* (New York: Simon and Schuster, 1975), 99, 417.

38. J. Robert Lilly, *Taken by Force: Rape and American GIs in Europe during World War II* (New York: Palgrave Macmillan, 2007), 31.

39. Though communist propaganda often charged US and UN forces with rape, I do not believe the WIDF report can be included in this category. The report is certainly one-sided, investigating only US, ROK, and UN war crimes, but the WIDF's long history as an interwar women's organization and the commission's careful detailing of names, dates, and locations of assaults lead me to accept the report as a credible piece of reportage. Women's International Democratic Federation, *We Accuse! Report of the Commission of the Women's International Democratic Federation in Korea, May 16 to 27, 1951* (Berlin: WIDF, 1951), esp. 16, 35, 36. For the background of the WIDF, see Francisca de Haan, "The Women's International Democratic Federation (WIDF): History, Main Agenda, and Contributions, 1945–1991," in *Women and Social Movements, International, 1840–Present*, ed. Kathryn Kish Sklar and Thomas Dublin, Alexander Street Press, http://alexanderstreet .com/products/women-and-social-movements-international; Francisca de Haan, "Continuing Cold War Paradigms in Western Historiography of Transnational Women's Organisations: The Case of the Women's International Democratic Federation (WIDF)," *Women's History Review* 19, no. 4 (2010): 547–73; Suzy Kim, "Crossing Borders: A Feminist History of Women Cross DMZ," *Asia-Pacific Journal* 13, no. 1.33 (2015): 1–31. For the debate over the report's presentation to the United Nations, see "Malik Pushes Report on Korea 'Atrocities,'" *New York Times*, June 23, 1951; "US Replies to Reds," *New York Times*, July 6, 1951; US Mission to the United Nations, "Non-governmental Organizations, Consultative Status with Economic and Social Council—Women's International Democratic Federation, 4 Oct. 1946–10 April 1953 (A)," press release 1224, June 22, 1951, folder 8, box: "S-0441-0016, Registry Section/Archives and Records Service/OGS, Branch Registries—Volume I–IV, 1946–1959," UN Archives and Records Management Section, New York, New York.

40. George Barrett, "Koreans Watch U.N. Murder Trial as Test of Curb on Unruly Troops," *New York Times*, August 21, 1951; "Navy Steward's Case to Judge Advocate," *Memphis World*, February 27, 1953; "Ask New Trial in Navy Case," *Baltimore Afro-American*, February 28, 1953. Crosslin was convicted to a ten-year term in 1951; the NAACP's lawyers petitioned to reopen the trial in 1953.

41. Yuh, *Beyond the Shadow*, 242n36. Cumings reported that wartime rape was an enduring memory for Korean survivors of the war in an interview by Dean Lawrence Velvel on the television program *Books of Our Time* (Massachusetts School of Law/Comcast, March 20, 2011), mslawmedia.org (accessed May 2, 2013).

42. Yuh, *Beyond the Shadow*, 242n36; Chungmoo Choi, "Nationalism and Construction of Gender in Korea," in *Dangerous Women: Gender and Korean Nationalism*, ed. Elaine H. Kim and Chungmoo Choi (New York: Routledge, 1998), 15.

43. Choi, "Nationalism," 15–18.

Boko Haram, Refugee Mimesis, and the Archive of Contemporary Gender-Based Violence

Benjamin N. Lawrance

Nigerian Isa Muazu came to the United Kingdom in 2007. He overstayed his visitor's visa and was detained. Muazu applied for asylum protection based on his fear of death at the hands of the West African Islamist entity Boko Haram (BH), which he claimed had already killed members of his family.[1] Muazu's fears were allegedly grounded in unsubstantiated claims that BH adherents had previously subjected his wife and daughters to persecutory harms that somehow extended to his person. The Home Office rejected his application and deported him in 2013.[2] Regardless of his claims' veracity and verifiability, Muazu may have been Britain's first asylum seeker fearing BH.

Asylum seekers today witness western migration fortresses' exclusionary walls rising ever higher.[3] Protection categories in the 1951 Refugee Convention seem frustratingly immutable; access to protection in developed countries is inexorably constricted. Refugees engaging newer analytical frameworks of gender-based persecution, such as domestic violence, or even established paradigms such as genital cutting, face heavy scrutiny for credibility. Whereas in the 1990s and 2000s exotic stories of what feminist migration theorists identify as "gendered persecutory harms" gained critical attention, they have been now displaced by sensational stories about security and terrorism.[4]

Radical History Review
Issue 126 (October 2016)   DOI 10.1215/01636545-3594505
© 2016 by MARHO: The Radical Historians' Organization, Inc.

Asylum seekers, cognizant of the incredulity greeting their personal testimonies, employ creative strategies to anchor their narratives and render them exotically
familiar.[5] Since the kidnapping of several hundred girls in Chibok in Borno State in
April 2014, asylum claims increasingly cite BH. Far from exposing BH's "weakness,"
as pundit Andrew Noakes claimed, the kidnappings lend new agency to grander,
expansive fears of abduction, rape, and forced marriage now filtering into asylum
claims.[6] Although migration authorities recognize BH's extreme violence, asylum
anxieties narrated in immigration courts often assert hypothetical future jeopardy, not enacted historical trauma.[7] By reshaping personal testimonies of gender-
based violence to foreground persecution by BH, Nigerian asylum seekers actuate
a mimetic strategy engaging powerful—and problematic—tropes about Africa and
Africans. Absent mimesis, and as Plato conjectured, the poetics of asylum seekers
risk being exposed as little more than "simple narration."[8]

Many of the asylum seeker testimonies I review in my capacity as expert witness contain unique and otherwise inaccessible first-hand accounts of historical and
contemporary gender-based violence. This analysis explores asylum seeking as an
emergent archival form to highlight how the strategies in asylum claiming conceal a
potentially rich archive of gender-based violence. Nigerian claims illustrate one such
strategy, namely, how gender-based-violence asylum claimants mimetically emphasize BH as a vehicle for resistance to endemic bureaucratic suspicion, doubt, and
disbelief. Echoing Luise White's inspiring analysis of rumor to reconstruct complex
historical "truths," attention to strategy illustrates how mimetic asylum texts may
be read as archives of gender-based violence.[9] In the mimetic invocation of BH
jeopardy, a spectrum of historical and projected persecutory fears adapts current
anxieties of gender-based violence. Nigerians highlight horror stories about BH to
instrumentalize stereotypes of African cultures—often as primitive and endemi-
cally violent—rendering gender-based violence into exotically familiar prejudices
of Africa. Asylum seekers' invocations of BH operate as a mimetic enterprise, a
forward-looking strategy whereby tired, often racist historical paradigms of Africa
collapse into presentist anxieties of gender-based violence.

Asylum as an Archive of Gender-Based Violence

Asylum seeking is emerging as an important site of historical research.[10] African
historians turn to asylum claimants, experiences narrated outside Africa, as a creative way to "think more critically and imaginatively" about "Africa's post-colonial
archive."[11] Asylum narratives allow historians to take the pulse of the contemporary
African gendered experience; they offer new and insightful paths to see and know
gender-based violence. Asylum seekers provide rich insights into the discrete worlds
of grassroots resistance to patriarchy and gender-based violence and alternative sexualities, part of the rubric of an "emergent and tentative new conceptual bundle" of
sexual rights "unfolding" in transnational globalized migrant networks.[12] Framing

asylum claims as archives responds to Ann Laura Stoler's attention to archival form, notably "genres of documentation," "arts of persuasion," and "affective strains."[13]

Asylum seeking has the potential to function as an archive in several ways. First, asylum seeking offers a valuable documentation genre for evaluating lived social experiences. While asylum narratives are first-person accounts, collectively asylum claiming offers a contemporary oral historical archive of gender-based violence. Asylum claiming—including but not limited to applicant testimonies, government response letters, judgments, and other documentation—operate as "rich documentary archives tethered to discrete legal contexts," which speak to "analytical categories, constructed identities, and personal narratives of fear, trauma and violence."[14] Testimonies are multilayered: each time an asylum seeker narrates an experience, or revisits an earlier statement or interview, a contemporary archive of persecution expands. Asylum narratives—and the snowballing of documentation as claims move toward adjudication—provide a window on the changing contexts of gender-based violence.[15]

Second, asylum narratives offer a critical perspective to revisit methodological debates about gender violence histories, such as establishing the basis of complaint.[16] As asylum claims are increasingly supported by expertise, they constitute a category of persuasive art. Reports by historians, and other experts, translate narratives of "personal trauma" into persuasive acts "of political aggression," anchored to Refugee Convention articles.[17] The discipline of history, modes of historical writing, and the methodologies of historicization have powerful explanatory facility for asylum adjudicators.[18] Experts are contracted to provide analysis of the empirical details of specific claims, ranging from current state protections and capacity for enforcement to the disjuncture between objectives and on-the-ground reality. The expert may be a foil to adjudicators, evaluating the legal basis for persecution claims and the history of specific persecutory forms.[19] By comparing claims with publicly available evidence about real and purported legal remedy, experts provide a hypothetical basis for advancing a claim.

Third, as a tightly regulated formula for affecting empathy, asylum claiming demands engagement with a register of strategies. The omission of gender from the international language of refugee protection gives rise to strategies to overcome this error. Understanding asylum-seeking strategies holds the possibility of unlocking a vast archive of persecution and trauma. The routinely hostile reception granted gender-based-violence claims ironically tenders an avenue for uncovering their very meaning.[20] Asylum seekers and their advocates fashion gender-based narratives into persuasive concepts and established frameworks; as an archive they are highly problematic, and some may be of questionable reliability.[21] Asylum narratives constitute personal lived truths, buttressed by fears, hearsay, and rumors, hence the significance of identifying and problematizing one such strategy, mimesis. Disassembling strategies—as they engage, resist, and seek to subvert criticisms of claims—reveal not only the lived experience of the personal and intimate but also how refugee convention definitions restrain and conceal gender-based violence.

From Credibility to Mimesis

Asylum operates within an unbounded legal domain, and in a constant state of flux, the unanchored nature of which is revealed by policies, procedures, standards, practices, and legal challenges. Claims are co-constituted in a climate of fear in which expert, claimant, advocate, and immigration authority all operate. Assessing credibility is one key site of contestation; it reveals the unbounded, unanchored dimensions of the refugee's legal predicament. Attacks on credibility turn asylum narratives into what April Shemak calls "sites of surveillance and policing of national boundaries."[22] Mimesis has emerged as one strategy refugees themselves use to resist attacks on credibility.

Mimesis is an affective strategy of resistance and subversion of the constraints imposed on survivors of gender-based violence. Asylum seekers' strategies are inextricable from their own personal testimony and tack closely to testimony and testimonial form. The woman fleeing genital cutting has only her personal narrative of violence and persecution. When decision makers question her credibility, she adopts techniques to broaden the significance *qua* seriousness of her specific claim. One response is to stretch, embellish, or invent narratives that conform to asylum law.[23] Another is to draw on the added burden of trauma many refugees suffer, and the difficulties of communicating across both linguistic barriers and cultural dissonance add complexity to elicit empathic responses on the part of adjudicators.[24] Mimesis is another such response to incredulity.

Mimetic practices have a rich history and present throughout sub-Saharan Africa. Mimetic affect is a mechanism to assimilate, perform, mask, dissolve, and reshape.[25] Mimetic performance is neither reenactment nor deceit but self-transformative in a context of upheaval and instability.[26] In gender-based violence narratives mimesis becomes a tool to reframe the personal narrative, within a broader canvas of jeopardy. Mimesis rebuts attacks on the credibility of asylum seekers by collapsing lived experiences or future jeopardies with presentist anxieties. The recourse to mimesis in asylum seeking as a direct response to the pressures of credibility attacks and fear of incredulity was seemingly anticipated by Jean-François Lyotard when he described the violent "double bind" as a *dommage* (a tort or wrong) "accompanied by the loss of means to prove the damage."[27] Because of the "improvability" of testimony, the asylum seeker is routinely perceived as mendacious.[28] As asylum seekers are often convinced their stories will never be believed, they reframe them within a broader presentist canvas populated by terrifying fears.

Boko Haram Mimesis

BH is a real danger in parts of Nigeria. Since 2009, twenty thousand deaths have been attributed to BH, and more than two million have been displaced by bombings, kidnappings, and armed invasions of villages. In 2015, BH was the world's deadliest extremist group in the Global Terrorism Index.[29] BH mimesis resists bureaucratic incredulity via four frameworks: representation, embodiment, transformation, and presentism. Each anchors asylum claims to specific Refugee Convention requirements. Representation operates as a documentary stage whereby a specific narrative is tied to established BH practices: the new unknown is tethered to the known. Via a discussion of documented events, embodiment designates BH as the physical manifestation of the potential gender-based persecution: the specific fear broadens to a known organization. Building on embodiment, transformation converts BH from general threats into historical persecutory patterns. And finally, presentism reifies BH by collapsing historical persecution with current anxieties; the danger is thus clear, present, and ongoing.

Representation constitutes a documentary stage whereby a link between the claimant and the larger scope of persecution materializes via "real" or purported prima facie evidence. Two examples illustrate how representation tethers an otherwise unverifiable instance to known BH practices with the mediation of expertise. In September 2014, one applicant produced a letter from a BH leader as evidence of a credible direct threat to one individual. Signed on letterhead, it purported to be from a known militant. A second individual in June claimed to have been "receiving threatening calls from BH" since 2007, which prompted flight.[30] The individual submitted logs of calls to a (since disconnected) Nigerian cell phone. In both instances, attorneys sought an expert witness to verify or authenticate the purported link between their client and the threat.

Such documents represent BH by explicitly mirroring the organization's known communication forms. The representation framework plays with specific ideas of BH as unknown or illicit, decentralized, acephalous, and quixotic. Communications never seem to emanate directly from a central command but are mediated by the Internet, news networks, or third parties, arriving unannounced and often unverified or unverifiable. For example, speculation that the Chibok girls were to be sold as wives rested on a video released in October 2014 by BH's self-proclaimed leader, Abubakar Shekau.[31] The October video was coupled with news of another mass kidnapping, bride abduction, and forced marriage in two northeast towns. Residents of Wagga told Agence France-Presse that suspected "Islamist gunmen" had gone "door-to-door" looking for young women and girls, abducting forty. Lazarus Baushe, a Wagga elder, said "they left 1,500 naira (£5.67) and some kola nuts in each home where they seized a woman, apparently as a bride price."[32] Asylum seekers may reference such anecdotes to corroborate mysterious letters or anonymous calls.

Embodiment, the second stage of mimesis, transcends the specific, uncorroborated alleged threats and reshapes the narrative into a general physical and/or moral threat, again through the mediation of the expert witness. Two examples are illustrative. In mid-2014, a lawyer described the predicament of a Christian Yoruba single mother with four children. She explained that two young girls were at risk of genital cutting, because they had not been cut. She herself had been cut (not by BH). She then cited a "general risk of Boko Haram" aligned with "religious conflict issues" as one of four possible protection grounds.[33] BH was listed fourth, after three others that narrated concrete physical threats of gender-based violence. In this way, BH was reframed as an implied physical threat and a purveyor of gender-based violence. Although neither the client nor her lawyer identified BH explicitly as a potential "cutter," the threat hierarchy left little doubt that cutting and BH were interlocked. An expert may then possibly document the possible, plausible, or hypothetical types of gender-based violence or threats.

In a similar case reported in the media, Afusat Saliu, from Lagos in southern Nigeria, unsuccessfully fought deportation of herself and her two daughters from Britain. She claimed, that as a "victim" of "female genital mutilation" herself, "she fears her daughters will also be mutilated and spoke of her fear that, as Christians, they could be targeted by the Nigerian Islamic extremist group Boko Haram, which recently kidnapped more than 200 schoolgirls."[34] Saliu arrived in 2011 and claimed to have fled Nigeria when her stepmother told her that her oldest daughter would be cut (not by BH). In another reported version, she claimed she feared "she will be forced into a marriage against her will."[35] Neither Saliu nor her attorney explained how BH might reach her children in Lagos.

Embodiment reorders specific gender-based violence by redefining jeopardy as a state's failure generally to protect its citizenry. BH becomes a macrocategory of gender violence against which the state has no capacity to protect. In a third reported iteration, Saliu claimed that she "could be targeted by Boko Haram militants, . . . because of her conversion to Christianity. . . . Ms Saliu's father was allegedly killed by the group."[36] Embodiment appeals to those trying to "understand" BH and its goals but does so by playing into misconceptions, biases, and ugly narratives of Islam, Africa, and Africans. Earlier wrongheaded and ill-conceived calls tied the Chibok kidnappings to terrorism; BH was enveloped by the rhetoric of counterterrorism.[37] Similarly, pundits have made wholly unsupported claims that BH practices genital cutting.[38]

A third formula of BH mimesis is transformation, a process of historicization whereby the generalized jeopardies are made comprehensible by reference to past experience and located within a larger pattern of persecution. An example from May 2014 illustrates how assumptions about what BH is and what it is capable of are embedded in a historical narrative of earlier forms of violence and terror. The senior protection officer of the UN High Commissioner for Refugees in Tokyo sought help to "understand how ordinary Christians" or "general supporters of the Nigerian government" may be "targets for persecution by Boko Haram." A query was posed thus: "Whether incidents committed by other persons or organizations were reported as Boko Haram actions."[39] In this example, BH is transformed into an aberration and persecutory enterprise targeting normalcy and stability. Moreover, past events are revisited, albeit hypothetically, as actions of BH.

From the perspective of the historian, the significance of transformation cannot be understated because transformation converts new things into historical practices. Protean fears, newness, and novelty are indeed a cornerstone of contemporary African asylum practice. Each instance of jeopardy embedded within any asylum application constitutes a distinct component of the archive of postcolonial African social and family life. This archive is alive and gives rise to new understandings about cultures and practices, behaviors and moralities.[40] While asylum seekers' narratives may appear, at least to western adjudicators, novel, unusual, and contested, digital information technology makes it possible for claimants to ground their need for protection in rich documentation about the absence of legal remedy or safeguards.[41]

This third mimetic formula highlights the role of experts to sustain contentions about BH. Experts mediate asylum narratives by comparing them with publicly available reports by news media, nongovernmental organizations, and government agencies. While such sources are highly problematic historical documents, adjudicators require experts to consider up-to-date "objective evidence": even historians who serve as experts must dispense with a disciplinary skepticism of such materials.[42] In so doing experts may reinvigorate established paradigms, such as slavery and witchcraft, or contribute to the emergence of perceived new analytical and social categories, such as statelessness and fraudulence.[43] In one case a BH narrative formed part of a successful asylum case. Michael C.'s lawyers transformed a confused narrative of religious and ethnic violence—hard to pin down as targeted and thus falling within Refugee Convention grounds—into a historical pattern of religious terrorism wherein BH was the teleological conclusion and future jeopardy. Michael C., a Berom man from Jos, in northern Nigeria, testified that he faced "near constant threats over more than a decade from Hausa Fulani and Boko Haram."[44] Yet allegedly Michael's cousin was killed in a 2001 massacre, an event predating BH's formation; in 2008, his home was burned in a larger attack on Berom Christians (far from any known BH activities); and in 2010, his youngest brother was allegedly killed near the family church.[45]

The fourth iteration of mimesis is presentism, whereby historical jeopardy is collapsed with current anxieties, thus making the claimant's narrative clear and real. Presentist narratives of BH deny the possibility of the recovery of the kidnapped girls by providing updates of additional kidnappings and chaos writ large. The Yoruba single mother, for example, having asserted BH's role in broad gender-based violence and the Nigerian state's failure to protect women, described the "possibility of internal relocation" in the narrowest terms. Here BH is instantiated as a nation-wide presence, in spite of considerable counterevidence.[46] In a second example, a Nigerian male—born to a Muslim father but himself a Christian convert—described how "his mother" was "killed in a Boko Haram attack." This uncorroborated allegation segued to a claim of fear of the "current situation" regarding Boko Haram.[47] In this second example BH encompasses the entire predicament of jeopardy.

Michael C.'s experience similarly illustrates the collapsing of history with presentist anxiety. Whereas he left Nigeria for Israel in 2011, returned in 2013, and then fled to the United States in February 2014, the only Jos violence with any alleged BH link was in May 2014, after his departure.[48] But the press release celebrating his triumph claimed, "Michael's case highlights the dangers Christians face in parts of Nigeria controlled by Muslim extremists including Boko Haram, which captured the world's attention last spring when it kidnapped hundreds of schoolgirls."[49] In reality, Michael C. lived far from Chibok, and the kidnappings were unrelated to his social and religious persecution. But as Chibok was in the news daily, the horrifying descriptions of rapes, forced marriage, and fears about the future children born of pregnant girls who escaped were collapsed into a presentist narrative of endemic violence into which no one may be returned.[50]

Presentism is a powerful mimetic technique because the mass abductions of 2014 invoke a general BH jeopardy, whereby the original story breathes life into other deep-seated fears. Asylum seekers may support their statements with journalistic field accounts, updates from nongovernmental organizations, and a range of so-called objective evidence that includes Amnesty International press releases, *New York Times* articles, and global terrorism surveys—the more current the better. Some submit videos from YouTube or Vimeo as substantiating "evidence." Alternatively, presentism can involve using parallel testimonies from others. Texan lawyer Linda Corchado, who represents a Nigerian preacher, claims her client fears "for her life" after "the Islamist group began killing Christians in her village." She plans to "reach out to folks from Nigeria, witnesses that were actually there when the attack happened, to help present the case in the best way possible."[51]

Presentism emphasizes continuing failures of Nigeria to protect its citizens, playing into stereotypes of failed states or worse. Presentism directs attention to alternate Nigerian state preoccupations and collapses historical failures with ongoing incompetence combating BH. Anxieties about further kidnapping are metonyms whereby Nigerian state actors explain many contemporary issues, including political paralysis. A vivid illustration of the collapsing discourse of presentism comes from self-described journalist Andrew Noakes, who wrote, "There are two insurgencies in Nigeria. There's the real insurgency that has claimed the lives of thousands of Nigerians, and then there's the insurgency that exists in the minds of much of Nigeria's political elite, to be unleashed as a tool to gain political advantage over their opponents."[52]

Conclusion

Recovering the archive of gender-based violence requires a new look at asylum seeking. Asylum narratives provide an avenue to connect to personal testimony in powerful ways. Asylum archives contain surprising histories about gender and violence, offering up stories that challenge axiomatic invocations of gender, power, and state and nonstate actors. African historians are continually frustrated by the difficulties of conducting research in the postcolonial African context. But if we look outside Africa, and to African exiles, such as asylum seekers and refugees, we will find rich personal archives of the contemporary African experience.

At the same, however, asylum claims alleging gender-based persecutory harms cannot be taken at face value. Because asylum seekers encounter institutional suspicion and bureaucratic disbelief, they employ various strategies to advance their claims. Narratives must be carefully scrutinized to preserve their archival value. Not unlike Luise White's vampire narratives that rendered the exotic familiar, Nigerian asylum seekers mimetically invoke BH to render the implausible into familiarly exotic and terrifying. Mimetic invocations of BH may or may not safeguard an asylum claim. Irrespective of success or failure, mimesis instrumentalizes unpleasant stereotypes about Africans and deep-seated racist generalizations.

Seeking asylum is no easy task, and refugees respond to credibility challenges in thoughtful and creative ways. Mimesis masks, reshapes, and reforms unsubstantiated, or unsubstantiatable, personal narratives into terrifying, shocking, present danger to affect empathy among decision-makers. Pliny the Elder's immortal proverb *ex Africa semper aliquid novi*—"always something new out of Africa"—is doubly instructive here insofar as it conveys first the idea that, at least where Africa is concerned, experiences are routinely framed as new or novel. But asylum seekers embrace this mimetically and reshape and reform their jeopardies and fears. Mimesis is not mendacity, fraud, or deceit; it is a conscious strategy to broaden a personal experience into something that may garner attention and, at its most optimistic, refugee status. Where gender-based violence is concerned, simple narration is all too often woefully inadequate.

Notes

1. "Isa Muazu Granted More Time in UK," *Guardian*, December 6, 2013.
2. "Hunger Strike Asylum Seeker Isa Muazu Deported to Nigeria," BBC News, December 18, 2013.
3. Vicki Squire, *The Exclusionary Politics of Asylum* (Basingstoke, UK: Palgrave-Macmillan, 2009).
4. For gendered persecutory harms, see Jenni Millbank and Catherine Dauvergne, "Forced

Marriage and the Exoticization of Gendered Harms in United States Asylum Law," *Columbia Journal of Gender and Law* 19, no. 3 (2011): 6. For security displacing gendered harms, see Magnus Taylor, "Africa in the News: Weekly Analysis from the RAS: How Africa Became All about 'Security,'" *Royal African Society* (blog), June 5, 2015.

5. Gregory Mann, "An Africanist's Apostasy: On Luise White's 'Speaking with Vampires,'" *International Journal of African Historical Studies* 41, no. 1 (2008): 120.

6. Andrew Noakes, "Boko Haram's Weakness Exposed by Girls' Abduction," Think Africa Press, May 2014, accessed June 30, 2015, https://www.facebook.com/notes/ameer-taawun -dawood-imran/boko-harams-weakness-exposed-by-girls-abduction/322774844555534/.

7. See, e.g., UK Home Office, "Operational Guidance Note: Nigeria," 3.18, December 2013, www.gov.uk/government/uploads/system/uploads/attachment_data/file/310454/Nigeria _operational_guidance_2013.pdf.

8. Plato, *Republic*, Book III, 393–94.

9. Luise White, *Speaking with Vampires: Rumor and History in Colonial Africa* (Berkeley: University of California Press, 2000).

10. Benjamin Lawrance, Iris Berger, Tricia Hepner Redeker, Joanna Tague, and Meredith Terretta, "Law, Expertise, and Protean Ideas about African Migrants," in *African Asylum at a Crossroads: Activism, Expert Testimony, and Refugee Rights*, ed. Iris Berger, Tricia Redeker Hepner, Benjamin N. Lawrance, Joanna Tague, and Meredith Terretta (Athens: Ohio University Press), 29–30.

11. Jean Allman, "Phantoms of the Archive: Kwame Nkrumah, a Nazi Pilot Named Hanna, and the Contingencies of Postcolonial History-Writing," *American Historical Review* 118, no. 1 (2013): 106.

12. Ara Wilson, "Transnational Geography of Sexual Rights," in *Truth Claims: Representation and Human Rights*, ed. Mark Philip Bradley and Patrice Petro (New Brunswick, NJ: Rutgers University Press, 2002), 252.

13. Ann Laura Stoler, *Against the Archival Grain: Epistemic Anxieties and Colonial Common Sense* (Princeton, NJ: Princeton University Press, 2009), 20.

14. Lawrance et al., "Law, Expertise," 2.

15. Benjamin N. Lawrance, "Asylum and the 'Forced Marriage' Paradox: Petitions, Translation, and Courts as Institutional Perpetrators of Gender Violence," in *Modern Slavery and Global Change*, ed. Joel Quirk and Anne Bunting (Vancouver: University of British Columbia Press, 2017). See also Benjamin Lawrance, "Historicizing as a Legal Trope of Jeopardy in Asylum Narratives and Expert Testimony of Gendered Violence," in *Politics and Policies in Upper Guinea Coast Societies: Change and Continuity*, ed. Jacqueline Knörr, Christian Kordt Højbjerg, and William P. Murphy (New York: Palgrave, 2016).

16. Emily Burrill, "Disputing Wife Abuse: Tribunal Narratives of the Corporal Punishment of Wives in Colonial Sikasso, 1930s," *Cahiers d'Études Africaines* 187–88 (2007): 603–22.

17. Amy Shuman and Carol Bohmer, "Representing Trauma: Political Asylum Narrative," *Journal of American Folklore* 117, no. 466 (2004): 396.

18. Lawrance, "Historicizing."

19. See Benjamin N. Lawrance and Galya B. Ruffer, "Witness to the Persecution? Expertise, Testimony, and Consistency in Asylum Adjudication," in *Adjudicating Refugee and Asylum Status: The Role of Witness, Expertise, and Testimony*, ed. Benjamin N. Lawrance and Galya Ruffer (Cambridge: Cambridge University Press, 2015), 1–24.

20. White, *Speaking with Vampires*, 43.

21. Benjamin N. Lawrance and Charlotte Walker-Said, "Resisting Patriarchy, Contesting Homophobia: Expert Testimony and the Construction of African Forced Marriage Asylum

Claims," in *Marriage by Force? Contestation over Consent and Coercion in Africa*, ed. Anne Bunting, Benjamin N. Lawrance, and Richard L. Roberts (Athens: Ohio University Press, 2016), 199–224.

22. April Shemak, *Asylum Speakers: Caribbean Refugees and Testimonial Discourse* (New York: Fordham University), 24.

23. Meredith Terretta, "Fraudulent Asylum-Seeking as Transnational Mobilization," in Berger et al., *African Asylum*, 58–74.

24. Bruce Einhorn and S. Megan Berthold, "Reconstructing Babel: Bridging Cultural Dissonance between Asylum Seekers and Asylum Adjudicators," in Lawrance and Ruffer, *Adjudicating Refugee and Asylum Status*, 27–53.

25. Joseph Hellweg, "Manimory and the Aesthetics of Mimesis: Forest, Islam and State in Ivoirian Dozoya," *Africa* 76, no. 4 (2006): 461–84; Markus V. Hoehne, "Mimesis and Mimicry in Dynamics of State and Identity Formation in Northern Somalia," *Africa* 79, no. 2 (2009): 252–81; Ann-Marie Tully, "Becoming Animal: Liminal Rhetorical Strategies in Contemporary South African Art," *Image and Text* 17 (2011): 64–84; Sasha Newell, "Godrap Girls, Draou Boys, and the Sexual Economy of the Bluff in Abidjan, Côte d'Ivoire," *Ethnos* 74, no. 3 (2009): 379–402.

26. Sasha Newell, "Brands as Masks: Public Secrecy and the Counterfeit in Côte d'Ivoire," *Journal of the Royal Anthropological Institute* 19, no. 1 (2013): 138–54; Sasha Newell, "Le Goût des Autres: Ivoirian Fashion and Alterity," *Etnofoor* 24, no. 2 (2012): 41–56; Christina McMahon, "Mimesis and the Historical Imagination: (Re)Staging History in Cape Verde, West Africa," *Theatre Research International* 33, no. 1 (2008): 20–39.

27. Jean-François Lyotard, *The Differend: Phrases in Dispute*, trans. George van den Abbeele (Minneapolis: University of Minnesota Press, 1988), 5–6.

28. Lawrance et al., "Law, Expertise," 27.

29. Associated Press, "Nigeria's Boko Haram Kills Forty-Nine in Suicide Bombings," *New York Times*, November 18, 2015.

30. Private e-mail correspondence in possession of the author.

31. "Missing Nigerian schoolgirls 'married off,'" *Al Jazeera*, November 1, 2014, www.aljazeera.com/news/africa/2014/10/boko-haram-says-schoolgirls-married-20141031222536853563.html.

32. David Smith, "Sixty More Women and Girls Reported Kidnapped in Nigeria," *Guardian*, October 24, 2014.

33. Private e-mail correspondence in possession of the author.

34. Kevin Rawlinson, "Nigerians Due to Be Deported, Despite Claim of Female Genital Mutilation Risk," *Guardian*, May 29, 2014.

35. Kevin Rawlinson, "Deportation Reprieve for Nigerians amid Female Genital Mutilation Fears," *Guardian*, May 30, 2014.

36. Heather Saul, "FGM Victim Afusat Saliu and Her Daughters 'Will Be Deported to Nigeria Tonight' Despite Fears for Their Safety," *Independent* (London), June 3, 2014.

37. See Jacob Zenn and Elizabeth Pearson, "Women, Gender, and the Evolving Tactics of Boko Haram," *Journal of Terrorism Research* 5, no. 1 (2013): 46–57.

38. E.g., Phyllis Chesler, "The Boko Haram Girls May Already Have Been Mutilated," May 12, 2014, Breitbart News, www.breitbart.com/national-security/2014/05/12/the-boko-haram-girls-may-already-have-been-mutilated/.

39. Private e-mail correspondence in possession of the author.

40. Lawrance et al., "Law, Expertise," 2–5.

41. Anthony Good, "Anthropological Evidence and 'Country of Origin Information' in British

Asylum Courts," in Lawrance and Ruffer, *Adjudicating Refugee and Asylum Status*, 122–44.

42. Anthony Good, "Expert Evidence in Asylum and Human Rights Appeals: An Expert's View," *International Journal of Refugee Law* 16 (2004): 358–80.

43. See several essays in Berger et al., *African Asylum*: Terretta, "Fraudulent Asylum-Seeking"; E. Ann McDougall, "'The Immigration People Know the Stories. There's One for Each Country': The Case of Mauritania," 121–40; Kate Luongo, "Allegations, Evidence, and Evaluation: Asylum-Seeking in a World with Witchcraft," 182–202; and John Campbell, "Expert Evidence in British Asylum Courts: The Judicial Assessment of Evidence on Ethnic Discrimination and Statelessness in Ethiopia," 102–20.

44. Columbia Law School, "Nigerian Man Who Faced Persecution by Boko Haram Wins Asylum in U.S.," press release, September 18, 2014, www.law.columbia.edu/media _inquiries/news_events/2014/september2014/irc-asylum-nigerian-2014.

45. Christian-Muslim violence in Jos in 2010 left 350–1,000 dead. Adam Nossiter, "Christian-Muslim Mayhem in Nigeria Kills Dozens," *New York Times*, January 19, 2010; Human Rights Watch, "'Leave Everything to God': Accountability for Inter-communal Violence in Plateau and Kaduna States, Nigeria," Human Rights Watch, December 12, 2013, https://www.hrw.org/report/2013/12/12/leave-everything-god/accountability-inter-communal -violence-plateau-and-kaduna.

46. UK Home Office, "Operational Guidance Notes."

47. Private e-mail correspondence in possession of author.

48. BH's role in the Jos bombing has never been established. See "Nigeria Violence: 'Boko Haram' Kill Twenty-Seven in Village Attacks," BBC News, May 21, 2014. BH leader Abubakar Shekau cited "incidents of cannibalism" of Jos Muslims for Christmas Day bombings. "Boko Haram: Nigerian Islamist Leader Defends Attacks," BBC News, January 11, 2012.

49. Columbia Law School, "Nigerian Man."

50. See Tulip Mazumdar, "Chibok Girls 'Forced to Join Nigeria's Boko Haram,'" BBC News, June 29, 2015.

51. Julián Aguilar, "Against the Odds, Finding Refuge in El Paso," *Texas Tribune*, September 19, 2014.

52. Andrew Noakes, "Nigeria's Boko Haram Ceasefire Deal: Too Good to Be True?," *African Arguments*, October 22, 2014, africanarguments.org/2014/10/22/nigerias-boko-haram -ceasefire-deal-too-good-to-be-true/.

Four Images of False Positives

A Visual Essay

Luis Morán (drawings) and Claudia Salamanca (text)

In first decade of the twenty-first century, Colombia moved from being a failed state to a sovereign nation, a turnaround that some US media outlets have called "the Colombian miracle."[1] Characterizing Colombia as a case of successful nation building and counterinsurgency tactics, US military analysts have praised Colombia's approach to stabilization as a strategy for the United States to emulate in other unstable areas around the world.[2] For Colombia, the success has been the result of "an uncompromising 'hard hand' against the insurgents," and the implementation of its Democratic Security and Defense (DSD) policy, an effort to consolidate state control by enhancing the technological capacity, intelligence and equipment of the Colombian armed forces.[3]

In 2008, a scandal known today as False Positives (FPs) tarnished this so-called military success. FPs are extrajudicial executions of civilians, whose corpses are made to look like guerrillas or members of illegal groups killed in combat. Perpetrated by the Colombian Army during the years of the DSD policy (2002–10), FPs inflated statistics of enemy combatants killed in action. Although this abhorrent practice has been part of the military culture in Colombia for more than twenty-five years, as reported by the CIA in 1994, the instances of FPs under the DSD policy show a systematic execution model.[4] "Recruiters" targeted Colombian males between the ages of sixteen and thirty-seven, choosing young men belonging to vulnerable populations living in marginalized areas, those with mental disabilities or substance abuse problems, and/or who were unemployed and desperate for money.

Radical History Review
Issue 126 (October 2016)   DOI 10.1215/01636545-3594517
© 2016 by MARHO: The Radical Historians' Organization, Inc.

With promises of work in countryside, recruiters lured the victims into leaving and transported them three hundred to four hundred miles away from their homes. Once in the countryside, these young men were handed over to a military unit and executed.[5] Their corpses would be dressed in fatigues, and weapons would be placed next to their bodies, which would then be photographed. A mandatory photographic record of the casualties and/or video taken at the location of the combat was part of the military armed forces protocol; those photographs were released to the press and kept in the archives for deceased and N.N. (*nomen nescio*, "name unknown") persons. Autopsy reports show that victims died between twelve and twenty-four hours from the time they were last seen by their family members.[6] Evidence suggests that these extrajudicial executions were rigorously planned and committed by a large number of military units around the country with disturbing frequency and are not, as the Colombian government asserts, the result of a few bad apples within the Colombian Army who misinterpreted the policies and goals of the DSD policy.[7]

To date, the exact number of FPs is still unconfirmed. Approximately four thousand cases have been reported to various state institutions, including the Office of the Attorney General, the Office of the Inspector General, and the Ombudsman.[8] However, organizations like the United Nations and Human Rights Watch estimate that more cases remain unreported. Relatives lack information about where and how to file FPs, and many have concerns about their own personal safety should they raise complaints against agents of the state. Relatives of many victims have received death threats to coerce them into dropping charges; some have been injured and killed for pursuing legal action, and others have relocated due to the constant fear of retribution.[9]

International organizations, such as the United Nations,[10] Amnesty International,[11] Human Rights Watch,[12] and the International Federation for Human Rights,[13] have explained FPs as the result of the formal and informal benefits, including monetary rewards, that the DSD policy set out in a series of classified directives issued by the Ministry of Defense, in exchange for successful military operations.[14] The DSD policy encouraged civilians, through its program of informants, to report the location and identity of enemy combatants in exchange for cash rewards.[15] This policy extended to the military through secret directives, based on which military units received bonuses for capturing or killing enemy combatants or for seizing any property or element that can contribute to weakening the enemy's position. In this context, FPs can be seen as instances of the body count mentality or the body count syndrome within an economy that rewards death.[16]

Although the system of benefits and rewards created by the DSD policy explains a great deal about FPs, analyzing these events based solely on the rewards and benefits given in exchange for systematic killing, and placing responsibility only on those who pulled the trigger, obscures the historical categories and social relations through which the body of a young man is turned into a commodity and his

Figure 1. Drawing by Luis Morán, 2014, copy of a photograph taken by the Colombian police. A cardboard booth with a sign that reads "rewards" and a hole in the middle is the device in which an informant poses to the press while receiving money for providing information that led to a successful military operation.

corpse photographed to create an image of the enemy. By considering the intersection between an economy of death and the construction of alterity through a fabricated image of the enemy's body, we see how the Colombian Army made these images essential for the process of claiming monetary rewards and benefits.

As part of the regular protocol, military operations are defined and planned in advance, and the information (video, photographs, and reports) related to them is an effort to further account for them.[17] The representation of an event is part of a process of accountability, explanations that come after the military operation in the field. In the case of the FPs, I argue that the photographic record was not an afterthought as it is seen in regular protocol or a side effect of the extrajudicial executions. The uniforms, boots, grenades, rifles, carbines, machine guns, and corpses were props used to fabricate an image; they were bought and prepared before the execution. Those young men were recruited and executed to construct images of dead enemy combatants, an enemy fabricated out of young unemployed males in need of money who lived on the outskirts of big cities. Those young men were fashioned into guerrillas, gang members, or paramilitary forces; identities outside the discourse of legality were inscribed on their bodies. The fabricated image of the enemy was not an afterthought but the paradigmatic image of terror. The killers

**Figure 2. Drawing by Luis Morán, 2014, copy of a photograph taken by the Colombian Army.
Anomaly no. 1: a corpse wears new rubber boots on the wrong feet.**

of these young men knew beforehand that they were going to create an image with dead bodies; they collapsed the killing of these men—the event—and its representation. My intention is to question the status of these images, which are often trapped within the walls of accountability, transparency, and documentation as in regular protocol. As poorly staged tableaus of military victory, these images reveal apparent mistakes in the crime scenes. I want to explore what these anomalies tell us about the process of creating an imagined enemy: is this how an enemy should look and, if so, why?

Figures 2, 3, 4, and 5 reproduce actual photographs taken by the security forces of the state. These drawings are accurate reproductions of the original photographs published in the Colombian magazine *Semana* on July 17, 2010, in an article titled "The Forgotten Cases of False Positives."[18] These drawings do not add any elements or aestheticize the violence they show. These copies omit the background that appears in the photograph and highlight the foreground, which is the corpse of the victim. These drawings were commissioned specifically for my research on FPs as a tool through which I could see the violence depicted in them as the result of the imagination, as well as painfully real. Created by artist Luis Morán, these drawings compel us to separate the purported "factuality" of photography from the subject matter and Colombia's fabricated narrative of success. In other words, the photo-

Figure 3. Drawing by Luis Morán, 2014, copy of a photograph taken by the Colombian Army. Anomaly no. 2: finger on the trigger.

graphs taken by the security forces of the state exist in a framework of transparency; the state released them as proof of their success, as evidence of their actions and an account of how a military operation succeeded by killing members of illegal organizations. We see a corpse, which is connected with an explanation that signals it as a guerrilla, paramilitary, or gang member. But when these photographs are turned into drawings, the referent and the narrative of success are suspended and we get to see the elements of the image in an exercise of seeing that is different from the one we exert when confronted with a photograph issued by the state.

In viewing the photographs taken by the Colombian Army, the siblings of FP victims both recognize their loved ones and reject the person portrayed in the image. Here, there is a process of recognition through misrecognition, a disjuncture between what is apparently real and its representation. The certainty of the referent is disputed: while the corpses are indeed those of boyfriend, husband, brother, son, or father, at the same time those images do not correspond to the people. For example, in the documentary "False Positives, a Story That Could Have Been Avoided,"[19] Viviana Andrea Salcedo tells the story of her brother while holding an image of him with crutches. She says her brother went out to have a beer with a friend in a nearby store and never returned. After searching for him for two days, she went to the Technical Investigation Team office, a branch of the Office of the Attorney General of Colombia. They showed her photographs of what they claimed were images of

Figure 4. Drawing by Luis Morán, 2014, copy of a photograph taken by the Colombian Army. Anomaly no. 3: two hand grenades in his pants pockets hanging from their safety levers.

dead guerrillas killed in combat. Recognizing her brother in one of the photos, she remarked that that was impossible—her brother was not a guerrilla but a member of the Colombian Army who was on a combat-related injury leave.

The photographs of the corpses attempt to erase the signs of their previous identities. Relatives of FP victims, however, constantly point out the untruths created about their loved ones: they were not delinquents; they were not rebels; they were not members of illegal organizations; they were not drug traffickers; they were not N.N. These claims assert that the young men's lived realities did not match the ways in which they died. In "Family Portraits," Alexandra Cardona's documentary on the mothers of some of FP victims, one of the mothers states, "They [the "recruiters"] thought these kids did not have mothers, brothers, or sisters who were going to look for them."[20] This mother is voicing an identity anchored in a social context, one that could not be erased in the photographs taken by the Colombian Army. The mothers and siblings of FP victims contest images created by the security forces of the state by pointing to what is outside the frame. Very often, mothers and relatives of FP victims provide evidence that their loved ones were not members of illegal organizations with their own photographs of the victims, in high school graduation pictures, as babies, and in military uniform during the year of mandatory military

Figure 5. Drawing by Luis Morán, 2014. Copy of a photograph taken by the Colombian Army. Extra magazines are hidden inside the rubber boots.

service: anecdotes and dreams of their dead sons that speak of a living presence in another time and with others. These personal narratives and photographs contest the status of evidence and truth that the images taken by the security forces of the state seem to carry. The photographs in the family albums, as well as the pictures carried by relatives and friends of FPs during the protests against human rights violations committed by the state, open a debate by questioning the photograph taken by the state as evidence and subverting the intentions of those who took the picture.

The photographs issued by the Colombian Army exhibit a presence: a dead body on the ground. However, the absence of life enables the possibility of fabrication, a malleability that creates something other from the available corpse. The poses of those corpses in the photographs could only have taken shape as the bodies of the victims became posthumously manipulatable. Photographing the dead makes possible a situation in which corpse and image coincide, an instance of total control over the pose.

Figures 2, 3, and 4 show obvious flaws in the combat scenes. The photographs correspond to a FP attributed to the Seventh Army Division, which reported that it "neutralized six suspected members of the criminal gang Bacrim in combat" during a "military operation" in "the rural area of La India in the municipality of Chigorodó, Uraba."[21] In figure 4, we see a supposed rebel with two hand grenades in his pants pockets hanging from their safety levers; if a combatant were running with hand grenades hung from his pants like this, they could explode at any moment. In figure 2, a corpse wears new rubber boots on the wrong feet. The corpse in figure 3 has his finger on the trigger of a machine gun, but it is not squeezed as if he were shooting when shot. Should these anomalies be categorized as mistakes? Poor fabrications? The corpses generally appear with something that signals a viable threat: wires, bomb triggers, guns, explosives, and/or other weapons next to the corpses. Two grenades in each pocket, finger on the trigger, and extra magazines hidden inside the rubber boots (figure 5) are attempts to prove that killing these men was the only available recourse. These images insist on resisting ambiguity by asserting that that corpse in the ground was in fact a threat, an enemy of the state. These images, evidence of "successful" combats, attempt to substitute for verbal explanation by stating the preeminence of the referent. These photographs assert, "here is the rebel," "here he is holding a gun and wearing military fatigues," "there he is," "he was dangerous," "he is dead." These images want to teach us how an enemy looks like and to show us that he in fact is dangerous. My contention is that these images exhibit an effort to narrate the impending fear of the future; the enemy is depicted in this photograph as a potential threat that needed to be eliminated. Indeed, these images are a testimony to the past—a successful operation; nevertheless, their narration could be explained in terms of a moralizing pedagogy for future citizens and ideal spectators.

The image of the corpse, in other words, as the embodiment of a neutralized Other, is not a mere side effect of the FP. Those young men were recruited and executed solely to manufacture an image of dead enemy combatants. The uniforms, boots, grenades, the rifles, carbines, machine guns, and the corpses were props in this endeavor. The distance that these young men traveled from their hometowns to the sites of their murder enacts the distance between the real and representation. Therefore, the image is not an afterthought; it uses terror in the service of a structure of the real and its representation, embedded in modes of explanations that register violence as a means to an end outside of the violence itself. FPs use the image as a pedagogical tool, to fabricate a country with a symbolic discourse of citizenship through images of young men supposedly to be understood as the enemy, an enemy that has been killed and thus represents military victory in an unending war.

Notes

1. "After Taint of Drugs, Colombia Reinvents Itself," *Morning Edition*, National Public Radio, April 12, 2012, search.proquest.com/docview/993564663?accountid=13250; Frida Ghitis, "The Colombian Miracle: Gaining Belated Notice," *World Politics Review*, July 4, 2008, www.worldpoliticsreview.com/articles/2383/the-colombian-miracle-gaining-belated -notice; Max Boot and Richard Bennet, "The Colombian Miracle: How Alvaro Uribe with Smart U.S. Support Turned the Tide against Drug Lords and Marxist Guerrillas." *Weekly Standard*, December 14, 2009, www.weeklystandard.com/Content/Public/Articles/000 /000/017/301nyrut.asp.

2. Robert Haddick, "Colombia Can Teach Afghanistan (and the United States) How to Win," *Air and Space Power Journal* 24, no. 2 (2010): 52–56.

3. Juan Forero, "Hard-Liner Elected in Colombia with a Mandate to Crush Rebels," *New York Times*, May 27, 2002, www.nytimes.com/2002/05/27/world/hard-liner-elected-in-colombia -with-a-mandate-to-crush-rebels.html.

4. Central Intelligence Agency, Office of African and Latin American Analysis, "Colombian Counterinsurgency: Steps in the Right Direction—Intelligence Memorandum," January 26, 1994, National Security Archive, www2.gwu.edu/~nsarchiv/NSAEBB/NSAEBB266 /19940126.pdf.

5. Philip Alston, "Report of the Special Rapporteur on Extrajudicial, Summary or Arbitrary Executions," UN General Assembly, Human Rights Council, Fourteenth Session (March 31, 2010), 11, www2.ohchr.org/english/bodies/hrcouncil/docs/14session/A.HRC.14.24.Add.2 _en.pdf.

6. "Una Tesis Macabra, Conflicto Armado," *Semana*, October 4, 2008, www.semana.com /nacion/conflicto-armado/articulo/una-tesis-macabra/95879-3.

7. Alvaro Uribe Vélez, "Declaración del Presidente Álvaro Uribe, Este Jueves, desde Canadá," Presidencia de La República de Colombia, Secretaría de Prensa, June 11, 2009, web .presidencia.gov.co/sp/2009/junio/11/01112009.html.

8. Philip Alston, "Report of the Special Rapporteur"; "Las Cuentas de los Falsos Positivos," *Semana*, January 27, 2009, www.semana.com/nacion/justicia/articulo/las-cuentas-falsos -positivos/99556-3; "Más de 4 Mil Casos de Falsos Positivos Son Investigados por la Fiscalía," *El Espectador*, September 27, 2014, www.elespectador.com/noticias/judicial /mas-de-4-mil-casos-de-falsos-positivos-son-investigados-articulo-519238.

9. Both of Carmenza Gómez's sons have been killed. First Víctor Fernando Gómez disappeared in August 23, 2008, and was found dead two days later four hundred miles away from his home; he was a victim of the FPs. Five months later, her son John Nilson was killed as a result of searching for the truth about his brother's death. He received several death threats warning him to not pursue legal action. For a second case, similar to this one, see the Amnesty International, "Colombia: Murdered Man's Brother Threatened," November 5, 2009, www.amnesty.org/en/library/asset/AMR23/026/2009/en/ef9541c8-088e-4a25-857a -e2d9e87541c8/amr230262009en.html.

10. Alston, "Report of the Special Rapporteur."

11. Amnesty International: "Colombia: Murdered Man's Brother Threatened"; "Colombia: Assisting Units That Commit Extrajudicial Killings: A Call to Investigate US Military Policy toward Colombia," April 9, 2008, www.amnesty.org/en/library/asset/AMR23/016/2008 /en/116d47ce-236b-11dd-89c0-51e35dab761d/amr230162008eng.html; "Colombia: Seeking Justice: The Mothers of Soacha," January 30, 2010, www.amnesty.org/en/library /asset/AMR23/002/2010/en/ec375877-5fbf-4d3c-a074-258a79c82c9b/amr230022010en

.html; "Colombia: Impunity Perpetuates Ongoing Human Rights Violations: Amnesty International Submission to the UN Universal Periodic Review," February 14, 2013, www .amnesty.org/en/library/asset/AMR23/005/2013/en/3aaa9d53-02f5-459b-8864-dbc5e367fda7 /amr230052013es.html.

12. *Human Rights Watch World Report 2012: Events of 2011* (New York: Seven Stories, 2012), 228–35; *Human Rights Watch World Report 2011: Events of 2010* (London: Seven Stories, 2011), 227–32.

13. International Federation of Human Rights, *Colombia: The War Is Measured in Litres of Blood*, June 2012, www.fidh.org/IMG/pdf/rapp_colombie__juin_2012_anglais_def.pdf.

14. Ministerio de Defensa Nacional, República de Colombia, "Directiva 29, 2005. La Polémica Directiva de Recompensas," *La Silla Vacía—Noticias, Historias, Debate, Blogs y Multimedia sobre el Poder en Colombia*, http://lasillavacia.com/sites/default/files/media /docs/historias/Directiva_29_2005-comentado.pdf.

15. "Información de Cooperantes Permitió Realizar 21 Mil Operativos en 2005," www .mindefensa.gov.co/irj/go/km/docs/Mindefensa/noticiasold/Noticias/2006/03/C _Informacion_de_cooperantes_permitio_realizar_21_mil_operativos_en_2005.html (accessed January 17, 2013).

16. International Federation for Human Rights, *Colombia.*

17. See David Kilcullen, "New Paradigms for Twenty-First-Century Conflict," *Foreign Policy Agenda* 12, no. 5 (2007), www.america.gov/st/peacesec-english/2008/May/20080522172835 SrenoDo.8730585.html.

18. "The Forgotten Cases of False Positives," *Semana*, July 17, 2010, http://www.semana.com //nacion/articulo/los-casos-olvidados-falsos-positivos/119416-3. Quoted in Hollman Morris, "Falsos Positivos: Una Historia Que Se Pudo Evitar," *Contravía*, January 22, 2010, www .contravia.tv/Falsos-Positivos.

19. Alexandra Cardona Restrepo, *Retratos de Familia* (Karamelo Producciones, n.d.) 2013. https://vimeo.com/86939560.

20. Morris, "Falsos Positivos."

21. Ibid.

Rethinking the Egalitarian Potential of Postapartheid South Africa:

Zanele Muholi's Intervention

Efeoghene Igor

In her portrait (figure 1), Pam Dlungwana's solemn gaze defiantly confronts the camera—her eyes meet the viewer's, making her appear confident. Wearing her hair in a short bleached-blond cut with hoop earrings, she reads as youthful. In the tightly framed picture, her shoulders are bare, suggesting comfort with the photographer. Staged against a patterned backdrop, her individuality is emphasized. The photograph of Pam is a part of the series *Faces and Phases* (2006–14) by photographer Zanele Muholi. Muholi deliberately obscures the background in order to highlight the singularity of Pam's lived experience. In text accompanying the portrait in the publication *Zanele Muholi Faces + Phases 2006–14* Pam reveals to the audience that she had been raped.[1] Many black queer individuals included in Muholi's series have been raped because of their sexuality. The morning after the crime, instead of hurrying to the clinic or calling the police, Pam completed an exam at school. The seeming indifference to such a violation—by continuing her day as if nothing was wrong—underscores the frequent threat of sexual violence that confronts queer black individuals in South Africa. Juxtaposing the highly expressive portrait with the haunting narrative of sexual violence, Pam's photograph threatens the confidence of queer South Africans lobbying for recognition within an ongoing struggle to achieve an egalitarian society.

Radical History Review

Issue 126 (October 2016)   DOI 10.1215/01636545-3594675

© 2016 by MARHO: The Radical Historians' Organization, Inc.

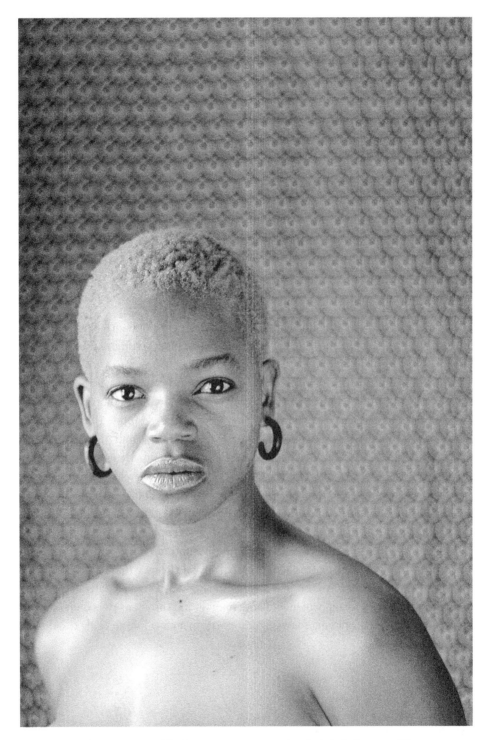

Figure 1. Pam Dlungwana in Vredehoek, Cape Town, 2011. © Zanele Muholi. Courtesy of Stevenson, Cape Town/Johannesburg, and Yancey Richardson, New York

Faces and Phases disables the regime of social and governmental silence by rendering visual and thus legible a community exiled from popular imagination. The series showcases portraits in sober tonalities of black and white, muted backdrops, and stoic facial expressions. These images strive to normalize the presence of black queer people within the landscape. Occupying space is a critical political and ideological question within South African history. As Jennifer Beningfield posits, "There remains, however, in contemporary South Africa, a sense that the land (unmediated, untouched and natural) can still be a resource for a political reworking of the image of South Africa—a way to unify its different citizens, to connect body and nation, to enable a different conception of country and continent to emerge from the past that tainted it."[2] Muholi introduces us to the potential and ambiguity of the landscape by situating her participants in place. This effort is to preserve the lives of black queer individuals by associating them with the land. Consequently, this article examines how Muholi's work shifts the focus solely from *sight* (visibility of lesbian, gay, bisexual, transgender, and intersex persons) to *site* (the places that the photographs are taken).

By co-opting documentary style photography, a visual language perhaps most associated with antiapartheid popular politics, Muholi provides crucial introspection on the antiracist rhetoric employed by the official liberation movement during apartheid. She upsets the liberal narrative by acknowledging the antiqueer rhetoric that persists in contemporary South Africa. Rape is a technology of violence that is used to punish transgressive sexuality and gender nonconformity. As Njabulo Simakahle Ndebele artfully articulates, rape is "transformed into lasting violation. The physical invasion once ended becomes a prolonged occupation, the continuing effect of violation snuffing out a woman's life in the eternity of living it."[3] Muholi's series helps audiences acknowledge black queer individuals as the casualties of the South African liberation movement's inner contradictions.

Conventionally, the sources of antiapartheid narratives were men. Although women did rise to prominent positions within the movement, they did so within a circumscribed social field. They were typically casts as supportive and nurturing caregivers. For instance, Winnie Mandela before her political demise in the early 1990s was mythologized as the mother of South Africa.[4] The apartheid system magnified racial, gender, and sexual differences, subsequently marginalizing black queer persons from mainstream liberation efforts. The fragmentary nature of the liberation movement made race and sexuality mutually exclusive terrains.[5] Perhaps the best example of the masculinist nature of the antiapartheid struggle was the Black Consciousness Movement (BCM). The South African Students' Organization, a black student group established in 1969, emerged as a "critical center" of the antiapartheid struggle because of its ability to create a positive self-image for black (male) South Africans.[6] Steve Biko, the leader of the BCM, in an editor's note explained oppression in gendered language. To uplift the black race he suggests,

"The first step therefore is to make the black man come to himself; to pump back life into his empty shell; to infuse him with pride and dignity, to remind him of his complicity in the crime of allowing himself to be misused and therefore letting evil reign supreme in the country of his birth. . . . This is the definition of 'Black Consciousness.'"[7] BCM's alternate form of nationalism betrayed its commitment to emancipation because it demanded an unrealistic monolithic black community—that of just black men.[8] Alternatively, Muholi's work troubles the status of the heterosexual black man as an easy metaphor for the liberated national subject.

In recognizing the state's failure to protect its citizens, Muholi acknowledges the multiple ways in which the black LGBTI community is exiled from mainstream liberation discourse. She explains, "Currently, we look to our Constitution for protection as legitimate citizens in our country. However, the reality is that black lesbians are targets of brutal oppression in the South African townships and surrounding areas. We experience rape from gangs, rape by so-called friends, neighbors, and sometimes even family members."[9] Muholi's intervention is crucial in this respect as she disrupts the historical archive by harnessing the stylistic conventions of the antiapartheid movement but transforms their intentions. However, as Patricia Hayes reminds us, it is too simplistic to suggest that the polysemous South African photographic archive is homogeneous. Although there was a script that made pictures of the antiapartheid struggle desirable, it was both the demand from the West and the gendered nature of violence that dictated the limited role of women in South Africa's visual economy.[10]

Photojournalism was preoccupied with black and white realist photography; it was, as Hayes suggests, associated with "certainty and evidence."[11] The previous outlet, the newspaper, had different requirements than the gallery, which is the present-day forum for activists. Whereas photojournalism is preoccupied with perceived objectivity, the gallery is concerned with subjectivity. During postapartheid reconstruction, public history became the domain to problematize homogenizing narratives that further oppressed formally disenfranchised communities. Ciraj Rassool explains, "In South Africa after 1994, beyond the boundaries of the academy, histories began to erupt into the public sphere in museums and other arenas through the 'visuality of the spectacle.' These visual histories have tended to be understood merely as 'revelations of hidden heritage,' previously submerged by apartheid."[12] Muholi helps us reckon with this oversight by reflecting on LGBTI lived experiences without being confined to the liberal politics of outreach. There is no intention of "liberating" the person being photographed. Rather, the emphasis is on brokering an exchange between LGBTI persons and the audience.

Alongside activists during the antiapartheid struggle, Muholi strives to create an alternative visual archive by documenting from within her community. Self-identifying as a visual activist, Muholi suggests, "The series articulates the collective pain we as a community experience due to the loss of friends and acquaintances through disease and hate crimes."[13] Appropriating a documentary style of photography, she attempts to bring to the fore black LGBTI issues to a popular audience that highlight that legal equality has not translated into radically different social, economic, and political conditions for black queer individuals in the postapartheid era. Although South Africa legalized gay and lesbian marriage in 2006, the blanket declaration that South Africa is a tolerant country obscures more sophisticated mechanisms that condone homophobic rhetoric and violence. Rachel Holmes reminds us, "Within the recent history of South African politics, there is no neat teleology within which the triumph of the African National Congress (ANC) has *inevitably* led to the liberation of lesbian and gay sexual identities and to the enshrinement of lesbian and gay civil rights through the implementation of the new postapartheid political settlement."[14] Thus, Pam's willingness to be photographed prompts thoughts of irresolution; her portrait troubles the selective ways in which liberation is articulated and constructed in the postapartheid era. Operating within an evocative cultural space, the series points to the inequalities that persist in contemporary South Africa.

Yet despite photographic efforts to render legible injustices, there is no robust framework for justice and accountability for antiqueer violence in contemporary South Africa. The absence of statistical information to help gauge the severity of hate crimes, for instance, is just one example of infrastructural deficiencies in the country.[15] In May 2015 Lydia Smith of the *Telegraph* reported that "at least 32 women have been raped and murdered in the last 15 years" because they were lesbians.[16] This number is likely a gross underestimation of the severity of the violence. "Curative" rapes are a violent tactic used by perpetrators to "restore" the "natural social order," whereby men occupy the top rung of the social strata.[17] Through the series *Faces and Phases*, Muholi has begun to document hate crimes committed against LGBTI individuals. Her exhibit at the Brooklyn Museum (May 1– November 8, 2015) titled *Isibonelo/Evidence* opens by acknowledging the violent death of Disebo Gift Makau. On Friday, August 18, 2014, *Mamba Online* reported that Disebo was found dead, with a shoelace and wire wrapped around her neck and a running water hose shoved into her throat, in the Tshing location. *Mamba Online*, a local South African news outlet, reported that she appeared to have been raped.[18] Family members believe that she was murdered because she was a lesbian.[19] Transforming landscapes of knowledge relations, the lifeless body of Disebo and others murdered can be read as an assertion of dominance within a space, which signals to other potential "transgressors" the narrow gender script prescribed by patriarchy. *Faces and Phases* acts as an alternative form of reckoning, another way to imagine the possibilities of social justice by making living people rather than lifeless bodies visible.

Anelisa Mfo's portrait attests to the protracted struggles that arrest development in the postapartheid era (figure 2). The weighted absence of black LGBTI persons in the mainstream national archive is highlighted by Anelisa's presence in

Figure 2. Anelisa Mfo in Nyanga, Cape Town, 2010. © Zanele Muholi. Courtesy of Stevenson, Cape Town/Johannesburg, and Yancey Richardson, New York

Faces and Phases.[20] The close-up portrait invites reflection on the ineffective state and civil response to homophobia. Muholi's work brings to light the complexities in the construction and reconstruction of a cohesive national postapartheid South African identity. During the opening of the Innovative Women exhibition in August 2009, the former minister of arts and culture Lulama "Lulu" Xingwana left the engagement unexpectedly before her scheduled speech. She found Muholi's images of lesbian couples nakedly embracing each other distasteful.[21] The minister stated the exhibition "was immoral, offensive and going against nation-building."[22] Subsequently the minister received criticism for her actions. Meditating on Anelisa's image, here we see Muholi critique the willed amnesia that forces LGBTI individuals into hiding. Holmes astutely remarks, "Such amnesia can leave people vulnerable to new narratives of national identity that either advertently or inadvertently foster the illusion of inclusion."[23]

In anticipation of remarks similar to those made by the minister, Muholi places black queer South Africans at the vanguard of contemporary liberation struggles. Anelisa's self-confident stance and calm expression create connection but also safe distance between her and the viewer. The scar on her left side invites questions: Who hurt her? Is the scar the remains of a violent encounter? Is she is a survivor of a hate crime? The photograph is dense with visual complexity that remains unresolved. Nevertheless, Anelisa's photograph is a significant affirmation of black LGBTI existence within a hostile national terrain. The photograph's explicit mediation on space suggests that LGBTI individuals can no longer be relegated to nonexistence. Our scrutiny follows from Anelisa's political aspiration of coming out to a mainstream South African and international audience. The obscured background faintly registers a corrugated wall. The minimal greenery suggests that the photograph was taken outdoors, like most of Muholi's portraits. Anelisa appears grounded—asserting herself within a pubic space. Within the photograph Muholi blurs the line between the public and private, disrupting the enforced privacy and secrecy of black queer life. One must note that hate crimes against LGBTI persons reported in South African and international newspapers typically include the discovery of the victim's body in a public space.

In *Faces and Phases*, we witness a desire for public recognition as well as an assertion of belonging as a rights-bearing citizen. In the statement accompanying the photograph Muholi lets the audience know that the portrait of Anelisa was taken in Cape Town. Muholi's explicit naming of the space anchors Anelisa within a specifically historicized and culturally informed place, making her presence indicative of South Africa's sexual and racial diversity. The affective charge of the image is embedded in the practice of naming, while the interplay between the visual and textual successfully unsettles normative expectations of who occupies the South African landscape. *Faces and Phases* shares Muholi's aspirational vision of the future where egalitarianism in South African society is considered in relation not just to race but to genders and sexualities as well.

The administrative grip the apartheid regime had on the (in)visibility of particular communities makes Muholi's artistic renderings seductive. The ability to control how one is represented in the public domain imbues the photographs with an emancipatory zeal. Often displayed in public galleries, national and international audiences are impelled to reflect on South Africa's diversity, thus transforming the gallery into a theater of learning. Shaun de Waal and Anthony Manion have noted that visibility is essential to countering long histories of concealment and disavowal.[24] The ways in which gender, race, and sexuality intersect to produce exclusionary practices in contemporary South Africa evoke a history of apartheid violence. The Sexual Offences Act of 1957 further criminalized homosexuality, making LGBTI South Africans part of the constellation of oppressed communities targeted by the apartheid state. This repression stemmed from the need to police white masculinity as an embodiment of the ideal national subject.[25] The brutal racist system routinized forms of domination by attempting to eradicate nonmonogamous, nonreproductive, interracial, and same-sex relationships.[26] Mainstream lesbian and gay resistance to apartheid state repression was sidelined, much as feminist politics were.

However, in the 1980s growing national and international pressure compelled the movement to become multiracial. At the same time, the ANC emerged as a key player in the transition toward a democracy.[27] Although the ANC codified the protection of gay and lesbian rights, there was homophobic opposition from members within the organization.[28] The post-1994 moment inaugurated a new epoch in South African sexual politics, yet black South African LGBTI individuals would inhabit the queer archive in limited ways, if at all. *Faces and Phases* recognizes that liberatory tactics in many ways have perpetuated the subordination of black queer individuals.[29] By marking and mapping the public presence of LGBTI people and specifically black lesbians and trans men to mainstream audiences, Muholi's series reconfigures our social world to include and celebrate black queer life. She thus operationalizes the shift from nominal visibility in the constitution to material visibility in the gallery space.

The portrait of Busi Sigasa in Braamfontein, Johannesburg, commemorates her life and death (figure 3). The desolate background is slightly out of focus to further punctuate her singularity. Posed off center, she appears self-assured and insubordinate. Her gaze cast off to the distance as though preoccupied with something else. Although the black-and-white image appears timeless, her contemporary clothing prevents the viewer from displacing Busi into a distant past. Through naming, we witness the reappropriation of hostile environments that have often violated black LGBTI community members. The photograph now acts as a memorial. An

Figure 3. Busi Sigasa in Braamfontein, Johannesburg, 2006. © Zanele Muholi. Courtesy of Stevenson, Cape Town/Johannesburg, and Yancey Richardson, New York

artist in her own right, Busi was a poet and political activist. She had contracted the HIV virus after being viciously raped by so-called friends.[30] However, it is not through scrutiny of the photograph that the viewer is made aware of her diagnosis; rather, it is the blog posts and news articles surrounding her life that reveal the status of her health. The choice of subject, framing, and focus by Muholi calls attention to the empowering agency that the act of remembering and telling stories engenders. Similar to ethnographic art, the repetition of form in the series creates a sensory accessibility that conjures a sense of familiarity. Nevertheless, Muholi does not completely elide the problematic influence of ethnographic art but, rather, samples it to make room for her participants in the mainstream South African national archive. Thus these enigmatic photographs present a creative tension—they are both a parody and copy. Muholi's work provides an opportunity to examine life on the margins and reevaluate the legacy of the antiapartheid movement and liberation in the postapartheid era.

By adopting visual cues from other genres like documentary and ethnographic photography and portraiture, the images in Muholi's series take what Patricia Yaeger calls "neobaroque" form. This genre "plays with the hybrid as the source of the haunted, contemplates cultural and stylistic excess, exposes (formally and economically) the violent, decorative acquisitions of New World imperialism, and suggest the dizzying interpretation of the past and present."[31] Ultimately, *Faces and Phases* disrupts the narrative of being the possession of another that is conventional in ethnographic images of African people. Muholi's participants are neither available nor accessible in that way. Although Muholi uses an ethnographic format—unspecified backgrounds with the subjects in focus in the foreground—to build an inventory of black LGBTI persons, her work resists the conventional codes that insistently position African women against a primitive nature. Ultimately, she refuses to offer up her participants as specimens to be viewed by curious voyeurs. The portrait format signals to the audience that participants actively crafted an identity in conversation with the artist. Her optics point viewers in a more personal and subjective direction, one that incites renewed interest in aesthetic experimentation in the postapartheid moment. We do not see the undressed, eroticized, feminized, and submissive object of colonial fantasy.[32]

Instead, Muholi's series mocks the "art-in-service-to-science" narrative embedded in previous colonial images.[33] Beth Fowkes Tobin's articulation of the imperial design of eighteenth-century botany indicates "the white border and snipped twig of late-eighteenth-century botanical illustration reinforced the idea that a plant could be plucked from one cultural and ecological context and inserted into another with ease and with little regard for negative consequences."[34] The violent destruction of appropriated botany sought to erase the social, cultural, and environmental context to emphasize the *discovery* made by Western scientists. To delicately gesture toward to the violent explosion of black queer individuals in national imaginary, Muholi quotes this format to again call upon the history of representation. However, the strategic layout of Muholi's images seeks to resist the colonial normalizing gaze. The captions are essential when encountering Muholi's portraits. Without the names, places, and dates, the viewer could draw incorrect conclusions about the photographs, aligning it with imperialist photography. Borrowing Beningfield's language, Muholi's "remaking the land can therefore become a kind of remembering, but a remembering which is increasingly forced to confront the physical traces of the past."[35] In this way, Muholi's images help rewrite the history of land occupation and racial terror. Her work strives to transform the politics of inclusion in South African political discourse.

CURATED SPACES provides a focus on the relationship between visual culture and social, historical, or political subject matter.

Notes

I am grateful to Zanele Muholi and the participants of *Faces and Phases* for their continued activism and courage sharing their stories. I am also indebted to professors Daniel Magaziner, Erica James, Brian Beaton, and Bill Rankin for their encouragement and thoughtful critiques. I am thankful for the editorial support of my friends and colleagues Ayan Kassim, Beans Velocci, Jason Bell, Naomi Sussman, and Nichole Nelson. Lastly, I thank editor Conor McGrady for his encouragement and comments. Earlier versions of this article were presented at Rutgers University and Northwestern University.

1. Zanele Muholi, *Zanele Muholi Faces + Phases 2006–14* (Göttingen: Steidl Gerhard, 2014), 146-48.

2. Jennifer Beningfield, *The Frightened Land: Land, Landscape and Politics in South Africa in the Twentieth Century* (London: Routledge, 2006), 6.

3. Njabulo Simakahle Ndebele, *The Cry of Winnie Mandela: A Novel* (Oxfordshire: Ayebia Clarke, 2003), 52.

3. Rachel Holmes, "Queer Comrades: Winnie Mandela and the Moffies," *Social Text*, no. 52/53 (1997): 175.

5. Tamar Garb and Martin Barnes, *Figures and Fictions: Contemporary South African Photography* (Göttingen: Steidl Gerhard, 2011), 41.

6. Daniel R. Magaziner, *The Law and the Prophets: Black Consciousness in South Africa, 1968–1977* (Athens: Ohio University Press, 2010), 3–4.

7. Steve Biko and Aelred Stubbs, *I Write What I Like: Selected Writings* (Chicago: University of Chicago Press, 2002), 29.

8. Pumla Dineo Gqola, "Contradictory Locations: Blackwomen and the Discourse of the Black Consciousness Movement (BCM) in South Africa," *Meridians* 2, no. 1 (2001): 135.

9. Zanele Muholi, "Faces and Phases," *Transitions*, no. 107 (2012): 113.

10. Patricia Hayes, "The Form of the Norm: Shades of Gender in South African Photography of the 1980s," *Social Dynamics* 37, no. 2 (2011): 263–74.

11. Ibid., 265.

12. Ciraj Rassool, "Power, Knowledge and the Politics of Public Pasts," *African Studies* 69, no. 1 (2010): 86.

13. Muholi, "Faces and Phases," 114.

14. Holmes, "Queer Comrades," 162.

15. Tiffani Wesley, "'Corrective' Rape as Hate Crime," *Open Society Initiative for Southern Africa*, November 25, 2012, www.osisa.org/buwa/south-africa/classify-'corrective'-rape-hate-crime.

16. Lydia Smith, "Corrective Rape: The Homophobic Fallout of Post-apartheid South Africa," *Telegraph*, May 21, 2015, www.telegraph.co.uk/women/womens-life/11608361/Corrective-rape-The-homophobic-fallout-of-post-apartheid-South-Africa.html.

17. Thabo Msibi, "Not Crossing the Line: Masculinities and Homophobic Violence in South Africa," *Agenda* 23, no. 80 (2009): 51.

18. "2014 Aug. 19: Makau Family Mourns the Brutal Murder of Their Beloved," Inkanyiso, August 20, 2014, inkanyiso.org/2014/08/20/2014-aug-19-makau-family-mourns-the-brutal-murder-of-their-beloved/.

19. "Sick! SA Lesbian Hate Crime Hosepipe Killing," *Mamba*, August 18, 2014, www.mambaonline.com/2014/08/18/sick-sa-lesbian-hate-crime-hosepipe-killing/.

20. Struggle photography is a photographic form that prioritized liberation over aesthetic conventions. Darren Newbury, "'Lest We Forget': Photography and the Presentation of History at the Apartheid Museum, Gold Reef City, and the Hector Pieterson Museum, Soweto," *Visual Communication* 4, no. 3 (2005): 264.

21. Danielle de Kock, "Faces and Phases: Zanele Muholi at FRED London Ltd," *Art Throb: Contemporary Art in South Africa*, accessed June 19, 2015, artthrob.co.za/Reviews/2009/07/Danielle-de-Kock-reviews-Faces-and-Phases-by-Zanele-Muholi-at-Brodie/Stevenson.aspx.

22. "Lulu Xingwana Describes Lesbian Photos as Immoral," *Mail and Guardian: Africa's Best Read*, March 3, 2010, mg.co.za/article/2010-03-03-lulu-xingwana-describes-lesbian-photos-as-immoral.

23. Holmes, "Queer Comrades," 162.

24. Shaun de Waal and Anthony Manion, introduction to *Pride: Protest and Celebration*, ed. Shaun de Waal and Anthony Manion (Johannesburg: Jacana Media, 2006), 9.

25. Ashley Currier, *Out in Africa: LGBT Organizing in Namibia and South Africa* (Minneapolis: University of Minnesota Press, 2012), 29–30.

26. Ibid., 28.

27. Ibid., 25.

28. Ibid., 39–40.

29. Gabeba Baderoon, "Composing Selves: Zanele Muholi's Faces and Phases as an Archive of Collective Being," in *Zanele Muholi Faces + Phases 2006–14*, by Zanele Muholi (Göttingen: Steidl Gerhard, 2014), 328.

30. Andrea K. Scott, "Outlook: A South African Photographer Brings Her life's Work to Brooklyn," *New Yorker*, May 18, 2015, www.newyorker.com/magazine/2015/05/18/out-look.

31. Patricia Yaeger, "'Black Men Dressed in Gold'"—Eudora Welty, Empty Objects, and the Neobaroque," *PMLA* 124, no. 1 (2009): 14.

32. The visual legacy left by the images of Saartjie Baartman is salient to note here. The violence that has fixed Baartman in the colonial archive points us to the lineage of institutional power quoted in Muholi's series. One of Baartman's audiences among many was the scientific community, along with artists—together, they confirmed her status as

an ethnographic specimen. The spectacle went beyond entertainment. Needless to say, Baartman's inferiority was a figment of collective imagination—she became a phantasmal figure used to naturalize the subordination of black people. Witnessing here is a part of colonial violence. Her images remain a poignant relic of conquest.

33. Lisa Gail Collins, *The Art of History: African American Women Artists Engage the Past* (New Brunswick, NJ: Rutgers University Press, 2002), 13.

34. Beth Fowkes Tobin, *Picturing Imperial Power: Colonial Subjects in Eighteenth-Century British Painting* (Durham, NC: Duke University Press, 1999), 179.

35. Beningfield, *Frightened Land*, 6.

Lisa Arellano is an associate professor of American studies and women's, gender, and sexuality studies at Colby College. Her research focuses on comparative social movements, critical historiography, and violence studies. Her book, *Vigilantes and Lynch Mobs: Community, Nation and Narrative*, was published in 2012. Arellano's current book manuscript, "Disarming Imagination: Violence and the American Political Left," focuses on rape revenge cases, antiviolence activism, militant political movements, and dis/utopian political literature.

Erica L. Ball is professor of American studies at Occidental College. She is author of *To Live an Antislavery Life: Personal Politics and the Antebellum Black Middle Class* (2012) and the coeditor of the forthcoming "Reconsidering *Roots*: Race, Politics, and Memory." She is currently completing an interpretive biography of Madam C. J. Walker.

Josh Cerretti teaches in the history department at Western Washington University, where he is also affiliated faculty with women, gender, and sexuality studies. He earned his PhD in global gender studies at SUNY University at Buffalo in 2014, where he organized around issues of sexual justice, prison abolition, and affordable public education. His work has appeared in the *Feminist Wire* and *Peace and Conflict Monitor* and is forthcoming in *Gender and History*.

Jonathan Culleton is a lecturer in sociology and criminal justice studies at Waterford Institute of Technology. His main research interests are the interactions between conceptions of race and national identities. Culleton has considerable experience of working with various marginalized social groups, including religious and ethnic minority communities, former (and current) prisoners, and Travelers. Jonathan also coordinates the Wexford-Savannah Axis Research Project, an archival study in Irish migration, at WIT.

Amanda Frisken, professor of American studies at SUNY College at Old Westbury, is author of *Victoria Woodhull's Sexual Revolution: Political Theater and the Popular Press in Nineteenth Century America* (2004). Her current book project is tentatively titled "Sensationalism and Modern Culture." "'A Song without Words:' Anti-Lynching Imagery in the 1890s African American Press," based on a chapter of that book, was published in the *Journal of African American History* in 2012.

Raphael Ginsberg is associate director of the University of North Carolina at Chapel Hill's Correctional Education Program, which brings UNC-Chapel Hill courses into prisons for credit. He is also a lecturer in UNC-Chapel Hill's Department of Communication Studies and teaches through the Correctional Education Program. He received his PhD in communication studies from the University of North Carolina at Chapel Hill, focusing on cultural studies.

Deana Heath is senior lecturer in Indian and colonial history at the University of Liverpool. She is the author of *Purifying Empire: Obscenity and the Politics of Moral Regulation in Britain, India, and Australia* (2010), and coeditor of *Communalism and Globalisation in South Asia and its Diasporas* (2011) and "South Asian Governmentalities: Michel Foucault and the Question of Postcolonial Orderings" (forthcoming). She is currently working on a book on torture in colonial India.

Efeoghene (Efe) Igor is currently a doctoral student in the departments of history and women's, gender, and sexuality studies at Yale University. Her work examines the interplay between race, aesthetics, form, and identity in apartheid South Africa. Her dissertation pays attention to the particular ways in which the scientific gaze informed aesthetic conceptions of the black body.

Catherine O. Jacquet is assistant professor of history and women's and gender studies at Louisiana State University. She is currently revising her book manuscript, which examines social movement activism in response to rape in the United States, 1950–80. She has previously published "The Giles-Johnson Case and the Changing Politics of Sexual Violence in the 1960s United States" in the *Journal of Women's History* (Fall 2013).

Jessie Kindig is visiting assistant professor of history at Indiana University and an assistant editor at the *Journal of American History*. Her current book project tracks the emergence of US empire across the post-1945 Pacific by interrogating political and cultural struggles over the meaning and visibility of the Korean War's violence. She is a founding member of the Histories of Violence Collective.

Benjamin N. Lawrance is Conable Chair in International Studies and professor of history and anthropology at the Rochester Institute of Technology. His research examines trafficking, citizenship, and asylum. His recent books include *Amistad's Orphans* (2014), the collection *Adjudicating Refugee and Asylum Status* (2014, edited with Galya Ruffer), *Citizenship in Question* (2016, edited with Jacqueline Stevens), and the collection *Marriage by Force?* (2016, edited with Annie Bunting and Richard L. Roberts).

Jen Manion is associate professor of history at Amherst College. Manion is author of *Liberty's Prisoners: Carceral Culture in Early America* (2015) and coeditor of *Taking Back the Academy: History of Activism, History as Activism* (2004) and has published in *Signs: Journal of Women in Culture and Society*, *Journal of the Early Republic*, and *TSQ: Transgender Studies Quarterly*.

Xhercis Méndez is an assistant professor in philosophy and African American and African studies at Michigan State University. As a scholar-activist her research brings together women of color and decolonial feminisms, sexuality studies, and Afro-Latinx/diasporic religion and philosophies in an effort to explore alternative grounds for the (re)making of social relations, histories, intimacies, and resistant possibilities. She is the author of "Notes toward a Decolonial Feminist Methodology: The Race/Gender Matrix Revisited" (2015) and "Transcending Dimorphism: Afro-Cuban Ritual Praxis and the Rematerialization of the Body" (2014). She is currently working on her manuscript, "An Other Humanity: Decolonizing Feminism through Methodological Interventions from the Dark Side."

Luis Morán is an artist interested in fiction and visual studies. His work in illustration, graphic novels, and video focuses on experimental forms of narrative.

Claudia Salamanca is an artist, writer, and researcher whose work engages geopolitics and visual studies. She holds a PhD in rhetoric from the University of California, Berkeley and is currently assistant professor at Pontifical Xavierian University in Bogotá, Colombia, in the Department of Visual Arts. Her most recent research analyzes the modes of perception of the territory in the Colombian war conflict during 2002–10. She is also interested in experimental forms of writing specifically within the arts.

Tomoko Seto is an assistant professor of modern Japanese history at the Underwood International College, Yonsei University, South Korea. Her research interests include early socialism and anarchism, gender relations in social movements, and popular media such as gossip newspapers, theater performances, and oral narratives. She is currently working on a book that deals with the relationship between the late Meiji socialist movement and popular culture in Tokyo.

Carla Tsampiras is a historian inhabiting the position of senior lecturer in medical humanities in the Primary Health Care Directorate at the University of Cape Town. She is currently writing a book on the early years of AIDS in South Africa.

Jennifer Yeager is a lecturer in social, abnormal, and forensic psychology at the Waterford Institute of Technology. Her research focuses on how victimology and trauma are remembered and narrated by survivors and wider society. She has worked extensively with survivors of sexual assault across multiple projects and is the principal investigator of the Waterford Memories Project, an oral-history-driven study in digital humanities.

DOI 10.1215/01636545-3594699

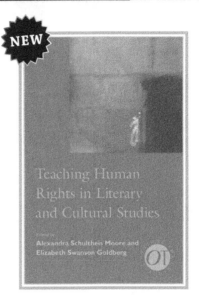

The Near Futures Series from Zone Books

Examining the impact of neoliberal thought on contemporary society

Musicians in Transit
Argentina and the Globalization of Popular Music
MATTHEW B. KARUSH
20 illustrations, paper, $24.95

"Karush reveals the individual footpaths and transnational bridges essential for decoding the relationship between music, capital, and nation."
—***Eric Zolov***

Punk and Revolution
Seven More Interpretations of Peruvian Reality
SHANE GREENE
63 illustrations, 8 page color insert, paper, $23.95

"[A] screamed prose-theory-anthropology-zine-poem to punk, and a daring mosh pit stage dive of an experimental ethnography."—***Orin Starn***

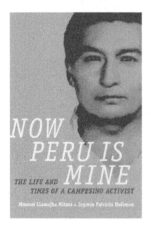

Now Peru Is Mine
The Life and Times of a Campesino Activist
MANUEL LLAMOJHA MITMA
and **JAYMIE PATRICIA HEILMAN**
Narrating Native Histories
24 illustrations, paper, $23.95

"Now Peru Is Mine makes a brilliantly original contribution to the study of twentieth-century Peru."—***Paulo Drinot***

dukeupress.edu | 888-651-0122 | 🐦 @DUKEpress

DUKE UNIVERSITY PRESS

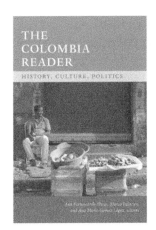

The Colombia Reader
History, Culture, Politics
**ANN FARNSWORTH-ALVEAR,
MARCO PALACIOS,** and
ANA MARÍA GÓMEZ LÓPEZ, editors
The Latin America Readers
103 illustrations (incl. 8 page color insert), paper, $29.95

*"In this stunning textual and visual compilation of
daily historical moments, the Colombian people
come alive, so that they may finally be understood
alongside their fellow Latin Americans."*
—**Herbert Braun**

We Dream Together
Dominican Independence, Haiti, and the
Fight for Caribbean Freedom
ANNE ELLER
11 illustrations, paper, $26.95

*"This is the book that tells the story of the Dominican
Republic's independence."*— **Laurent Dubois**

Man or Monster?
The Trial of a Khmer Rouge Torturer
ALEXANDER LABAN HINTON
22 illustrations, paper, $26.95

*"[A] finely observed and elegantly meditative study
of the Duch trial before the Khmer Rouge Tribunal...
Man or Monster? is a singular achievement."*
—**Lawrence Douglas**

dukeupress.edu | 888-651-0122 | 🐦 @DUKEpress

DUKE UNIVERSITY PRESS

The Rise of the American Conservation Movement

Power, Privilege, and Environmental Protection

DORCETA E. TAYLOR

paper, $29.95

"This book will inspire you to reconsider nearly everything you think you know about environmental history."—**David Naguib Pellow**

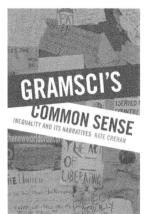

Gramsci's Common Sense

Inequality and Its Narratives

KATE CREHAN

6 photographs, paper, $23.95

"An essential text in Gramscian studies, Gramsci's Common Sense will generate transdisciplinary interest across the humanities and social scientists."—**Marcus E. Green**

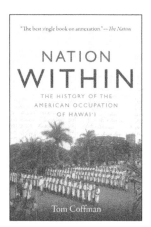

Now published by Duke University Press:

Nation Within

The History of the American Occupation of Hawai'i

TOM COFFMAN

68 illustrations, paper, $26.95

"This book gives us the untold story, the history we were not given in school, placing Hawai'i inside the larger picture of U.S. expansion into the Pacific. What we learn is sobering and fascinating."—**Howard Zinn**

dukeupress.edu | 888-651-0122 | 🐦 @DUKEpress

DUKE UNIVERSITY PRESS

Printed and bound by CPI Group (UK) Ltd, Croydon, CR0 4YY

13/04/2025

14656485-0004